Finance and Derivatives

Finance and Derivatives
Theory and Practice

Sébastien Bossu
Philippe Henrotte

John Wiley & Sons, Ltd

Original title: Exercices de Finance des Marchés: Théorie de la finance
Copyright © Dunod, Paris, 2002

Authorized English translation by Sébastien Bossu © 2006
Published by John Wiley & Sons Ltd, The Atrium, Southern Gate,
　　　　　　　Chichester, West Sussex PO19 8SQ, England
　　　　　　　Telephone　(+44) 1243 779777

Email (for orders and customer service enquiries): cs-books@wiley.co.uk
Visit our Home Page on www.wileyeurope.com

All Rights Reserved. No part of this publication may be reproduced, stored in a retrieval system or transmitted in any form or by any means, electronic, mechanical, photocopying, recording, scanning or otherwise, except under the terms of the Copyright, Designs and Patents Act 1988 or under the terms of a licence issued by the Copyright Licensing Agency Ltd, 90 Tottenham Court Road, London W1T 4LP, UK, without the permission in writing of the Publisher. Requests to the Publisher should be addressed to the Permissions Department, John Wiley & Sons Ltd, The Atrium, Southern Gate, Chichester, West Sussex PO19 8SQ, England, or emailed to permreq@wiley.co.uk, or faxed to (+44) 1243 770620.

Other Wiley Editorial Offices

John Wiley & Sons Inc., 111 River Street, Hoboken, NJ 07030, USA

Jossey-Bass, 989 Market Street, San Francisco, CA 94103-1741, USA

Wiley-VCH Verlag GmbH, Boschstr. 12, D-69469 Weinheim, Germany

John Wiley & Sons Australia Ltd, 42 McDougall Street, Milton, Queensland 4064, Australia

John Wiley & Sons (Asia) Pte Ltd, 2 Clementi Loop #02-01, Jin Xing Distripark, Singapore 129809

John Wiley & Sons Canada Ltd, 22 Worcester Road, Etobicoke, Ontario, Canada M9W 1L1

Wiley also publishes its books in a variety of electronic formats. Some content that appears in print may not be available in electronic books.

Library of Congress Cataloguing-in-Publication Data

Bossu, Sébastien.
　[Exercices de finance des marchés. English]
　Finance and derivatives : theory and practice / Sébastien Bossu, Philippe Henrotte.
　　p.　cm.
　Includes bibliographical references and index.
　ISBN-13: 978-0-470-01432-5 (cloth : alk. paper)
　ISBN-10: 0-470-01432-6 (cloth : alk. paper)
　ISBN-13: 978-0-470-01433-2 (pbk. : alk. paper)
　ISBN-10: 0-470-01433-4 (pbk. : alk. paper)
　1. Investments–Mathematical models　2. Derivative securities.　I. Henrotte, Philippe.　II. Title.
　HG4515.2.B6713　2005
　332.63'2'0151—dc22

2005017618

British Library Cataloguing in Publication Data

A catalogue record for this book is available from the British Library

ISBN-13 978-0-470-01432-5 (HB) 978-0-470-01433-2 (PB)
ISBN-10 0-470-01432-6 (HB) 0-470-01433-4 (PB)

Typeset in 10/12pt Garamond by TechBooks, New Delhi, India
Printed and bound in Great Britain by Antony Rowe Ltd, Chippenham, Wiltshire
This book is printed on acid-free paper responsibly manufactured from sustainable forestry in which at least two trees are planted for each one used for paper production.

Published with the financial help of the Ministére de la Culture—Centre national du livre.

The contents of this book only reflect the views of the authors and do not constitute any recommendation from their respective institutions. The authors and their institutions expressly disclaim any responsibility for any remaining errors and any use to which the contents of this book are put.

Contents

Preface ix

Foreword xi

Acknowledgements xiii

1 Interest rate 1

    1.1 Measuring time 1
    1.2 Interest rate 2
    1.3 Discounting 5
    Exercises 7
    Solutions 9

2 Investment decision criteria 13

    2.1 Rate of return; time of return 13
    2.2 Net present value 14
    2.3 Internal rate of return 15
    2.4 Other investment criteria 16
    Further reading 16
    Exercises 17
    Solutions 19

3 Bonds 23

    3.1 Financial markets 23
    3.2 Bonds 26
    3.3 Yield 27
    3.4 Zero-coupon yield curve; arbitrage price 30
    Further reading 34
    Exercises 35
    Solutions 39

4 Derivatives — 47

4.1 Introduction — 47
4.2 Forward contracts — 48
4.3 'Plain vanilla' options — 51
Exercises — 54
Solutions — 58

5 Portfolio theory — 65

5.1 Summary of portfolio valuation — 65
5.2 Risk and return — 66
5.3 Gains of diversification; portfolio optimization — 71
5.4 Capital Asset Pricing Model — 72
Further reading — 73
Exercises — 74
Solutions — 77

6 Binomial model — 85

6.1 Introduction — 85
6.2 Binomial trees — 85
Further reading — 90
Exercises — 91
Solutions — 94

7 Lognormal model — 103

7.1 Lognormal model — 103
7.2 Closed-form formulas — 105
7.3 Monte-Carlo method — 106
Further reading — 108
Exercises — 109
Solutions — 113

8 Dynamic hedging — 125

8.1 Introduction — 125
8.2 Delta-hedging — 126
8.3 Other risk parameters: the Greek letters — 127
Further reading — 132
Exercises — 133
Solutions — 136

Contents

9   Models for asset prices in continuous time 141

    9.1   Continuously compounded interest rate 141
    9.2   Introduction to models for the behaviour of asset prices in continuous time 142
    9.3   Introduction to stochastic processes 144
    9.4   Introduction to stochastic calculus 147
    References and further reading 148
    Exercises 149
    Solutions 154

10 The Black–Scholes model 167

    10.1   The Black–Scholes partial differential equation 167
    10.2   Black–Scholes formulas 170
    10.3   Volatility 171
    References and further reading 174
    Exercises 175
    Solutions 178

Appendix A: Probability review 185

Appendix B: Calculus review 193

Appendix C: Finance formulas 197

Index 203

Preface

This is the revised edition in English of *Exercices de Finance des Marchés*, published in Paris by Dunod in 2002. The first textbook of its kind to compile course notes and exercises with solutions in the field of quantitative finance, it is designed as a complement to an MBA sequence in finance or an MS class in financial mathematics. It may also serve as a self-teaching guide for beginning practitioners and confirmed financiers who wish to catch up with financial theory and its applications.

From basic notions on interest rates to option pricing theory through portfolio optimization, we wanted this book to cover the essential theoretical and practical knowledge in the field, and yet be accessible to neophytes. As such, the only required background is an undergraduate level in mathematics – no prior knowledge in finance is assumed, except for a general understanding of basic economic concepts found in the press. A probability and calculus review is included in an appendix for those readers who need to refresh their memory in these particular areas.

We had to make some choices on the extent of the concepts we could cover, and the level of mathematical machinery we could employ. Our approach was to focus on first principles such as arbitrage or the risk-return trade-off; key concepts such as yield or Greek letters; and the major numerical methods such as binomial trees or Monte-Carlo simulations. We strived to keep the course notes as concise and straightforward as possible, while covering a fair amount of fundamental results illustrated with 'real-life' examples. We left non-essential proofs or advanced concepts in the exercises of higher difficulty, which we identified with an asterisk (*).

The result is ten chapters in ascending order of difficulty, which we recommend you to read in sequence:

- Chapters 1 and 2 deal with the time value of money and correspond to a core finance course;
- Chapters 3 and 5 cover bonds, arbitrage and risk-return, which are usually taught in an advanced core finance course;

- Chapters 4 and 6 introduce derivative securities and their valuation, which are taught in an advanced core finance course or in an elective;
- Chapters 7 and 8 cover the advanced valuation and management of options, corresponding to an intermediate MBA elective or a core MS course;
- Chapters 9 to 10 introduce continuous-time finance which would be taught in an advanced MBA elective or a core MS course.

We hope that our book will prove insightful and useful to students and practitioners. We are committed to continually improve successive editions and we will appreciate all feedback from our readers.

Foreword

As revolutions go, the one in finance over the last thirty years may not seem to be that dramatic. It's been quite a lengthy revolution, led by the least likely revolutionaries, mathematicians. But nevertheless this revolution has had an enormous impact on the financial markets, and on the entire world. Not so long ago the financial markets were governed by middle-aged men with undergraduate degrees in History, a wardrobe of Savile Row suits and dandruff. In their place are now the freshly minted Physics PhDs, in chinos and Ferraris.

The change in emphasis from finance being a social science to a more hardcore science began with Paul Samuelson, and later Fischer Black, Myron Scholes and Robert Merton. With this change, and because of the large financial rewards associated with the City and Wall Street, the number of people wanting to join in the fun has exploded. And all of these people are scrambling to learn the subject ASAP. This is where the book by Bossu and Henrotte comes in. *Finance and Derivatives* teaches all of the fundamentals of quantitative finance clearly and concisely without going into unnecessary technicalities. You'll pick up the most important theoretical concepts, tools and vocabulary without getting bogged down in arcane derivations or enigmatic theoretical considerations.

But Bossu and Henrotte have an important responsibility with so much money being controlled by spotty scientists just out of school. When educating people in this field you must always remember to emphasise that this is not really a hardcore science – that a model that worked for the past decade could stop working, tomorrow, with an impact which could cause financial earthquakes on a global scale. So, pick up the tools of the trade from this book, but also appreciate the experience of its authors, it's the practice that makes perfect, not the theory.

Paul Wilmott

Acknowledgements

We thank Denes Kelecsenyi for his contribution to the translation of the French edition into English.

SB would like to thank Jim McCurley, Ryan Schiffbauer, Olivier Lopez and Scott Kemp for their help in proof-reading the manuscript or their support at various stages of the publication process.

1 Interest rate

1.1 Measuring time

In finance the most common unit of time is the year, perhaps because it is one that everyone presumes to know well. Although, as we will see, the year can actually create confusion and give an edge to the better-informed investor. How many days are there in 1 year? 365. But what about the 366 days of a leap year? What fraction of a year does the first 6 months represent? Is it 0.5, or 181/365 (except, again, for leap years)?

Financial markets have regulations and conventions to answer these questions. The problem is that these conventions vary by country. Worse still, within a given country different conventions may be used for different financial products.

We leave it to readers to become familiar with these day count conventions while in this book we will use the following rule, which professionals call **30/360**. Note that the first day starts at noon and the last day ends at noon. Thus, there is only 1 whole day between 2 February 2007 and 3 February 2007.

Rule	Result	Example: from 15 January 2006 to 13 March 2009
1. Count the number of whole years	Y	3 (from 15 January 2006 to 15 January 2009)
2. Count the number of remaining months and divide by 12	M/12	1/12 (from 15 January 2009 to 15 February 2009)
3. Count the number of remaining days (the last day of the month counting as the 30th unless it is the final date) and divide by 360	D/360	28/360 (under the 30/360 convention there are 16 days from 15 February 2009 at noon to 1 March 2009 at noon and 12 days from 1 March 2009 at noon to 13 March 2009 at noon)
TOTAL	Y + M/12 + D/360	$3 + 1/12 + 28/360 = 3.161111\ldots$

From this rule, we can arrive at the following simplified measures:

Semester (half year)	0.5 year
Quarter	0.25 year
Month	1/12 year
Week	7/360 year
Day	1/360 year

> **In practice...**
>
> The Excel function DAYS360(*Start_date, End_date*) counts the number of days on a 30/360 basis.

1.2 Interest rate

In the economic sphere there are two types of agents whose *interests* are by definition opposed to each other:

- **Investors**, who have money and want that money to make them richer while they remain idle.
- **Entrepreneurs**, who don't have money but want to get rich actively using the money of others.

Banks help to reconcile these two interests by serving as an intermediary, placing the money of the investor at the entrepreneur's disposal and assuming the risk of bankruptcy. In exchange, the bank demands that the entrepreneur pay *interest* at regular intervals, which serves to pay for the bank's service and the investor's capital.

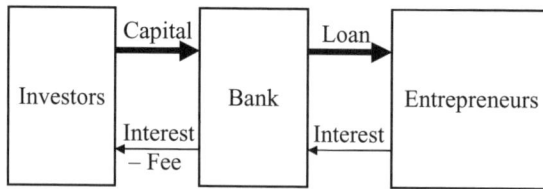

1.2.1 Gross interest rate

If I is the *total* interest paid on a capital K, the **gross interest rate** *over the considered period* is defined as:

$$r = \frac{I}{K}$$

Interest rate

Examples

- €10 of interest paid over 1 year on a capital of €200 corresponds to an annual gross interest rate of 5%.
- $10 of interest paid *every year* for 5 years on a capital of $200 corresponds to a 25% gross interest rate over 5 years, which is five times the annual rate in the preceding example.

We must emphasize that **an interest rate is meaningless if no time period is specified**; a 5% gross interest rate every 6 months is far more lucrative than every year.

This rate is called 'gross' because it does not take into consideration the **compounding of interest**, which is explained in the next section.

1.2.2 Compounding: compound interest rate

Hearing the question 'How much interest does one receive over 2 years if the annual interest rate is 10%?', a distressing proportion of individuals reply in a single cry: '20%!' However, the correct answer is 21%, because **interest produces more interest.** In fact, a good little capitalist, rather than foolishly spend the 10% interest paid by the bank after the first year, would immediately reinvest it the second year. Therefore, his total capital after 1 year is 110% of his initial investment on which he will receive 10% interest the second year. His gross interest over the 2-year period is thus: $10\% + 10\% \times 110\% = 21\%$.

More generally, starting with initial capital K one can build a **compounding table** of the capital at the end of each interest period:

Compounding table of capital K at interest rate r over n periods

Period	Capital	Example: $r = 10\%$
0	K	$2000
1	$K(1+r)$	$2000 \times (1 + 10\%) = \$2200$
2	$K(1+r)^2$	$2200 \times (1 + 10\%) = \$2420$
...	...	...
n	$K(1+r)^n$	$2000 \times (1 + 10\%)^n$

From this table we obtain a formula for the amount of accumulated interest after n periods:

$$I_n = K(1+r)^n - K$$

We may now define the **compound interest rate** over n periods, corresponding to the total accumulated interest:

$$r^{[n]} = \frac{I_n}{K} = (1+r)^n - 1$$

(To avoid confusion we prefer the notation $r^{[n]}$ over r_n to indicate compounding over n periods, as r_n typically denotes a series of time-dependent variables.)

Example. The total accumulated interest over 3 years on an initial investment of $2000 at a semi-annual compound rate of 5% is: $I_6 = 2000 \times (1+0.05)^6 - 2000 = \$680$. The compound interest rate over 3 years (six semesters) is $r^{[6]} = 34\%$. Note that this result would be different with a 10% *annual* compound rate.

1.2.3 Conversion formula

Two compound interest rates over periods τ_1 and τ_2 are said to be **equivalent** if they satisfy:

$$\left[1 + r^{[\tau_1]}\right]^{\frac{1}{\tau_1}} = \left[1 + r^{[\tau_2]}\right]^{\frac{1}{\tau_2}}$$

Here τ_1 and τ_2 are two positive real numbers (for instance, $\tau_1 = 1.5$ represents a year and a half) and $r^{[\tau_1]}$ and $r^{[\tau_2]}$ are the equivalent interest rates over τ_1 and τ_2 years respectively.

This formula is very useful to convert a compound rate into a different period than the 'physical' interest payment period. A good way to remember it is to think that for a given investment all expressions of type $[1 + r^{[\text{period}]}]^{\text{frequency}}$ are equal, where frequency is the number of periods per year.

Example. An investment at a semi-annual compound rate of 5% is equivalent to an investment at a 2-year compound rate of:

$$r^{[2]} = (1 + 5\%)^{\frac{2}{0.5}} - 1 \approx 21.55\%$$

1.2.4 Annualization

Annualization is the process of converting a given compound interest rate into its annual equivalent. This allows one to rapidly compare the profitability of investments whose interests are paid out over different periods.

In this book, unless mentioned otherwise, all interest rates are understood to be on an annual basis or annualized. With this convention, the compound interest rate over T years can always be written as:

$$r^{[T]} = (1 + r^{[\text{annual}]})^T - 1$$

Example. The annualized rate equivalent to a semi-annual rate of 5% is:

$$r^{[1]} = (1 + 5\%)^{\frac{1}{0.5}} - 1 = 1.05^2 - 1 = 10.25\%$$

From which we obtain the 2-year compound rate found in the previous example:

$$r^{[2]} = (1 + 10.25\%)^2 - 1 \approx 21.55\%$$

1.3 Discounting

'*Time is money.*' In finance, this principle of the businessman has a very precise meaning: **a dollar today is worth more than a dollar tomorrow**. Two principal reasons can be put forward:

- **Inflation**: the increase in consumer prices implies that one dollar will buy less tomorrow than today.
- **Interest**: one dollar today produces interest between today and tomorrow.

With this principle in mind the next step is to determine **the value today of a dollar tomorrow** – or generally the **present value** of an amount received or paid in the future.

1.3.1 Present value

The **present value** of an amount C paid or received in T years is the equivalent amount that, invested today at the compound rate r, will grow to C over T years: $PV \times (1 + r)^T = C$. Equivalently:

$$PV = \frac{C}{(1 + r)^T}$$

Example. A supermarket chain customarily pays its suppliers with a 3-month delay. With a 5% interest rate the present value of a delivery today of €1 000 000 worth of goods paid in 3 months is:

$$\frac{1\,000\,000}{(1 + 5\%)^{0.25}} \approx €987\,877$$

The 3-month payment delay is thus implicitly equivalent to a €12 123 discount, or 1.21%.

Discounting is the process of computing the present value of various future cash flows. Similar to annualization, it is a key concept in finance as it makes amounts received or paid at different points in time comparable to what they are worth today. Thus, an investment which pays one million dollars in 10 years is 'only' worth approximately $614 000 assuming a 5% annual interest rate.

1.3.2 Discount rate and expected return

In practice, the choice of the **discount rate** r is crucial when calculating a present value and depends on the **expected return** of each investor. The minimum expected return for all investors is the interest rate offered by such 'infallible' institutions as central banks or government treasury departments. In the USA, the generally accepted benchmark rate is the yield[1] of the 10-year Treasury Note. In Europe, the 10-year Gilt (UK), OAT (France) or Bund (Germany) are used, and in Japan the 10-year JGB. However, an investor who is willing to take more risk should expect a higher return and use a higher discount rate r in her calculations. In investment banking it is not uncommon to use a 10–15% discount rate when assessing the profitability of such risky investments as financing a film production or providing seed capital to a start-up company.

[1] See Chapter 3 for the definition of this term.

Exercises

Exercise 1

Calculate, in years, the time that passes between 30 November 2006 and 1 March 2008 on a 30/360 basis. What is the annualized interest rate of an investment at a gross rate of 10% over this period?

Exercise 2: savings account

On 1 January 2005 you invested €1000 in a savings account. On 1 January 2006 the bank sent a summary statement indicating that you received a total of €40 in interest in 2005.

1. What is the gross annual interest rate of this savings account?
2. How much interest will you receive in 2006?
3. How much interest would you have received in 2005 if you had closed your account on 1 July 2005?

Your bank calculates and pays your interest every month based on your balance.

Exercise 3

Ten years ago you invested £500 in a savings account. The last bank statement shows a balance of £1030.52. What will your savings amount to in 10 years if the interest rate stays the same?

Exercise 4: from Russia with interest

You are a reputed financier and your personal credit allows you to borrow up to $100 000 at a rate of 6.5% (with a little bit of imagination). The annual interest rate offered on deposits by the Russian Central Bank is 150%. The exchange rate of the Russian ruble against the US dollar is 25 RUB/USD and your analysts believe that this exchange rate will remain stable during the coming year. Can you find a way to make money? Analyse the risks that you have taken.

Exercise 5

Sort the interest rates below from the most lucrative to the least lucrative:

(a) 6% per year;
(b) 0.5% per month;
(c) 30% every 5 years;
(d) 10% the first year then 4% the following 2 years.

Exercise 6: overdraft

To help you face your long-overdue bills your bank generously offers you an unlimited overdraft at a 17% interest rate per year. Interest is calculated and charged on your balance every month.

1. Calculate the effective interest rate charged by the bank if you pay off your balance after 1 month, 1.5 years or 5 years.
2. Draw the curve of the interest rate as a function of time.
3. When will the interest charged exceed the initial balance?

Exercise 7*: continuous interest rate

To solve this exercise, you must be familiar with limits and Taylor expansions.

1. Let (u_n) be the sequence: $u_n = \left(1 + \frac{1}{n}\right)^n$ ($n \geq 1$). Show that (u_n) has limit e (Euler's constant: $e \approx 2.71828$). Hint: $x^y = e^{y \ln x}$, $\ln(1+h) \approx h - \frac{h^2}{2} + \frac{h^3}{3} - \ldots$ for small h.
2. If A_2 is a savings account with an annual interest rate of 5% split into two payments of 2.5% every 6 months, what is the corresponding annualized interest rate r_2?
3. More generally, A_n is a savings account with an annual interest rate of 5% split into n payments. Determine the corresponding annualized interest rate r_n.
4. Find the limit r of r_n as n goes to infinity. What significance can be given to r?

Exercise 8: discounting

Using a discount rate of 4% per year, what is the present value of:

(a) €100 000 in 1 year?
(b) €1 000 000 in 10 years?
(c) €100 000 10 years ago?

Exercise 9: expected return

After hesitating at length Mr Smith, an accomplished investment banker, eventually renounced an investment project whose cost was 30 million pounds against a promised payoff of one billion pounds in 20 years. Can you estimate his expected return?

Exercise 10: today's value of one dollar tomorrow

On 14 April 2005 the annualized interest rate on an overnight dollar deposit in dollars (i.e. between 14 April and 15 April 2005) was 2.77%. Calculate 'the value today of a dollar tomorrow', that is the present value as of 14 April 2005 of one dollar collected on 15 April 2005.

Solutions

Exercise 1

Rule	Result	From 30 November 2006 until 1 March 2008
1. Count the number of whole years	Y	1 (from 30 November 2006 until 30 November 2007)
2. Count the number of remaining months and divide by 12	M/12	3/12 (from 30 November 2007 until 29 February 2008)
3. Count the number of remaining days (the last day of the month counting as the 30th unless it is the final date) and divide by 360	D/360	1/360 (there is 1 day between 29 February 2008 and 1 March 2008)
TOTAL	Y + M/12 + D/360	1 + 3/12 + 1/360 = 1.2527...

According to the conversion formula:

$$r^{[1]} = (1 + 10\%)^{1/1.2527} - 1 \approx 7.90\% \text{ per year}$$

Exercise 2: savings account

1. The gross annual interest rate is:

$$r = \frac{I}{K} = \frac{40}{1000} = 4\%$$

2. The interest received in 2006 will be €41.60, as shown in the compounding table below:

Date	Balance	Interest
1 January 2005	€1000	—
1 January 2006	1000 × (1 + 4%) = €1040	€40
1 January 2007	1040 × (1 + 4%) = €1081.60	€41.60

3. From the annual rate $r^{[1]}$ of 4% we can infer through the rate conversion formula that the monthly rate $r^{[1/12]}$ used by the bank to pay monthly interest is:

$$r^{[1/12]} = (1 + 4\%)^{1/12} - 1 \approx 0.327\%$$

Thus the compound interest over 6 months is:

$$r^{[1/2]} = (1 + 0.327\%)^6 - 1 \approx 1.98\%$$

The interest received after 6 months is thus €19.80, which is slightly less than €40/2 = €20 because of compounding. Note that we could have calculated the semi-annual interest rate directly:

$$r^{[1/2]} = (1 + 4\%)^{1/2} - 1 \approx 1.98\%$$

Exercise 3

The total amount of interest accumulated over the past 10 years was £530.52. The 10-year interest rate of this savings account is thus:

$$r = \frac{530.52}{500} \approx 106.11\%$$

Assuming the same interest rate, the savings in 10 years will amount to: $1030.52 \times (1 + 106.11\%) \approx £2124$.

Exercise 4: from Russia with interest

The fact is undeniable: 150% interest is a lot better than 6.5%! But you won't be able to buy the car of your dreams with rubles (unless you are a big Lada fan). How can you get what you want?

1. Borrow $100 000 at 6.5% interest for 1 year.
2. Convert this capital into RUB 2 500 000.
3. Invest the RUB 2 500 000 at 150% interest for 1 year.
4. At the end of 1 year, you get back RUB 6 250 000 (do not forget to thank the Russians).
5. Exchange the RUB 6 250 000 for $250 000 at the same rate of 25 RUB/USD (do not forget to thank your analysts).
6. Repay the $100 000 loan with interest, totalling $106 500.

Bottom line: you just made $143 500!

Oddly enough, the **exchange rate risk** is not necessarily the most significant risk in carrying out this strategy. The exchange rate would need to grow from 25 to $\frac{6\,250\,000}{106\,500} \approx 58.69$ RUR/USD to prevent you from paying off your $100 000 loan together with the $6500 interest. Such devaluation of the ruble is not impossible, but unlikely according to your analysts.

In reality the first incurred risk is the **default risk** (i.e. bankruptcy) of the Central Bank of Russia; it would be rather naïve to believe that a bank that offers a 150% interest rate can stay in business for very long. Note that **inflation risk** is implicit to the exchange rate risk: if the price of a hamburger stays the same in the USA but doubles in Russia, it is unlikely that dollar investors will want to pay twice for their Russian hamburger imports. In case of strong inflation in Russia, the demand for Russian hamburgers (and for rubles in general) will decrease and the exchange rate will deteriorate, i.e. go up in dollar terms (one will need more rubles to buy one dollar).

Exercise 5

With the conversion formula we can annualize all the given rates and observe that:

$$b > a > d > c$$

(Note that for **d** the compounding over three years is given as: $(1 + 10\%) \times (1 + 4\%)^2$.)

Exercise 6: overdraft

1. Using the conversion formula we have:

$$r^{[\tau]} = (1 + 17\%)^\tau - 1$$

Thus:
- $r^{[1/12]} \approx 1.3\%$;
- $r^{[0.5]} \approx 8.2\%$;
- $r^{[1.5]} \approx 26.6\%$;
- $r^{[5]} \approx 119.2\%$.

2. The curve of $r^{[\tau]}$ as a function of τ is exponential:

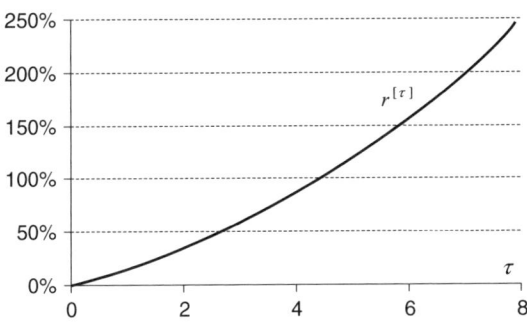

3. The interest charged will exceed the initial balance when the interest rate exceeds 100%. Denoting by τ the time when this happens, we have:

$$(1 + 17\%)^\tau = 1 + 100\% = 2$$

Taking the logarithm of both sides we obtain:

$$\tau = \frac{\ln 2}{\ln 1.17} \approx 4.41 \text{ years}$$

Exercise 7*: continuous interest rate

1. Using the exponential form, we have for all $n \geq 1$: $u_n = e^{n \ln(1+\frac{1}{n})}$.
   When n goes to infinity, $\frac{1}{n}$ goes to 0 and thus:

$$\ln\left(1 + \frac{1}{n}\right) = \frac{1}{n} - \frac{1}{2n^2} + \frac{1}{3n^3} - \cdots$$

Multiplying both sides by n yields:

$$n \ln\left(1 + \frac{1}{n}\right) = 1 - \frac{1}{2n} + \frac{1}{3n^2} - \ldots$$

Therefore $n \ln\left(1 + \frac{1}{n}\right)$ goes to 1 when n goes to infinity, from which we obtain:

$$\lim_{n \to +\infty} u_n = e^1 = e$$

2. Based on the conversion formula: $(1 + 2.5\%)^2 = 1 + r_2$, whence: $r_2 \approx 5.06\%$.
3. Similarly: $r_n = \left(1 + \frac{5\%}{n}\right)^n - 1$.
4. With the same reasoning as in question 1, one obtains that $r = \lim_{n \to +\infty} r_n = e^{5\%} - 1 \approx 5.13\%$. This is the annualized interest rate corresponding to an imaginary savings account for which the interest would be paid out continually during the year, at each fraction of a second. We say that the 5% interest rate is continuously compounded (see Chapter 9).

Exercise 8: discounting

Based on a 4% discount rate the present values are:

(a) $PV = \dfrac{100\,000}{1 + 4\%} \approx €96\,154$;

(b) $PV = \dfrac{1\,000\,000}{(1 + 4\%)^{10}} \approx €675\,564$;

(c) $PV = \dfrac{100\,000}{(1 + 4\%)^{-10}} = 100\,000 \times (1 + 4\%)^{10} \approx €148\,024$ (this is actually compounding).

Exercise 9: expected return

The fact that Mr Smith hesitated at length before cancelling the project indicates that the return was only slightly inferior to the expected return of the investment banker. Therefore, we can deduce that for Mr Smith, the value of one billion pounds in 20 years discounted at a rate r is inferior but close to 30 million pounds today, i.e.:

$$30\,000\,000 \approx \frac{1\,000\,000\,000}{(1 + r)^{20}}$$

i.e. : $r \approx 19\%$

Exercise 10: today's value of one dollar tomorrow

Today's value of one dollar tomorrow is:

$$\frac{1}{(1 + 2.77\%)^{\frac{1}{360}}} \approx \$0.999924105$$

2 Investment decision criteria

2.1 Rate of return; time of return

Consider an investment of cost or price P and earnings or income E for the period between $t = 0$ and $t = T$. The **gross rate of return** (**ROR**, also called return on investment or ROI) over the period is given as:

$$ROR = \frac{E}{P}$$

In the case of a financial security[1] $P = P_0$ is the price paid today and E is the difference between the value P_T at time T and the price P_0, plus any income I paid in between. With these notations, the gross rate of return becomes:

$$ROR = \frac{P_T - P_0 + I}{P_0}$$

Observe that the rate of return generalizes the notion of interest rate.

Example. The gross rate of return of $1000 invested at an annual rate of 5% is... 5% per annum!

The **time of return** is defined as the inverse of the rate of return:

$$TOR = \frac{P}{E} = \frac{1}{ROR}$$

The time of return measures the number of periods an investor will wait until her money is *returned* to her in earnings, assuming the latter remains constant and regular in time. Note that a time of return equal to 1 corresponds to a wait of T years. To express a time of return in years it must be multiplied by T.

Example. The rate of return of an investment which pays an income equal to the capital in 5 and 10 years and also returns the capital in 10 years is 200% over

---

[1] See Chapter 3 for the definition of this term.

10 years (here $P_T = P_0$: there are no capital gains or losses). The time of return is $\frac{1}{2}$, i.e. 5 years.

The advantage of these two investment decision criteria is that they are easy to calculate. Their disadvantage is that they only take one period into consideration.

2.2 Net present value

The first and foremost obsession of the financier clearly is his own money. His second biggest obsession is the money of others. And his main goal in life can be summarized by the statement: to transfer the money of others into his own pockets – this is the idea of **cash flow**.

Naturally one cannot always win: certain cash flows are positive (in-pocket) while others are negative (out-of-pocket).

At this point there does not seem to be much difference between a financier and an accountant. There is, however, one major difference: an accountant contemplates cash flows from the past while a financier fantasizes over *future* cash flows. When considering an investment the financier always starts with the **table of future cash flows**:

General form				Example				
Time	t_1	t_2	...	Date (31 Dec)	2006	2007	2008	2009
Cash flow	F_1	F_2	...	Cash flow (m €)	+100	−150	+200	+500

The next step is to discount the cash flows and calculate the **present value** of the investment as a whole, which is simply the sum of each cash flow's present value:

$$PV = \sum_{i=1}^{+\infty} \frac{F_i}{(1+r)^{t_i}} = \frac{F_1}{(1+r)^{t_1}} + \frac{F_2}{(1+r)^{t_2}} + \ldots$$

$$PV = \frac{100}{1+10\%} + \frac{-150}{(1+10\%)^2} + \frac{200}{(1+10\%)^3} + \frac{500}{(1+10\%)^4} \approx €458.71\text{m}$$

General form   Example with a discount rate $r = 10\%$

If the investment cost C_0 is already known, the **net present value (NPV)** is defined as the present value *net of* the initial cost:

$$NPV = -C_0 + \sum_{i=1}^{+\infty} \frac{F_i}{(1+r)^{t_i}} = -C_0 + \frac{F_1}{(1+r)^{t_1}} + \frac{F_2}{(1+r)^{t_2}} + \ldots$$

There are then three cases:

- NPV > 0: the investment is profitable and may be carried out.
- NPV < 0: the investment would be at a loss and should be rejected.
- NPV = 0: the investment is neutral (theoretical case).

Example. In the previous example, if the initial cost is €400m the net present value is +€58.71m: the investment project may be carried out.

As always, the problem of selecting the appropriate discount rate is difficult and raises the issue of the investor's expected return. Nevertheless, the NPV is a far more advanced measure of an investment's profitability than the gross rate of return since it takes into account the compounding of interest over multiple periods. It is the basic investment decision criterion used by professionals.

2.3 Internal rate of return

We can reverse the problem of the discount rate and calculate instead the **internal rate of return (IRR)** r which makes the NPV equal zero, in other words find the indifference point for the investor.

In mathematical terms the IRR is the solution r^* to the equation $NPV(r) = 0$, i.e.:

$$-C_0 + \sum_{i=1}^{+\infty} \frac{F_i}{(1+r)^{t_i}} = 0$$

Example. The IRR of the investment described in the previous section is 14.26%. Using a calculator one would verify that:

$$-400 + \frac{100}{1+14.26\%} + \frac{-150}{(1+14.26\%)^2} + \frac{200}{(1+14.26\%)^3} + \frac{500}{(1+14.26\%)^4} = 0$$

Note that the IRR is a criterion equivalent to the NPV and must be compared to the investor's expected return to decide whether the investment should be accepted or rejected.

In practice...

The Excel functions XNPV and XIRR calculate the NPV and IRR corresponding to a cash flow table.

You must install the Analysis ToolPack add-in through the Tools menu to access these functions.

	A	B	C	D	E	F
1	Date	1/1/2006	12/31/2006	12/31/2007	12/31/2008	12/31/2009
2	cash flow (m€)	-400	100	-150	200	500
3						
4	NPV (10%)	58.70		IRR	14.26%	
5		=XNPV(10%;B2:F2;B1:F1)			=XIRR(B2:F2;B1:F1)	
6						

2.4 Other investment criteria

Many accounting criteria are also used in finance to assess the suitability of an investment, particularly for company stocks. These criteria are beyond the scope of this book and we will only mention the most famous one: the **price-to-earnings ratio (PER or P/E)**, which is simply the time of return for a listed company. It is given as:

$$PER = \frac{\text{price (per share)}}{\text{earnings (per share and per annum)}}$$

A company with a PER of 20 means that its listed stock price is worth 20 years' of profits – in other words a new stockholder would have to wait for 20 years before the company earnings would pay back his investment (assuming earnings remain constant and entirely redistributed in the form of dividends).

Rapidly growing companies have a high PER: they reinvest their profits to sustain their growth and redistribute very little to stockholders. However, since the prices of these stocks often increase at a faster pace, holders of these stocks tend to be compensated through capital gains.

Conversely, companies which have reached their maximum expansion have a low PER: they do not need to further invest in their activity and therefore redistribute most of their profits to stockholders. Dividends become regular and predictable and the stock price is close to the present value of the dividend flow.

Further reading

Brealey, R.A., Myers, S.C. and Marcus, A.J. (2003) *Fundamentals of Corporate Finance*, 4th edn. McGraw Hill, New York.

Exercises

Exercise 1: rate and time of return

What is the annualized rate of return and time of return in years of:

(a) A security purchased at $350 which analysts estimate to be worth $400 in one and a half years?
(b) A winning lottery ticket purchased for €10 which will redeem €20 in one week?
(c) A security purchased at its value of £1000 which pays £100 in cash next year and whose value is thought to decrease by 5% after this payment?

Exercise 2: NPV and IRR

Miss Léclair offers an investment project with the following cash flows:

t (years)	2	4
Cash flow (% of invested amount)	−10	+150

1. Calculate the NPV of this investment using a 5% and a 15% annual discount rate. Comment on the difference.
2. Calculate the IRR.
3. What do you think of this investment?

Exercise 3: expected return

Mr Smith offers an investment project with the following cash flows:

Date	today	in 6 months	in 1 year	in 2 years and 3 months
Cash flow (m$)	−10	−50	+20	+60

1. What is the maximum price you would be willing to pay for this project knowing that the reference interest rate of the Federal Reserve is 4% per year?
2. Where does Mr Smith estimate your expected return?

Exercise 4*: perpetuity, dividends and stock value

1. Determine the present value of an investment called perpetuity which pays a constant annual cash flow C for ever as a function of the discount rate r. What is the IRR of a perpetuity bought at $100 which pays $5 every year?

2. At the annual stockholders' meeting of Sky Inc., a distribution of €3 dividend per share was voted. The CEO also announced that he was committed to a dividend growth rate of 1.5% every year. Calculate the theoretical value of Sky Inc.'s stock using a 4% annual discount rate.

Exercise 5: return and inflation

Determine the internal rate of return for a real-estate investment in a Parisian apartment bought for €425 000 and rented at €1500 per month for a 20-year period, then resold at its original sale price:

(a) Without taking inflation into account.
(b) Assuming a 2.5% annualized inflation rate (monthly rent and resale price).

Exercise 6: announcement effect

Today is 31 December 2005. The stock price of company M is €150. Analysts predict the following earnings per share (EPS) for M over the next 5 years:

2005	2006	2007	2008	2009	2010
20	40	47	55	15	12

Analysts also estimate that EPS after 2010 will be negligible.

1. What is company M's PER for 2005?
2. What is the stock value of M to an investor whose expected return is 10% per year?
3. What is the market's expected return for company M?
4. At a press conference, the managers of M announce a project that will cut 2006 earnings per share by €5 due to initial costs but will increase profits by 10% from 2008 onwards. Could you quantify the reaction of the market to this announcement?

Solutions

Exercise 1: rate and time of return

(a) $r^{[1.5]} = \dfrac{400 - 350}{350} \approx 14.29\% \to r^{[1]} = (1 + r^{[1.5]})^{\frac{1}{1.5}} - 1 \approx 9.31\%$.
TOR $= 1/9.31\% \approx 10.74$ years.

(b) $r^{[7/360]} = \dfrac{20 - 10}{10} = 100\% \to r^{[1]} = (1 + r^{[7/360]})^{\frac{360}{7}} - 1 \approx 3 \times 10^{17}\%$.
TOR ≈ 0.

(c) $r^{[1]} = \dfrac{100 + 950 - 1000}{1000} = 5\%$. TOR $= 20$ years.

Exercise 2: NPV and IRR

1. NPV with 5% and 15% discount rates:

$$NPV(5\%) = -C_0 + \dfrac{-0.1 \times C_0}{1.05^2} + \dfrac{1.5 \times C_0}{1.05^4} \approx 14.33\% \times C_0 > 0$$

$$NPV(15\%) = -C_0 + \dfrac{-0.1 \times C_0}{1.15^2} + \dfrac{1.5 \times C_0}{1.15^4} \approx -21.80\% \times C_0 < 0$$

Using a moderate expected return of 5% the investment looks tempting. Using a high expected return of 15% it is exactly the opposite. Thus, the indifference point which makes NPV zero (alias IRR) is to be found in the range 5–15%.

2. The IRR is the discount rate r^* such that $NPV(r) = 0$:

$$-C_0 + \dfrac{-0.1 \times C_0}{(1+r)^2} + \dfrac{1.5 \times C_0}{(1+r)^4} = 0$$

or: $(1+r)^4 + 0.1 \times (1+r)^2 - 1.5 = 0$

Introducing $x = (1+r)^2$ we obtain a second-order polynomial equation whose positive solution is:

$$x^* = \dfrac{-0.1 + \sqrt{0.1^2 + 4 \times 1.5}}{2} = 1.1758 \to r^* = 8.43\%$$

3. An 8.43% IRR is quite attractive. However, achieving this return relies entirely on the last cash flow of 150% in 4 years: the investor is thus making a risky bet.

Exercise 3: expected return

1. Using a 4% minimum expected return, the present value of the project is:

$$PV(4\%) = -10 - \dfrac{50}{1.04^{0.5}} + \dfrac{20}{1.04} + \dfrac{50}{1.04^{2.25}} \approx 5.98$$

Thus a rational investor would not pay more than $5 980 000 for this project.

2. Mr Smith estimates our expected return to be around the project's IRR:

$$-10 - \frac{50}{(1+r)^{0.5}} + \frac{20}{1+r} + \frac{50}{(1+r)^{2.25}} = 0$$

Using a financial calculator or a spreadsheet, we find: $r^* \approx 11.13\%$:

Exercise 4*: perpetuity, dividend and stock value

1. The present value on an investment paying a constant annual cash flow C ad infinitum is:

$$PV = \sum_{i=1}^{+\infty} \frac{C}{(1+r)^i} = \frac{C}{1+r} \times \frac{1}{1 - \frac{1}{1+r}} = \frac{C}{r}$$

(Remember that $\sum_{i=0}^{+\infty} q^i = \frac{1}{1-q}$ for all real q such that $|q| < 1$.)

Using $C = 5$ and $C_0 = 100$, we can calculate the IRR:

$$-100 + \frac{5}{r} = 0 \rightarrow r^* = 5\%$$

2. Stocks are securities which pay dividends every year. If the dividend today is €3 and future dividends increase by 1.5% per year, the table of dividend flow is:

t (years)	0	1	2	...	i	...
Cash flow (€)	+3	+3.045	+3.091	...	$3 \times (1 + 1.5\%)^i$	...

Using a 4% discount rate, the present value is:

$$PV = 3 + \sum_{i=1}^{+\infty} \frac{3 \times 1.015^i}{1.04^i}$$

$$= 3 \times \sum_{i=0}^{+\infty} \left(\frac{1.015}{1.04}\right)^i$$

$$= 3 \times \frac{1}{1 - \frac{1.015}{1.04}}$$

$$= €124.80$$

Exercise 5: return and inflation

(a) The cash flow table for this real-estate investment without taking inflation into account is:

t (years)	0	1/12	...	239/12	20
Cash flow (€)	−425 000	1500	...	1500	426 500

The IRR is the solution r^* to the equation:

$$-425\,000 + \sum_{i=1}^{240} \frac{1500}{(1+r)^{\frac{i}{12}}} + \frac{425\,000}{(1+r)^{20}} = 0$$

Substituting $x = \left(\frac{1}{1+r}\right)^{\frac{1}{12}}$ and $\sum_{i=1}^{240} x^i = x\left(\frac{1-x^{240}}{1-x}\right)$, we can write:

$$-425\,000\,(1 - x^{240}) + 1500x\,\frac{1-x^{240}}{1-x} = 0$$

Dividing both sides by $(1 - x^{240})$ and rearranging terms then yields:

$$\frac{x}{1-x} = \frac{425\,000}{1500} \rightarrow x = \frac{425\,000}{426\,500} \approx 0.9965 \rightarrow r^* \approx 4.32\%$$

(b) Taking a 2.5% annual inflation into account, the IRR equation becomes:

$$-425\,000 + 1500 \sum_{i=1}^{240} \left(\frac{1+2.5\%}{1+r}\right)^{\frac{i}{12}} + 425\,000 \left(\frac{1+2.5\%}{1+r}\right)^{20} = 0$$

Substituting $R = \frac{1+r}{1+2.5\%} - 1$, we find again the same equation as in (a), whose solution is $R^* \approx 4.32\%$. Thus, the IRR is $r^* = (1 + 4.32\%) \times (1 + 2.5\%) - 1 \approx 6.93\%$, which is approximately equal to the ex-inflation IRR plus 2.5%.

Exercise 6: announcement effect

1. PER for 2005:

$$PER_{2005} = \frac{150}{20} = 7.5$$

In other words, the stock price of M is equal to 7.5 times the earnings in 2005.

2. Stock value to an investor with a 10% expected return:

$$PV = \frac{40}{1.1} + \frac{47}{1.1^2} + \frac{55}{1.1^3} + \frac{15}{1.1^4} + \frac{12}{1.1^5} = €134.23$$

This value is lower than the stock price of €150: our investor would not invest in M.

3. The market's expected return for company M is equal to the IRR:

$$-150 + \frac{40}{1+r} + \frac{47}{(1+r)^2} + \frac{55}{(1+r)^3} + \frac{15}{(1+r)^4} + \frac{12}{(1+r)^5} = 0$$

Using a financial calculator or a spreadsheet we find: $r^* = 5\%$.

4. Taking into account the announcement and the expected return of the market, we can estimate the post-announcement value of M to be:

$$PV = \frac{35}{1.05} + \frac{47}{1.05^2} + \frac{60.5}{1.05^3} + \frac{16.5}{1.05^4} + \frac{13.2}{1.05^5} = €152.14$$

The stock price of M should thus increase by €2.14.

3 Bonds

3.1 Financial markets

3.1.1 Securities and portfolios

A **financial security** is a contract in which two or more parties exchange cash flows. As this book only deals with quantitative finance, our focus here will be on the last part of this definition: cash flows.

Examples

- A company's stock is a financial security whose cash flows are dividends.
- A fixed interest rate loan is a financial security whose cash flows are the interest and principal repayments.

A **portfolio** is a combination of n financial securities. A portfolio cash flow at time t is the sum of the securities' cash flows at time t weighted by their quantities:

Portfolio with 10 000 units of security A and 5000 units of security B

Security	Quantity	Time (years)	$t = 1$	$t = 2$
A	10 000	Cash flows A (¥)	100	200
B	5000	Cash flows B (¥)	—	50
Portfolio P	1	Cash flows P (¥)	1 000 000	2 250 000

3.1.2 Value and price

The **value** of a security is a positive or negative amount which represents the anticipated change in wealth of its owner. There are several valuation methods which will yield different values for the same security except in trivial cases. When there is no uncertainty on the cash flows, the standard valuation method is the present value introduced in Chapter 2.

Example. The 'gross value' of portfolio P in the previous example is ¥3 250 000 (the sum of all its cash flows). Its present value is ¥3 195 765 using a 1% discount rate and ¥3 041 790 with 4%.

The **price** of a security is the amount of money agreed upon by two parties to trade that security. Typically the buyer pays the price to the seller but it may happen that the seller must pay the buyer in order to get rid of a security with negative value. Note that the buyer and seller may not agree on 'the' value of the security; and even if they do, nothing forces them to set the price at such value.

Example. The owner of portfolio P believes that its value is ¥3 195 765 (present value using a 1% discount rate). However, all potential buyers believe that the value is ¥3 041 790 (present value using a 4% discount rate). Pressed to sell the portfolio by her manager, she arranges an auction among buyers. The best quote she receives is ¥3 000 000 and she decides to trade at that price.

3.1.3 Financial markets

Financial markets are marketplaces (either physical or virtual) where one can buy and sell financial securities. Investors are usually authorized to **short sell** securities they do not own.[1] In this way, market participants can buy and sell securities at any time according to their views and the law of supply and demand is continuously verified. Note that **in the case of short selling the seller must pay all the security cash flows to the buyer.**

Example. After a corporate announcement, investor S believes that the stock price of Bust Inc. will go down but she does not own it. There is a potential buyer B in the market showing a price which is 5% lower than the last traded price. S decides to short sell the stock to B. Two months later Bust Inc. pays a dividend of 20¢ per share to its stockholders. Since S is short of the stock she must pay the dividend to B.

3.1.4 Arbitrage

An **arbitrage opportunity** is a strategy for buying and selling securities which has no cost and yields positive profits with absolute certainty (either today or at a future date).

---

[1] In practice, a market agent who is short, say 1000 stocks, must immediately borrow them back on a short-term rolling basis from other market agents until he has repurchased the entire lot. This borrowing mechanism has a cost reflected in a lower interest rate paid by the security lender.

Example. Suppose there are two securities on the market which are both priced at €99: security A, paying off €100 in 6 months, and security B, paying off €110 in 6 months. In such a case, infinite amounts of money can be made by buying security B and selling security A:

| | Cash flows | |
Transaction	Today	6 months later
Sell A	+€99	−€100
Buy B	−€99	+€110
TOTAL	0 (no cost)	+€10 (positive profit)

Sadly, if unsurprisingly, arbitrage opportunities are extremely uncommon. This is why the **absence of arbitrage opportunities** is always assumed in financial theory. At any rate, if there is an arbitrage opportunity on the market it will only exist for a very short period of time: in the above example all rational investors would buy B and sell A, thus moving the price of A down and that of B up until the arbitrage disappears.

The absence of arbitrage assumption will allow us to derive rules for pricing certain securities.

3.1.5 Price of a portfolio

The distinction between value and price applies to portfolios of securities as well. However, under the assumptions of absence of arbitrage and infinite liquidity,[2] the **arbitrage price** of a portfolio of securities is simply the sum of each security's price multiplied by its respective quantity. This elementary principle is sometimes called the '**law of one price**'.

Example. Consider a portfolio P of two securities A and B with prices of €100 and €50 respectively and the following cash flows:

Security	Quantity	Unit price (€)	Time (years)	$t=1$	$t=2$
A	2	100	Cash flows A (€)	10	110
B	1	50	Cash flows B (€)	30	30
Portfolio P	1	250	Cash flows P (€)	50	250

---

[2] A security is liquid if it can be purchased and sold in large quantities without affecting its price. In this book we always use the hypothesis of infinite liquidity, in other words we assume that we can buy and sell any given security in any desired quantity.

The arbitrage price of P is €250. The proof is as follows:

- Suppose that P has a market price $X > 250$. In this case investors could carry out an arbitrage strategy by short selling P at price X and buying 2 units of A and 1 unit of B for €250. Such a strategy would result in a profit of $X - 250 > 0$ today without entailing any cost in the future:

Transaction	$t = 0$	$t = 1$	$t = 2$
Sell P	$+X$	-50	-250
Buy 2A	-200	$+20$	$+220$
Buy B	-50	$+30$	$+30$
TOTAL	$X - 250 > 0$	0	0

- Conversely, if we suppose that the market price of P is $X < 250$, investors could also make an arbitrage by buying P, short selling 2 units of A and 1 unit of B.
- Thus, in the absence of arbitrage opportunities, the market price of P must be €250, or the weighted sum of the prices of A and B.

3.2 Bonds

3.2.1 Treasury bonds

Bonds are debt securities. When dealing with debt the issue of capacity for repayment naturally arises. For this reason, Mr Smith will always prefer to lend money to the government rather than his aunt Claudine who is 85 years old and has a bad cough. In the unfortunate event of Claudine's death (in financial language one would say 'In the event of Claudine *defaulting*'), Mr Smith has no guarantee of recovering his money; and while the government can also default, the probability of this happening is incomparably lower.

In this book we will only consider bonds issued by the government and assume that they are default-free. We may now define a bond using just three parameters:

- A **face value** N (also called **par amount, principal amount** or sometimes **nominal amount**): the amount borrowed.
- A **maturity date** T: the date when the principal must be repaid.
- A series of **coupons** $C_{t_1}, C_{t_2}, \ldots, C_T$: interest amounts paid by the borrower at dates $t_1, t_2, \ldots, T$.

Typically all the coupons are equal and given as a percentage of the face value. When the face value N is not specified it is conventionally set at 100.

Cash flows of a bond				Example: UK Gilt Bond 8% 25 September 2009			
Time	t_1	t_2 ...	T	Date	25 Sep 06	25 Sep 07	25 Sep 08	25 Sep 09
Cash flow	C_{t_1}	C_{t_2} ...	$N + C_T$	Cash flow (£)	+8	+8	+8	+108

3.2.2 Zero-coupon bonds

Zero-coupon bonds, also called **zero-coupons,** are bonds which pay no coupon: only the principal is repaid at maturity. Short-terms bonds (whose maturity is shorter than 1 year) are usually zero-coupon bonds when issued.

3.2.3 Bond markets

Bonds are issued by a government's treasury department through auctions on the **primary market** at a price usually close to the par amount N. Once issued they are traded on the **secondary market** at a fluctuating price. At each coupon date (typically every anniversary date of the issue date) coupons are 'detached' and bondholders receive the coupon amount from the issuer. At maturity, bondholders surrender their securities to the issuer who repays the par amount N.

3.3 Yield

Bond analysis essentially deals with two problems:

1. Comparing two bonds given their prices (relative value analysis).
2. Valuing a bond without knowing its price (fundamental analysis).

The classical approach, still commonly used in practice, relies on the concept of **yield to maturity**.

3.3.1 Yield to maturity

Given the price of a bond one can calculate its internal rate of return (see Chapter 2) which is called **yield to maturity** or simply **yield**. A bond's yield y is thus the solution to the equation:

$$P = \frac{C_{t_1}}{(1+y)^{t_1}} + \frac{C_{t_2}}{(1+y)^{t_2}} + \cdots + \frac{N + C_T}{(1+y)^T}$$

Note that when the yield y increases the price P must decrease: '**when rates go up, prices go down**'.

Example. On the European market a 5-year bond with an annual coupon of 5% is quoted at €99 and a 3-year bond with an annual coupon of 3% is at €95. Even though the 5-year bond is more expensive, its yield (5.23%) is higher than that of the 3-year bond (4.83%). One can indeed verify that:

$$\frac{5}{1.0523} + \frac{5}{1.0523^2} + \frac{5}{1.0523^3} + \frac{5}{1.0523^4} + \frac{105}{1.0523^5} = €99$$

and:

$$\frac{3}{1.0483} + \frac{3}{1.0483^2} + \frac{103}{1.0483^3} = €95$$

3.3.2 Yield curve

Investors tend to prefer short maturity bonds for the following two reasons.

1. **Lower interest rate risk**: the yield of a bond will match the investor's actual wealth accrual only if (a) the investor is able to reinvest each detached coupon at the same yield and (b) the investor holds the bond until maturity. This could happen if the central bank did not change the interest rate and inflation remained low, in which case bond yields would remain stable over time. Since the central bank *does* change the interest rate to adjust to economic conditions, the price and yield of bonds fluctuate and an investor would normally prefer short-term bonds to avoid being locked up until maturity with say a 4% yield when the short-term interest rate is suddenly at e.g. 8%.
2. **Lower default risk**: even though governments have a very low default risk, the probability of default on a specific bond is still higher for long maturities (e.g. 30 years) than for short maturities.

Issuers, on the other hand, tend to prefer long maturities in order to postpone their debt repayments. This divergence between demand (investors) and supply (issuers) normally results in long-term maturity yields being higher than short-term ones. In other words the **yield curve** (also called the **interest rate term structure**, that is the structure of rates as a function of maturity or *term*), usually slopes upward.

In practice there are three typical shapes of the yield curve.

- **Flat**: $y \equiv r$ (where r is constant). This is a theoretical case in which all rates are assumed to be the same regardless of maturity.
- **Upward sloping**: this is the most common case, the longer the maturity the higher the interest rate and default risks for which the market demands a higher yield.
- **Downward sloping**: this is the case when the market expects rates to decrease in the future.

Yield

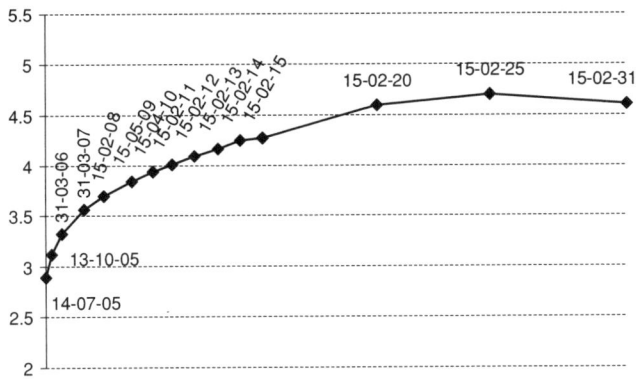

Maturity	Yield (%)	Maturity	Yield (%)	Maturity	Yield (%)
14-07-05	2.8989	15-05-09	3.8451	15-02-14	4.25
13-10-05	3.1287	15-04-10	3.9303	15-02-15	4.2744
31-03-06	3.3274	15-02-11	4.0035	15-02-20	4.5957
31-03-07	3.5647	15-02-12	4.0852	15-02-25	4.7015
15-02-08	3.697	15-02-13	4.1647	15-02-31	4.6083

Yield curve of US government bonds as of 19 April 2005

3.3.3 Approximate valuation

Using the yield curve one can compute the approximate value $\tilde{V}$ of a bond with maturity T whose price is unknown. To do this:

1. Linearly interpolate the yields of the two bonds with closest maturities:

$$\tilde{y} = y_1 + \frac{y_2 - y_1}{T_2 - T_1}(T - T_1)$$

2. Use the interpolated yield to compute the present value of the bond:

$$\tilde{V} = \frac{C_{t_1}}{(1+\tilde{y})^{t_1}} + \frac{C_{t_2}}{(1+\tilde{y})^{t_2}} + \cdots + \frac{N + C_T}{(1+\tilde{y})^T}$$

Example. On the European bond market the yield of a 5-year bond with an annual coupon of 5% is 5.23% and the yield of a 3-year bond with an annual coupon of 3% is 4.83%. The interpolated 4-year yield is thus:

$$\tilde{y} = \frac{4.83\% + 5.23\%}{2} = 5.03\%$$

and the approximate value of a 4-year bond with an annual coupon of 7% is:

$$\tilde{V} = \frac{7}{1.0503} + \frac{7}{(1.0503)^2} + \frac{7}{(1.0503)^3} + \frac{107}{(1.0503)^4} \approx €106.98$$

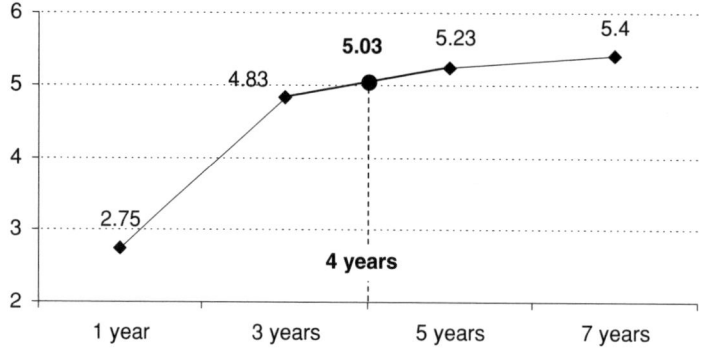

3.4 Zero-coupon yield curve; arbitrage price

3.4.1 Yield to maturity: limits

The concept of yield to maturity has only one merit: it induces gullible investors to think that bond analysis is easy. In the following example we show that reality is a bit more complex.

Consider two bonds A and B maturing in 2 years with a face value of $1000. Bond A pays a $100 coupon every year and bond B pays only one coupon of $1000 after 1 year. The cash flow table is as follows:

t	1	2
A	100	1100
B	1000	1000

Suppose that bond A is priced today at $1000 and bond B at $1735 – which bond should we recommend buying?

The classical approach tells us to compute and compare yields. However in this case the two bonds have the same yield: $y_A = y_B = 10\%$. Does this mean that we should be indifferent between buying A or B?

Zero-coupon yield curve; arbitrage price

To help answer this question, suppose that a better-informed investor also looks at bond C which matures in 1 year, has no coupon, a face value of $100 and is priced at $92. While gullible investors ponder over the pros and cons of investing in A or B, such a better-informed investor makes infinite amounts of money by implementing the following arbitrage strategy:

		Cash flows	
Transaction	$t=0$	$t=1$	$t=2$
Buy B	−1735	+1000	+1000
Sell $\frac{10}{11}$ A	+909.09	−90.91	−1000
Sell 9C	+828	−900	—
TOTAL	+2.09	+9.09	—

This example quickly demonstrates why there is more to bond analysis than computing a yield to maturity. In fact, arbitrage-free bond analysis relies on the concept of **zero-coupon yield**.

3.4.2 Zero-rate curve

The **zero-rate curve** is the arbitrage-free version of the yield curve. In mature markets such as US or French government bonds, the zero-rate curve is directly observable as zero-coupon bonds known as 'strips' are quoted on the market. In other markets it is inferred from standard bond prices through the bootstrapping method which we introduce in Section 3.4.4.

The **zero-rate** at maturity T is the yield of a zero-coupon bond which matures at time T:

$$z(T) = \left(\frac{N}{p(T)}\right)^{\frac{1}{T}} - 1$$

where N is the face value and $p(T)$ the price of the zero-coupon.

Examples

- If the 4-year zero-coupon bond has a price of $90, then the 4-year zero-rate is:[3]

$$z(4) = \left(\frac{100}{90}\right)^{1/4} - 1 = 2.67\%$$

- On the US bond market the zero-rate curve is directly observable:

---

[3] Recall that when the face value is not specified it is conventionally set at 100.

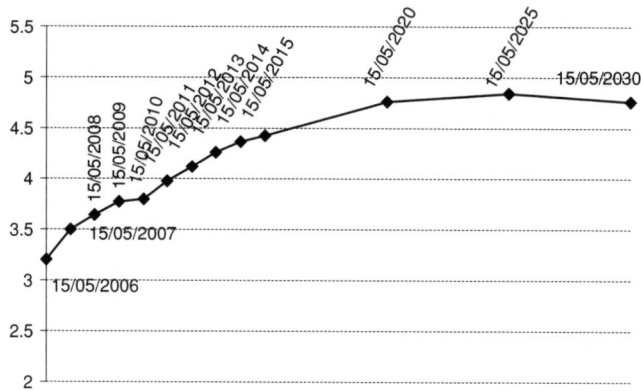

Maturity	Yield (%)	Maturity	Yield (%)	Maturity	Yield (%)
15-05-06	3.20	15-05-11	3.97	15-05-20	4.76
15-05-07	3.50	15-05-12	4.12	15-05-25	4.80
15-05-08	3.64	15-05-13	4.26	15-05-30	4.76
15-05-09	3.77	15-05-14	4.36		
15-05-10	3.79	15-05-15	4.42		

Zero-rate curve of US government bonds as of 19 April 2005

3.4.3 Arbitrage price

Given a zero-rate curve $z(t)$ we can determine the **arbitrage price** of any bond with face value N, maturity T and coupons $C_{t_1}, C_{t_2}, \ldots, C_T$ paid at dates $t_1, t_2, \ldots, T$:

$$P = \frac{C_{t_1}}{(1+z(t_1))^{t_1}} + \frac{C_{t_2}}{(1+z(t_2))^{t_2}} + \cdots + \frac{N + C_T}{(1+z(T))^T}$$

Example. Using the above zero-rate curve of US government bonds, we can calculate that the arbitrage price of a 5-year bond with 5% coupons is:

$$P = \frac{5}{1.032} + \frac{5}{1.035^2} + \frac{5}{1.0364^3} + \frac{5}{1.0377^4} + \frac{105}{1.0379^5} \approx €105.49$$

This formula is the generalization of the present value formula given in Chapter 2 and extends to any **fixed income security**[4] paying a series of n cash flows (F_t)

---

[4] A fixed income security is any financial security whose cash flows are known in advance. A standard bond with fixed coupons is a fixed income security. A stock is not a fixed income security as it pays dividends which vary with the company's profits.

Zero-coupon yield curve; arbitrage price

at future dates $t_1, t_2, \ldots, t_n$:

$$P = \sum_{i=1}^{n} \frac{F_{t_i}}{(1+z(t_i))^{t_i}}$$

The proof is based on a decomposition of the cash flows into a portfolio of zero-coupons (see Exercise 9).

3.4.4 Zero-rate calculation by inference

As mentioned in Section 3.4.2, we can infer the zero rates from standard bond prices if we assume that there is no arbitrage opportunity on the bond market. To do so merely requires solving a linear system, with the provision that all bond cash flow dates must coincide.[5] The methodology is often known as 'bootstrapping' – we illustrate it below with an example.

Consider three bonds A, B, C with the following cash flows:

Bond	Price at $t=0$	Cash flow at $t=1$	Cash flow at $t=2$	Cash flow at $t=3$
A	111.41	10	110	—
B	102.82	5	5	105
C	88.90	—	—	100

Find the zero-rates $z(1), z(2), z(3)$ which satisfy:

$$\begin{cases} \dfrac{10}{1+z(1)} + \dfrac{110}{(1+z(2))^2} = 111.41 \\ \dfrac{5}{1+z(1)} + \dfrac{5}{(1+z(2))^2} + \dfrac{105}{(1+z(3))^3} = 102.82 \\ \dfrac{100}{(1+z(3))^3} = 88.90 \end{cases}$$

Introducing the notation $x_i = \frac{1}{(1+z(i))^i}$ we see that this problem is equivalent to solving the linear system of equations:

$$\begin{cases} 10x_1 + 110x_2 = 111.41 \\ 5x_1 + 5x_2 + 105x_3 = 102.82 \\ 100x_3 = 88.90 \end{cases}$$

---

[5] In practice a variety of fixed income securities are used to determine the zero curve and their dates rarely match. A linear interpolation between the closest dates is commonly used to circumvent this problem.

whose solution is:

$$\begin{cases} x_1 = 0.9704 \\ x_2 = 0.9246 \\ x_3 = 0.8890 \end{cases}$$

Reverting to z through the definition of x we obtain the zero rates:

$$\begin{cases} z(1) = \dfrac{1}{x_1} - 1 = 3.05\% \\ z(2) = \left(\dfrac{1}{x_2}\right)^{1/2} - 1 = 4\% \\ z(3) = \left(\dfrac{1}{x_3}\right)^{1/3} - 1 = 4\% \end{cases}$$

Note that x_1, x_2, x_3, which are called **discount factors**, are the respective prices of the 1-year, 2-year and 3-year zero-coupons with a face value of 1.

Further reading

Fabozzi, F.J. (2005) *The Handbook of Fixed Income Securities*, 7th edn. McGraw-Hill Trade, New York.

Hull, J.C. (2005) *Options, Futures and Other Derivatives*, 6th edn. Prentice Hall, Englewood Cliffs, NJ.

Exercises

Exercise 1: yield

Compute the annual yield of the following bonds:

(a) Bond A – maturity: 30 years, annual coupon: 5%, price: €100.
(b) Bond B – maturity: 2 years, annual coupon: 6%, price: £106.
(c) Bond C – maturity: 1 year, zero-coupon, price: $95.
(d) Bond D – maturity: 13 years, face value: $1000, semi-annual coupon: $50, price: $1000.

Exercise 2: yield curve

Interpret the following yield curve:

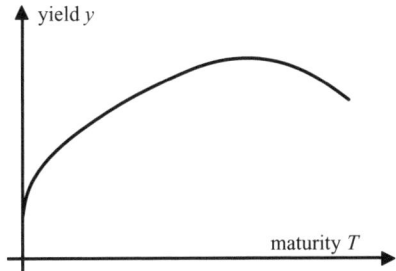

Exercise 3: yield to maturity and coupon rate

'On 1 January 2006 the 3-year yield is 4%. I can choose between a bond with maturity date of 15 November 2008 and a coupon of 3% and another bond with maturity date of 15 February 2009 and a coupon of 4.5%. I should buy the second one because its coupon rate is higher than the 4% market yield.' Comment on this argument.

Exercise 4: approximate valuation

Using the yield curve in Section 3.3.2, estimate the value of a bond with 5% coupon and maturity date of 15 August 2022. The next coupon payment is in 116 days and then annually for the following 17 coupon payments.

Exercise 5: arbitrage

On a market investors can buy and sell:

- Bond A – maturity: 1 year, zero-coupon, face value: £100, price: £90.

- Bond B – maturity: 2 years, face value: £1000, annual coupon: £50, price: £945.
- Bond C – maturity: 2 years, face value: £1000, annual coupon: 10%, price: £990.

Can you find an arbitrage strategy that has no cost today and will make a profit in 2 years?

Exercise 6: dividend announcement

Tankai Corp. is a high-technology company whose stock presently trades at ¥10 000 in Tokyo. At the annual stockholders' meeting, a dividend distribution of ¥400 per share was voted for the first time in the company's history. The dividend will be paid the following day to every owner of the stock at today's close of market, which will occur in 5 minutes. Can you predict the opening stock price of Tankai Corp. the following day? Choose one of the following scenarios and justify your decision:

(a) 4% increase;
(b) 4% decrease;
(c) unchanged;
(d) the market reaction is unpredictable.

Exercise 7: arbitrage price

Using the zero-rate curve in Section 3.4.2, calculate the arbitrage price of a 10-year bond with $500 face value and 6% coupon. *Assume that today is 15 May 2005.*

Exercise 8: zero-rate curve

On the market investors can buy and sell:

- Bond A – maturity: 1 year, zero-coupon, price: €97.
- Bond B – maturity: 2 years, constant annual coupon, yield: 4%, price: €100.
- Bond C – maturity: 3 years, annual coupon: 4%, price: €95.

Calculate the 1-, 2-, 3-year zero rates.

Exercise 9*: arbitrage price formula

Let A be a financial security that pays three annual cash flows F_1, F_2, F_3, and let X, Y, Z be the 1-, 2-, 3-year zero-coupon bonds with face value 1 and prices of P_X, P_Y, P_Z respectively.

1. Show that the arbitrage price of A is:

$$P = P_X F_1 + P_Y F_2 + P_Z F_3$$

2. Compare P with the arbitrage price formula in Section 3.4.3.

Exercises

Problem 1: price sensitivity, convexity

It is recommended to use a spreadsheet to solve this problem and to carry out calculations to the third decimal place.

The US zero-rate curve has the following shape:

Maturity (year)	1	2	3	4	5	6	7
Zero-rate	7.5%	8%	8.25%	8.25%	8%	8%	7.75%

Consider the following three bonds with face value $100:

Bond	Maturity	Annual coupon
X	4	8%
Y	7	9%
Z	5	—

1. Calculate the arbitrage price of each bond.
2. The price sensitivity of a bond (also known as DV01: dollar value of one basis point) is defined by its change in price when rates go up 1 basis point (i.e. a +0.01% parallel shift of the entire zero-rate curve). Compute the price sensitivity of each bond.
3. Calculate the price of each bond in the following scenarios:
   (a) 10 basis point rate increase (+0.10%);
   (b) 1 point rate increase (+1%).
4. Compare your results in question 3 to:
   (a) 10 times the price sensitivity;
   (b) 100 times the price sensitivity.
   Is price sensitivity a good indicator of the interest rate risk that bonds are exposed to?

5*. Suppose that the zero-rate curve is flat at rate r. Using a second-order Taylor expansion around r, identify a secondary indicator for the interest rate risk exposure of a bond.

Problem 2: zero-rate curve and expectations

The short-term zero-rate curve in the euro zone has the following shape:

Maturity	1 day	1 week	2 weeks	1 month	2 months
Zero-rate	2.78%	2.77%	2.75%	2.92%	3.08%

The reference rate of the European Central Bank (ECB) is 2.75% at present. This is the rate at which the main private banks can borrow funds from the ECB for 2 weeks. The Board of Governors of the ECB will meet in 2 weeks and potentially decide on a new rate R.

1. Simply looking at the yield curve and without making any calculation can you guess if the market expects the ECB to:
   (a) Lower the reference rate by 25 bps (i.e. $R = 2.5\%$)?
   (b) Leave the reference rate unchanged (i.e. $R = 2.75\%$)?
   (c) Raise the reference rate by 25 bps (i.e. $R = 3\%$)?
   (d) Raise the reference rate by 50 bps (i.e. $R = 3.25\%$)?
   (e) Any other scenario?
2. Lezard Brothers, a reputed investment bank, has a €100m treasury need for the coming month. Find two ways to cover this need and give the cost of each method, one of which involves R.
3. How does your answer to question 2 support or invalidate your answer to question 1?
4. Fadeberg News, a financial news agency, recently published the following survey of the chief economists of the top 30 investment banks regarding the ECB decision:

Rate R	Number of predictions
25 basis point drop	0
Unchanged	3
25 basis point hike	21
50 basis point hike	6

Having read this survey, Bernard Bull, a trader at Lezard Brothers, thinks that the 1-month zero-rate at 2.92% is overvalued and comes to you, the head of trading at Lezard Brothers, with the following strategy:

(i) Invest €100m at 2.92% for 1 month.
(ii) Borrow €100m at 2.75% for 2 weeks.
(iii) In 2 weeks, roll over and borrow €100m at rate R for 2 weeks.

(a) Bernard presents this strategy as an 'outstanding arbitrage opportunity'. What do you think?
(b) Calculate the profit or loss of this strategy for each of the scenarios mentioned in the survey.
(c) Do you greenlight Bernard's proposal? *There is no unique answer to this question.*

Solutions

Exercise 1: yield

(a) 5% (the yield of a bond with a price of 100 is always equal to the coupon).
(b) 2.87%.
The yield is the solution y^* to the equation:

$$-106 + \frac{6}{1+y} + \frac{106}{(1+y)^2} = 0$$

Substituting $x = \frac{1}{1+y}$, we obtain a familiar quadratic equation:

$$106x^2 + 6x - 106 = 0$$

which gives:

$$x = \frac{-6 \pm \sqrt{6^2 + 4 \times 106^2}}{2 \times 106} \rightarrow x^* \approx 0.9721 \rightarrow y^* \approx 2.87\%$$

(c) $z(1) = \frac{100}{95} - 1 \approx 5.26\%$.
(d) 10.25% (the yield of a bond with a price of 100 is always equal to the coupon which is 5% per semester; the annualized yield is thus $(1 + 5\%)^2 - 1 = 10.25\%$).

Exercise 2: yield curve

This curve is a hybrid of the upward and downward sloping cases. This kind of curve can be observed when the market expects rates to decrease in the medium term, but not immediately.

Exercise 3: yield to maturity and coupon rate

This argument confuses yield to maturity with coupon rate. The coupon rate is fixed when the bond is issued. The bond yield, on the other hand, fluctuates until maturity; it corresponds to the coupon rate of a newly issued bond that matures at the same time as the original bond. Only the yield can help decide whether a bond is 'cheap' or 'rich' as it takes into consideration both the price and the coupon rate.

In this example the 3-year yield is 4%. The two bonds (15 November 2008 and 15 February 2009) both have maturities close to 3 years so their yield should be close to 4% regardless of the coupon rate. However, we cannot conclude anything without knowing the exact yield of the bonds.

Exercise 4: approximate valuation

Using the yield curve in Section 3.3.2, we find the yield of the bonds with closest maturity to 15 August 2022:

Maturity	Yield (%)
15-02-20	4.5957
15-02-25	4.7015

Since 15 August 2022 is half-way between these two maturities, the interpolated yield is simply:

$$\tilde{y} = \frac{4.5957\% + 4.7015\%}{2} \approx 4.65\%$$

We can thus estimate the value of the bond to be:

$$\tilde{V} = \frac{5}{1.0465^{\frac{116}{360}}} + \frac{5}{1.0465^{1+\frac{116}{360}}} + \cdots + \frac{105}{1.0465^{17+\frac{116}{360}}} \approx 107.48$$

Exercise 5: arbitrage

Example of an arbitrage strategy that has no cost today and makes a profit in 2 years:

Bond		Cash flows	
	$t=0$	$t=1$	$t=2$
A	90	100	—
B	945	50	1050
C	990	100	1100
Buy 2C, sell 2B and 1A	0	0	100 > 0

Exercise 6: dividend announcement

The stock price of Tankai Corp. should drop by 4% to ¥9600, otherwise there would be an arbitrage opportunity. Suppose that the stock price S is above ¥9600 the following day; we can then implement the following arbitrage strategy:

Solutions

Transaction	Cash flow
Buy one stock just before close of market	−¥10 000
Collect the dividend	+¥400
Sell the stock at market opening the following day	+S
TOTAL	S − ¥9600 > 0

Similarly, if we assume $S < ¥9600$, we would have an arbitrage by reversing transactions and signs.

Exercise 7: arbitrage price

Arbitrage price of the bond:

$$P = \frac{30}{1.032} + \frac{30}{1.035^2} + \cdots + \frac{530}{1.0442^{10}} \approx \$567$$

Exercise 8: zero-rate curve

We want to find $z(1)$, $z(2)$, $z(3)$ that satisfy:

$$\begin{cases} \dfrac{100}{1+z(1)} = 97 \\ \dfrac{4}{1+z(1)} + \dfrac{104}{(1+z(2))^2} = 100 \\ \dfrac{4}{1+z(1)} + \dfrac{4}{(1+z(2))^2} + \dfrac{104}{(1+z(3))^3} = 95 \end{cases}$$

The classic approach is to substitute with $x_i = \dfrac{1}{(1+z(i))^i}$ in order to get a familiar linear system. However, here it is possible to solve these equations one after the other:

$$\begin{cases} \dfrac{100}{1+z(1)} = 97 \rightarrow z(1) = 3.09\% \\ \dfrac{4}{1+3.09\%} + \dfrac{104}{(1+z(2))^2} = 100 \rightarrow z(2) = 4.02\% \\ \dfrac{4}{1+3.09\%} + \dfrac{4}{(1+4.02\%)^2} + \dfrac{104}{(1+z(3))^3} = 95 \rightarrow z(3) = 5.96\% \end{cases}$$

Exercise 9*: arbitrage price formula

1. The cash flows of security A can be decomposed into a portfolio of X, Y, Z in quantities F_1, F_2, F_3 respectively. Under the assumptions of absence of

arbitrage opportunities and infinite liquidity, the arbitrage price of this portfolio is:

$$P = P_X F_1 + P_Y F_2 + P_Z F_3$$

2. If $z(1), z(2), z(3)$ denote the 1-, 2-, 3-year zero-rates respectively, the equation above can be rewritten as:

$$P = \frac{F_1}{(1+z(1))} + \frac{F_2}{(1+z(2))^2} + \frac{F_3}{(1+z(3))^3} = \sum_{t=1}^{3} \frac{F_t}{(1+z(t))^t}$$

This is the formula given in Section 3.4.3 when there are only three cash flows.

Problem 1: price sensitivity, convexity

1. Arbitrage prices of the bonds:

$$P_X = \frac{8}{1.075} + \frac{8}{1.08^2} + \frac{8}{1.0825^3} + \frac{108}{1.0825^4} = 99.260$$

$$P_Y = \frac{9}{1.075} + \frac{9}{1.08^2} + \frac{9}{1.0825^3} + \frac{9}{1.0825^4} + \frac{9}{1.085^5} + \frac{9}{1.086^6} + \frac{109}{1.0775^7} = 106.175$$

$$P_Z = \frac{100}{1.085^5} = 68.058$$

2. Price sensitivities of the bonds:

$$DV01_X = \frac{8}{1.0751} + \frac{8}{1.0801^2} + \frac{8}{1.0826^3} + \frac{108}{1.0826^4} - 99.260 = -0.033$$

$$DV01_Y = \frac{9}{1.0751} + \frac{9}{1.0801^2} + \cdots + \frac{109}{1.0776^7} - 106.175 = -0.055$$

$$DV01_Z = \frac{100}{1.0801^5} - 68.058 = -0.03$$

3. Bond prices in each scenario:
   (a) P_X goes down 32.7 cents from \$99.260 to \$98.933.
       P_Y goes down 54.4 cents from \$106.175 to \$105.631.
       P_Z goes down 31.4 cents from \$68.058 to \$67.744.
   (b) P_X drops \$3.206 from \$99.260 to \$96.054.
       P_Y drops \$5.277 from \$106.175 to \$100.898.
       P_Z drops \$3.065 from \$68.058 to \$64.993.
4. First-order comparison:
   (a) to 10-fold price sensitivity

Bond	DV01 × 10	Price change	Difference
X	−0.33	−0.327	0.003
Y	−0.55	−0.544	−0.006
Z	−0.3	−0.34	+0.004

Solutions

(b) to 100-fold price sensitivity

Bond	DV01 × 100	Price change	Difference
X	−3.3	−3.206	−0.094
Y	−5.5	−5.277	−0.223
Z	−3.0	−3.065	−0.035

Multiplying the price sensitivity by the basis point rate move will give a good approximation of the change in bond price when the move is small. However for large moves the approximation becomes less accurate and we notice that the actual change in price is lower than predicted by the $DV01$.

5*. When the zero-rate curve is flat at r, the price of a bond becomes a single variable function $P(r)$. A second-order Taylor expansion gives:

$$P(r+\delta) \underset{\delta \to 0}{\overset{(2)}{\approx}} P(r) + \delta \frac{\partial P}{\partial r}(r) + \frac{1}{2}\delta^2 \frac{\partial^2 P}{\partial r^2}(r)$$

For $\delta = 0.01\%$ we have:

$$DV01 = P(r+0.01\%) - P(r) \approx 0.01\% \times \frac{\partial P}{\partial r}(r) + \frac{1}{2}0.01\%^2 \frac{\partial^2 P}{\partial r^2}(r)$$

Since 0.01% is very close to 0, the second-order term is negligible and $DV01 \approx 0.01\% \times \frac{\partial P}{\partial r}(r)$, i.e.:

$$\frac{\partial P}{\partial r}(r) \approx DV01 \times 10\,000.$$

Thus, for a given parallel shift δ of the rate curve, the change in the bond price can be written:

$$P(r+\delta) - P(r) \underset{\delta \to 0}{\overset{(2)}{\approx}} 10\,000 \times \delta \times DV01 + \frac{1}{2}\delta^2 \frac{\partial^2 P}{\partial r^2}(r)$$

For example if $\delta = 1\%$:

$$P(r+1\%) - P(r) \approx 100 \times DV01 + \frac{1}{20\,000}\frac{\partial^2 P}{\partial r^2}(r)$$

This equation helps us to better understand the empirical finding in question 4 that $DV01$ is only an accurate indicator of the change in bond price for small rate moves. For large moves the second-order term will have an impact. This term, known as **bond convexity**, is therefore a natural complement to $DV01$ when measuring the sensitivity of a bond to interest rate risk.

Problem 2: yield curve and expectations

1. This question will trick most readers into the following 'common sense' argument: since the 2-week rate is 2.75% and the 1-month rate is 2.92% the market expects an increase of 2.92% − 2.75% = 0.17% to occur between 2 weeks and 1 month. Thus the majority of market participants must expect the ECB to raise the reference rate by 25 basis points.

   However this argument neglects the fact that the 2.92% rate also applies for the coming 2 weeks. Thus if the ECB only raised its reference rate to 3%, an investor would make profits by investing at 2.92% over the coming month, picking up 0.17% the first 2 weeks over the current reference rate of 2.75%, while only losing 0.08% the following 2 weeks when the reference rate is at 3%.

   If the market truly believed in a 25 basis point increase, most market participants would find this trade idea attractive, the demand for 1-month deposits would increase and push the 2.92% rate down to a less attractive level. As there is no mention of a market trend in the problem we must assume that the 2.92% rate is an equilibrium, which implies that the market expects R to increase by 25 to 50 basis points.

2. First method: Lezard Brothers borrows €100m for 1 month at 2.92%. Interest paid on this transaction would be:

$$100\,000\,000 \times (1 + 2.92\%)^{\frac{1}{12}} - 100\,000\,000 = €240\,136.21$$

   Second method: Lezard Brothers borrows €100m for 2 weeks at 2.75%, and rolls over this loan plus interest in 2 weeks' time at rate R for an additional 2 weeks. The total cost of this method is:

$$100\,000\,000 \times (1 + 2.75\%)^{\frac{1}{24}} \times (1 + R)^{\frac{1}{24}} - 100\,000\,000$$
$$= 100\,113\,100.02 \times (1 + R)^{\frac{1}{24}} - 100\,000\,000$$

   Equating the costs of the two previous methods, we find that the indifference point R^* is:

$$R^* = \left(\frac{100\,240\,136.21}{100\,113\,100.02}\right)^{24} - 1 \approx 3.09\%$$

3. Clearly Lezard Brothers is not the only market participant with funding needs, and they would all come to the same conclusion. Thus the rate of 3.09% can be interpreted as the market's expectation of the ECB's decision in 2 weeks. In other words, the market expects an increase between 25 and 50 basis points which is different from the naïve answer to question 1.

4. (a) First, Bernard is not accurate because in 2 weeks the amount he will need to borrow is $100\,000\,000 \times (1 + 2.75\%)^{\frac{1}{24}} = €100\,113\,100.02$ rather than €100 000 000. Taking this into account and writing down the exact cash flow

table of Bernard's strategy we have:

Transaction	Today	In 2 weeks	In 1 month
(i) Invest €100m at 2.92% over 1 month	−€100m		+€100 240 136.21
(ii) Borrow €100m at 2.75% for 2 weeks	+€100m	−€100 113 100.02	
(iii) In 2 weeks, borrow €100 113 100.02 at rate R for another 2 weeks		+€100 113 100.02	−€100 113 100.02 × $(1+R)^{\frac{1}{24}}$
TOTAL	0	0	+100 240 136.21 − 100 113 100.02 × $(1+R)^{\frac{1}{24}}$

For Bernard's strategy to be a pure arbitrage the final cash flow should always be positive. Clearly, this is not always the case here as the expression depends on R which is as yet unknown. It is thus necessary to carry out a risk analysis of Bernard's strategy along various scenarios for R.

(b) Profit or loss of Bernard's strategy in various scenarios for R:

Scenario	(a) −25 bps	(b) no change	(c) +25 bps	(d) +50 bps
Profit/loss	+€23 980.93	+€13 808.25	+€3659.26	−€6466.16

(c) Bernard's strategy would make a small profit of €3659.26 in the consensus scenario (25 basis point increase) but it would also entail a larger loss of €6466.16 in the case of a 50 basis point increase.

To know whether or not the risk is worth a try one may, for instance, calculate the expected gains using the results of the survey for probabilities:

Scenario	(a) −25 bps	(b) no change	(c) +25 bps	(d) +50 bps
Profit / Loss	+€23 980.93	+€13 808.25	+€3659.26	−€6466.16
Probability	0%	10%	70%	20%

Expected profit = +€2649.07.

From this calculation Bernard's strategy indeed looks attractive but it should be pointed out that the order of magnitude of the gains (a few thousand euros) is very different from the principal amounts employed (€100m). To be truly profitable, the strategy should be leveraged several times, which might pose some risk management problems.

4 Derivatives

4.1 Introduction

A derivative security is a financial security whose value depends on the value of other securities called underlying assets.[1]

Example. A contract to buy 1000 ounces of gold in a month's time at a pre-agreed price of $450 per troy ounce is a derivative security whose underlying asset is the ounce of gold. If gold increases from its current level at $400 to $500 in 1 month the buyer has made a good deal (he buys something worth $500 on the market for $450). More generally the value of this derivative contract increases with the price of the underlying (and conversely decreases if the underlying price falls).

For ease of analysis we will focus on derivatives with a single underlying asset. Formally, if D_t is the value of a derivative security at time $t \geq 0$ and S_t is the value of its underlying asset, there exists a function f of time t and S such that:

$$D_t = f(t, S_t)$$

Example. Denoting $T = \dfrac{1}{12} = 0.0833$ for the maturity of the gold contract above, we have:

$$D_T = (S_T - 450) \times 1000$$

Thus if gold trades at $500 at $t = T$, the value of the contract at maturity is $D_T = \$50\,000$, which is the profit that the buyer would make by immediately reselling the 1000 ounces of gold on the market for $500 000.

---

[1] Technically speaking an asset is any entity that has financial value, which covers securities as well as immaterial entities, such as brands. However, the term 'asset' is commonly used in finance as a synonym for 'security' and we will use these terms interchangeably in this book.

In general finding an expression for $D_t = f(t, S_t)$ at an arbitrary point in time $t < T$ is nontrivial. Economic assumptions must be made, in particular the absence of arbitrage opportunities. Fortunately the theory of derivatives pricing has been one of the most active and successful areas of economic research over the past 30 years, and its conclusions are widely accepted and implemented in practice. It is the aim of this book to introduce our readers to the main results of this theory.

There are two main categories of derivative securities:

- **Forward and futures contracts**,[2] where two parties agree to exchange an asset at a pre-agreed price and date. The gold contract in the above example falls in this category.
- **Options**, where one party has the right (but not the obligation) to exchange an asset at a pre-agreed price and date with the other party. This right is usually bought for a premium paid upfront to the option seller (comparable to a one-off insurance fee).

There are also more complex derivative securities called **exotic derivatives**, which we will come across in the exercises.

Although it is financially conceivable to create perpetual derivatives, in practice all derivatives have a final date called the **maturity date**, past which they cease to exist. The value of the derivative at maturity is called the **payoff**.

4.2 Forward contracts

The financial characteristics of a forward contract are:

- An **underlying asset** to be exchanged in the future.
- A **maturity date** T, the date when the underlying will be exchanged (or 'delivered').
- A **delivery price** or **strike**[3] K, the price to pay in exchange for the underlying asset.

Throughout this book we will denote the value of a forward contract at time t from the buyer's viewpoint as FC_t. Clearly the seller lives in a symmetric world where the contract value is $-FC_t$. Note that the value FC_t is for one unit of the underlying (e.g. one ounce of gold).

---

[2] Futures are traded on exchanges while forward contracts trade 'over-the-counter' (OTC). The margin call system of exchanges can result in a more or less significant price difference between these two types of derivatives, especially if long maturities are involved. However, we will ignore these differences and use the terms 'forward' and 'futures' interchangeably in this book.

[3] Technically the term 'strike' applies to options. In an era where the redundant expression 'ATM machine' does not bother anyone, we hope that the reader will not object to the perpetuation of this minor confusion.

4.2.1 Payoff

The **payoff** of a forward contract at maturity is:

$$FC_T = S_T - K$$

(Recall that for the seller the payoff is: $-FC_T = K - S_T$.)

This formula corresponds to the profit or loss for the buyer at maturity T: the buyer receives one unit of the underlying whose value is S_T and pays K to the seller. Note that such profit or loss is *latent* in the sense that to actually realize his gains or losses the buyer would need to immediately resell the underlying on the market.

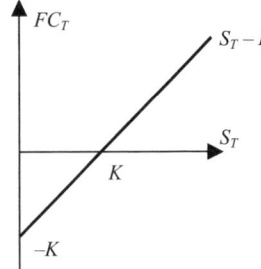 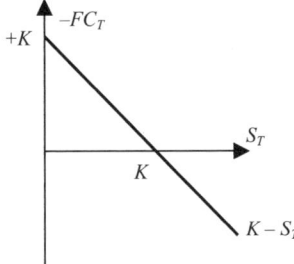

Payoff for the forward buyer at $t = T$ **Payoff for the forward seller at $t = T$**

4.2.2 Arbitrage price

We now focus on the value of the forward contract at an arbitrary point in time $t \leq T$ and particularly on today's value FC_0. As mentioned earlier, the valuation of derivatives is often difficult and requires some modelling assumptions. However, forward contracts are a nice category of derivatives for which only minimal assumptions are required.

Assume that:

- The underlying does not pay any cash flows[4] (in particular no dividends or coupons).
- Investors can borrow and lend money over T years at interest rate r.
- There are no arbitrage opportunities, securities are infinitely liquid and short selling is allowed.

Then **the arbitrage price at $t = 0$ of a forward contract is:**

$$FC_0 = S_0 - \frac{K}{(1+r)^T}$$

This formula is easily generalized for an arbitrary point in time t (see Exercise 6).

---

[4] This assumption is relaxed in Problem 1. Note that in practice gold pays interest in gold, a fact that we will ignore for ease of analysis.

Example. The price of gold is $400 per troy ounce and the 1-month zero-rate is 5%. The arbitrage price of a forward contract to buy an ounce of gold in 1 month for $450 is:

$$FC_0 = 400 - \frac{450}{(1+5\%)^{1/12}} \approx -\$48.17$$

The proof is as follows:

- Suppose $FC_0 > S_0 - \frac{K}{(1+r)^T}$, i.e.: $FC_0 + \frac{K}{(1+r)^T} > S_0$. One may then follow the arbitrage strategy below:

Transaction	Cash flow at $t = 0$	Cash flow at $t = T$
Buy the underlying today Sell the forward contract today	$-S_0$ $+FC_0$	— $-FC_T = K - S_T$
Borrow $\frac{K}{(1+r)^T}$ today at rate r until maturity	$+\frac{K}{(1+r)^T}$	$-\left[\frac{K}{(1+r)^T}\right] \times (1+r)^T = -K$
Sell the underlying at maturity	—	$+S_T$
TOTAL	$FC_0 + \frac{K}{(1+r)^T} - S_0 > 0$	0

Note that this strategy is perfectly covered since the arbitrageur owns the underlying at time of delivery.

- Suppose $FC_0 < S_0 - \frac{K}{(1+r)^T}$, i.e.: $FC_0 + \frac{K}{(1+r)^T} < S_0$. Again one may follow the arbitrage strategy:

Transaction	Cash flow at $t = 0$	Cash flow at $t = T$
Sell the underlying today Buy the forward contract today	$+S_0$ $-FC_0$	— $FC_T = S_T - K$
Invest $\frac{K}{(1+r)^T}$ today at a rate r until maturity	$-\frac{K}{(1+r)^T}$	$+\left[\frac{K}{(1+r)^T}\right] \times (1+r)^T = +K$
Buy the underlying at maturity	—	$-S_T$
TOTAL	$S_0 - FC_0 - \frac{K}{(1+r)^T} > 0$	0

Note that this strategy can be implemented only if either the arbitrageur already possesses the underlying at $t = 0$ (e.g. a gold mining company or a central bank with gold reserves), or short selling is allowed.

4.2.3 Forward price

In practice, when entering into a forward contract, the parties do not exchange any initial cash flows. This is made possible by choosing a delivery price K^* such that the contract has zero initial value, i.e.: $S_0 - \frac{K}{(1+r)^T} = 0$. Solving for K yields:

$$K^* = S_0(1 + r)^T$$

This price is called the **forward price** of the underlying at maturity T, while the current price of the underlying S_0 is called the **spot price**. The forward price, commonly denoted F_0 or $F(0, T)$, is not to be confused with S_T, the future spot price of the underlying at time $t = T$. F_0 is indeed determined at $t = 0$ while S_T is unknown until $t = T$ and has no particular reason to be equal to F_0 on that date.

Example. If gold currently trades at $400 per troy ounce and the 1-month zero-rate is 5%, the 1-month forward price of gold is:

$$F_0 = 400 \times (1 + 5\%)^{1/12} \approx \$401.63$$

4.3 'Plain vanilla' options

4.3.1 Definitions and notations

- A **European call** on an asset confers the right but not the obligation to buy this asset at a pre-agreed price and date.
- A **European put** on an asset confers the right but not the obligation to sell this asset at a pre-agreed price and date.
- An **American call** on an asset confers the right but not the obligation to buy this asset at a pre-agreed price *until* a certain date.
- An **American put** on an asset confers the right but not the obligation to sell this asset at a pre-agreed price *until* a certain date.

These four categories are referred to by practitioners as **plain vanilla options**, in contrast to **exotic options** which are more sophisticated (see exercises).

We will adopt the following notation in relation to options throughout this book.

- K: **exercise price** or **strike**, the price at which the underlying asset is exchanged.
- T: **expiry** or **maturity**, the date when or until when the underlying is exchanged.
- c_t, C_t^{US}: the value at time t of a European and American call.
- p_t, P_t^{US}: the value at time t of a European and American put.

As with forward contracts, an option value is expressed per unit of underlying asset and from the option buyer's viewpoint.

4.3.2 Payoff

Options can be viewed as one-sided forward contracts in the sense that 'the option owner can only win'. Consider, for example, a 1-month European call on an ounce of gold struck at $450. Let S_T be the market price of gold in 1 month. At this date the owner of the call must decide whether to exercise his right to buy the asset:

- If so, his relative gain is $S_T - 450$ (≥ 0 if a profit, <0 if a loss).
- If not, there is no profit or loss.

Clearly a rational individual will only exercise this option if it is profitable to do so, i.e. if gold trades above $450 at maturity. Therefore, the option payoff can be written as follows:

$$c_T = \max(0, S_T - 450)$$

Generally, the respective payoffs of the European call and put with strike K and maturity T are given as:

- For the call: $c_T = \max(0, S_T - K)$
- For the put: $p_T = \max(0, K - S_T)$

Visually:

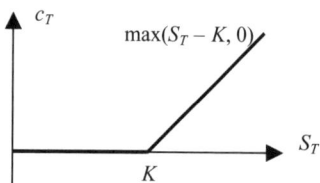
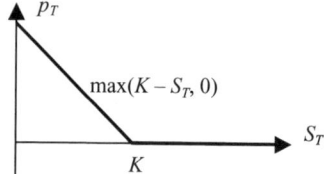

Payoff of the European call   **Payoff of the European put**

4.3.3 Put–call parity

European puts and calls with identical characteristics (underlying S, strike K, maturity T) satisfy the **put–call parity** equation:

$$c_0 - p_0 = FC_0 = S_0 - \frac{K}{(1+r)^T}$$

In other words: 'call minus put equals forward'. Note that **put–call parity does not hold for American options**. The technical proof of this equation is left to Exercise 8.

'Plain vanilla' options

Put–call parity shows that a European call is in fact exactly one half of a forward contract, the other half being a sold ('short') put as illustrated below:

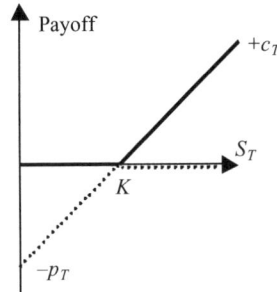

Put–call parity: buying a call and selling a put is the same as buying a forward contract

Exercises

Exercise 1

'The value of a derivative product is always positive.' Comment on this statement, with examples.

Exercise 2: forward price and price of the forward contract

Microshita Corp. is a fast-growing IT company which reinvests all of its profits in its business and pays no dividends to its stockholders. Its stock currently trades at ¥5200 in Tokyo. The risk-free interest rate is 1% per annum for all maturities.

1. Calculate the 1-year forward price of Microshita Corp.
2. Calculate the price of a 6-month forward contract on Microshita Corp. struck at ¥5000.

Exercise 3

Determine the payoff of buying an ounce of gold and selling a forward contract on that ounce. Can you also find the value of this strategy as of today? State your assumptions.

Exercise 4: option strategies

In this exercise all options are of European type.

Determine the payoff at maturity of the following option strategies:

(a) 'short put': selling a put;
(b) 'covered call': selling a call and buying the underlying;
(c) 'straddle': buying a call and a put with identical characteristics (underlying, strike, maturity);
(d) 'synthetic short forward': buying a put and selling a call with identical characteristics. What do you notice?

Exercise 5: strategy replication

Find two portfolios of European calls maturing at time T on the same underlying S whose payoffs are:

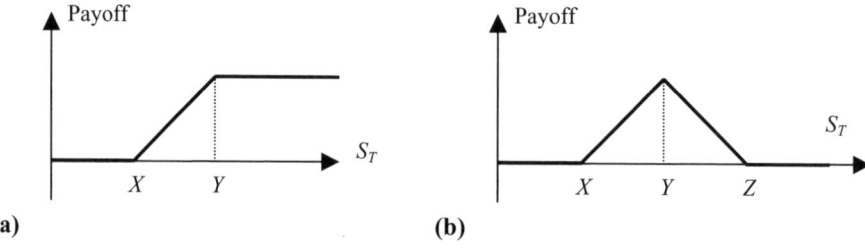

(a)   (b)

Exercise 6: forward price and price of the forward contract at an arbitrary time t

Generalize the formulas for the forward price and the arbitrage price of the forward contract at any point in time $t < T$.

Exercise 7: forward exchange rate

The spot exchange rate of the euro is S dollars, i.e. to buy 1 euro one must pay S dollars. The euro zone yield curve is flat at r_{EU} while the American yield curve is flat at r_{US}. A forward contract on the euro–dollar is an agreement to receive euros and pay dollars at a pre-determined date T and exchange rate F.

1. Starting with €1, find two ways to have dollars in a year's time by investing or borrowing in either currency and exchanging between currencies through the spot and forward markets. With an arbitrage argument show that the 1-year exchange rate of the euro must be:

$$F = S\frac{1+r_{US}}{1+r_{EU}}$$

2. $r_{EU} = 2\%$, $r_{US} = 4\%$, $S = \$1.30$ for €1. What is the 1-year forward exchange rate? Can you also find the 2-year exchange rate?
3. Interpret your results in terms of appreciation or depreciation of the *dollar*. Find at least one supporting argument for your interpretation and one opposing argument. Assuming both arguments will weigh equally on the evolution of the euro–dollar exchange rate through time, what would be your best guess of the exchange rate in a year's time? Can you find a way to make money if this forecast proves to be accurate? Is this an arbitrage?

Exercise 8: arbitrage arguments

Establish the following relationships using the economic assumptions in Section 4.2.2. *All option characteristics are the same (underlying S, maturity T, strike K)*.

(a) For all t, $0 \leq t \leq T$: $c_t \leq S_t$;
(b) $c_0 \geq S_0 - \dfrac{K}{(1+r)^T}$;
(c) $C_0^{US} \geq S_0 - K$;
(d) $c_0 - p_0 = FC_0$ (put–call parity).

Exercise 9*: exotic option

An example of an exotic option is the *European call on a call*, which is a European call whose underlying is a European call on an asset S.

1. Let T_1 denote the maturity of the call on a call, T_2 the maturity of the underlying call. What can you tell about the following cases:
   (a) $T_1 > T_2$;
   (b) $T_1 = T_2$;
   (c) $T_1 < T_2$?
2. How is put–call parity modified when considering a call on a call and a put on a call?

Problem 1: benefits and cost of carry

In this problem we consider a market where (i) investors can borrow and lend money at rate r for any maturity, (ii) there are no arbitrage opportunities, (iii) liquidity is infinite and (iv) short selling is allowed.

1. Using an arbitrage argument, show that if S_0 is the spot price of an asset which pays a cash flow I at time $\tau < T$ then the forward price of this asset at maturity T is:

$$F_0 = S_0(1+r)^T - I(1+r)^{T-\tau}$$

   Hint: Rewrite this equation as $F_0 + I(1+r)^{T-\tau} = S_0(1+r)^T$.
2. What is the 1-year forward price of Bonux SA, a company whose stock is currently trading at €430 in Paris and that is unanimously expected to pay a €40 dividend per share in 6 months? The risk-free rate is 5% per annum.
3. What is the 1.5-year forward price of a 2-year bond which will detach a 10% coupon in 1 year and a 15% coupon in 2 years? The yield curve is flat at 8%.
4. What is the forward price of 250 kg of oranges delivered in 1 month? The risk-free rate is 5% per annum, the price of 1 kg of oranges at your local supermarket is $5 and your neighbours offer to rent cold storage in their basement for just $99.99 a month.

Problem 2: forward rate

In this problem we consider a market where investors can invest and borrow money for any maturity T at the zero rate $z(T)$, liquidity is infinite and there are no arbitrage opportunities. Let $z(T, \tau)$ denote the *forward rate* which applies today to investments and loans starting at a future date T and ending at time $t = T + \tau$. For instance the '6-month × 1-year' forward rate, which corresponds to the rate agreed today on an investment or loan starting in 6 months and ending in a year and a half, is denoted $z(0.5, 1)$.

1. In this question the zero-rate curve is given as: $z(T) = 5\% + T \times 0.5\%$.
   (a) Draw z.
   (b) Suppose that $z(1, 2) = z(3)$. Determine two ways to invest or borrow money over 3 years and show that there is an arbitrage opportunity.

Exercises

(c) Calculate the rate $z(1,2)$ which eliminates the arbitrage and generally $z(1,\tau)$ for any investment period τ. Draw $z(1,\tau)$.

2. In this question the zero-rate curve $z(T)$ is arbitrary. Show that the forward rate $z(T,\tau)$ satisfies:

$$(1+z(T,\tau))^\tau = \frac{(1+z(T+\tau))^{T+\tau}}{(1+z(T))^T}$$

Verify your results in 1(c).

Solutions

Exercise 1

In the general case this statement is false: for instance forward contracts, which are clearly derivative securities, can have negative value (for example when the price of the underlying at maturity is lower than the delivery price). Plain vanilla options, however, always have positive value.

The correct statement is as follows: 'the value of a derivative security whose payoff is positive is always positive'.

Exercise 2: forward price and price of the forward contract

1. 1-year *forward price* of Microshita Corp. stock:

$$F(0, 1) = S_0(1+r)^T = 5200 \times (1 + 1\%)^1 = ¥5252$$

(The formula above is correct because Microshita Corp. does not pay any dividend.)

2. Price of the *forward contract* on Microshita Corp. stock:

$$FC_0 = S_0 - \frac{K}{(1+r)^T} = 5200 - \frac{5000}{(1+1\%)^{0.5}} = ¥224.81$$

Exercise 3

The payoff of a forward contract for the seller is $-FC_T = K - S_T$, so the payoff of the portfolio is: $S_T + K - S_T = K$. This is a fixed cash flow, whose present value is $\frac{K}{(1+r)^T}$, where r is the zero-rate for maturity T. No other assumption than the absence of arbitrage and infinite liquidity is required.

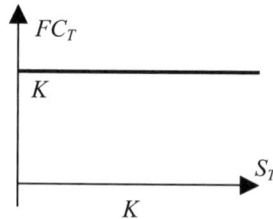

Exercise 4: option strategies

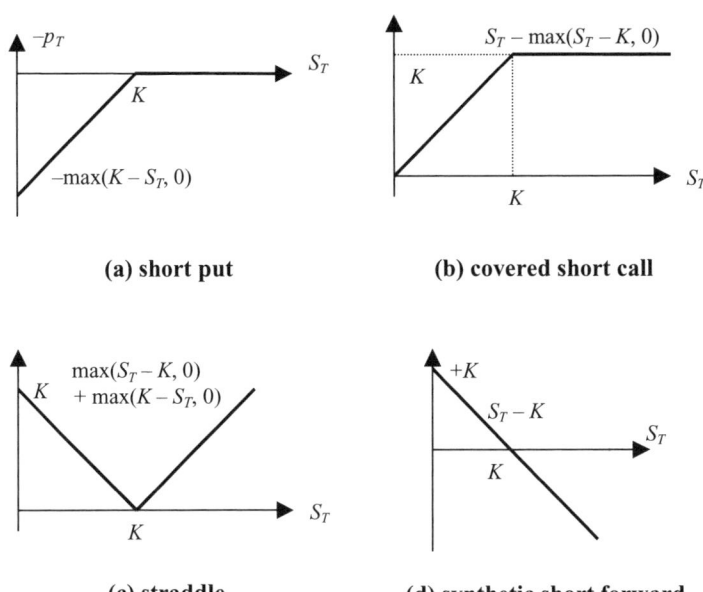

(a) short put

(b) covered short call

(c) straddle

(d) synthetic short forward

In (d), the combined payoff of buying a put and selling a call is the same as selling a forward contract. Consequently, the value of such a portfolio must be equal to $-FC_0$, otherwise there would be an arbitrage opportunity. This is in fact equivalent to put–call parity from the seller's viewpoint.

Exercise 5: strategy replication

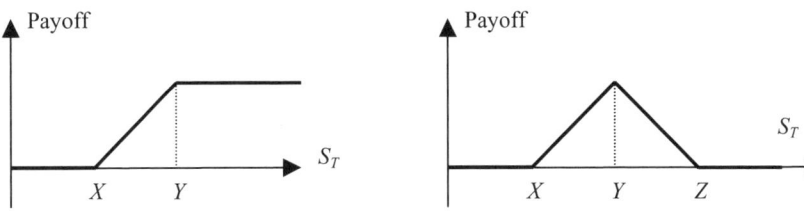

(a) 'call spread': buy call with strike X, sell call with strike Y

(b) 'collar': buy call with strike X, sell two calls with strike Y, buy call with strike Z

Exercise 6: forward price and price of the forward contract at an arbitrary time t

The formulas given in Section 4.2 are valid for $t = 0$. It is easy to see that looking at maturity T from an arbitrary point in time t is equivalent to looking at maturity $T - t$ from time $t = 0$. This observation instantly yields the generalized formulas:

(a) $FC_t = S_t - \dfrac{K}{(1+r)^{T-t}}$ (same proof as given in Section 4.2.2).

(b) $F_t = S_t(1+r)^{T-t}$ (obtained by solving equation $FC_t = 0$ for K).

Exercise 7: forward exchange rate

1. First method: exchange €1 for $\$S$ today and invest the dollars at rate r_{US} for a year; the final dollar amount in a year's time is $\$S(1 + r_{US})$.

   Second method: invest €1 at rate r_{EU} for a year and then exchange the compound capital of €$(1 + r_{EU})$ into dollars at the forward rate F agreed today; the final dollar amount in a year's time is $\$F(1 + r_{EU})$.

   Both methods are equivalent ways of exchanging euros into dollars in a year's time. Thus they must yield the same dollar amount per euro, under penalty of arbitrage. As a result: $S(1 + r_{US}) = F(1 + r_{EU})$, which proves the required formula.

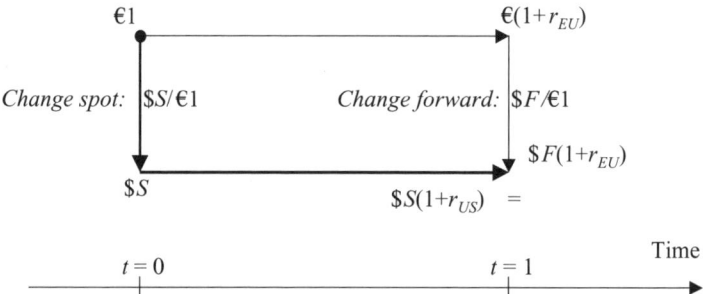

2. Using the formula for F found in question 1, we have:

$$F = 1.30 \times \frac{1 + 4\%}{1 + 2\%} \approx \$1.3255 \text{ for €1}$$

For the 2-year forward exchange rate, we can either repeat the argument in question 1 with an investment horizon of 2 years, or we can iterate the 1-year forward exchange rate formula a second time:

$$F(0, 2) = 1.30 \times \frac{(1 + 4\%)^2}{(1 + 2\%)^2} \approx 1.3255 \times \frac{1 + 4\%}{1 + 2\%} \approx 1.3515$$

Solutions

3. In both cases the number of dollars required to buy 1 euro through the forward markets is higher than through the spot market. The forward markets thus imply a depreciation of the dollar in time. This evolution can be justified by the fact that the higher interest rate in the USA probably reflects a higher inflation in consumer prices than in the euro zone: the demand for the dollar should thus decrease.

On the other hand, the higher interest rate in the USA should attract foreign investments from the euro zone into the dollar zone. The demand for the dollar should thus increase and the dollar appreciate.

Assuming both arguments will weigh equally on the spot exchange rate market throughout the coming year, the best forecast of the euro–dollar exchange rate in 1 year would be the current spot rate $S = 1.30$ rather than the forward rate $F = 1.3255$.

Thus, an investor with euros today could enter into a strategy to invest his euros at a 2% rate and simultaneously buy dollars cheap at 1.3255 through the forward markets. In a year's time, if the exchange rate is still at 1.30, he will have a profit of $1.3255 \times 1.02 - 1.30 = \$0.052$ for €1.

This strategy is clearly not an arbitrage since it would be at a loss in case the euro–dollar exchange rate in 1 year is above $\$1.3255 \times 1.02 = 1.3520$.

Exercise 8: arbitrage arguments

(a) Suppose that at a given point in time t we have $c_t > S_t$. Then buy the underlying asset and sell the call for a profit. At maturity the payoff of this strategy is $S_T - \max(0, S_T - K)$, which is always positive. Thus we have an arbitrage strategy, which contradicts the no-arbitrage assumption in Section 4.2.2.

(b) Suppose $c_0 < S_0 - \dfrac{K}{(1+r)^T}$. Then buy the call and sell a forward contract on the underlying asset with strike K for a profit. At maturity the payoff is $\max(0, S_T - K) - (S_T - K)$, which is always positive. Thus we have an arbitrage strategy, which contradicts the no-arbitrage assumption in Section 4.2.2.

(c) Suppose $C_0^{US} < S_0 - K$. Then buy the American call and exercise it immediately, receive $S_0 - K$, which is above the price of the call and make a profit. We just made an arbitrage, which contradicts the no-arbitrage assumption in Section 4.2.2.

(d) Suppose $c_0 - p_0 < FC_0$. Then buy the call, sell the put, and sell a forward contract with the same characteristics, for a profit. At maturity the payoff is nil. Thus we have an arbitrage, which contradicts the no-arbitrage assumption in Section 4.2.2, and similarly if $c_0 - p_0 > FC_0$. Therefore we have $c_0 - p_0 \geq FC_0$ and $c_0 - p_0 \leq FC_0$, which proves the put–call parity equation.

Exercise 9*: exotic option

1. (a) $T_1 > T_2$: the underlying call does not exist any more when the call on a call comes to maturity. This is nonsense!
   (b) $T_1 = T_2$: the value of the underlying call at T_2 is $c_{T_2} = \max(S_{T_2} - K_2, 0)$ (where S denotes the underlying asset of the underlying call) and the value of the call on a call at T_1 is $cc_{T_1} = \max(c_{T_1} - K_1, 0)$. If $T_1 = T_2 = T$ we have:

$$cc_T = \max(\max(S_T - K_2, 0) - K_1, 0) = \max(S_T - K_2 - K_1, 0)$$

   Thus, the call on a call is identical to a vanilla call on the underlying asset S with strike $K_1 + K_2$.
   (c) $T_1 < T_2$: this is the standard case and there is nothing particular to say.
2. 'Call minus put equals forward.' Here the underlying is a vanilla call. Therefore buying a call on a call and selling a put on a call will yield a forward on the underlying call. Since a call does not pay any cash flow before maturity we can use the formula for forward contracts from Section 4.2.2:

$$cc_0 - pc_0 = c_0 - \frac{K_1}{(1+r)^{T_1}}$$

Problem 1: benefits and cost of carry

1. Suppose that $F_0 + I(1 + r)^{T-\tau} > S_0(1 + r)^T$. We now have the following arbitrage strategy:

Transaction	$t = 0$	$t = \tau$	$t = T$
Buy the underlying today at the spot price S_0	$-S_0$	$+I$	—
Sell the underlying through a forward contract with strike set to the forward price F_0	—	—	$+F_0$
Borrow S_0 today at rate r for maturity T	$+S_0$	—	$-S_0(1+r)^T$
Invest I at time $t = \tau$ at rate r until maturity T	—	$-I$	$+I(1+r)^{T-\tau}$
TOTAL	0	0	>0

Similarly, if $F_0 + I(1 + r)^{T-\tau} < S_0(1 + r)^T$, we again have an arbitrage. This contradicts the no-arbitrage assumption (ii) and proves that $F_0 = S_0(1+r)^T - I(1+r)^{T-\tau}$.

2. 1-year forward price of a Bonux SA:

$$F_0 = 430 \times (1 + 5\%) - 40 \times (1 + 5\%)^{1-0.5} = €410.51.$$

3. To answer this question we must first determine the price of the bond. Using the formula from Section 3.4.3 we have:

$$P = \frac{10}{1 + 8\%} + \frac{110}{(1 + 8\%)^2} \approx 103.57$$

The 1.5-year forward price of the bond is then:

$$F_0 = 103.57 \times (1+8\%)^{1.5} - 10 \times (1+8\%)^{1.5-1} = 105.85$$

(Since $T = 1.5$, only the first 10% coupon must be taken into consideration.)

4. Here we have a negative income, which is the cost of renting the storage: $I = -\$99.99$. Thus:

$$F_0 = 250 \times 5 \times (1+5\%)^{1/12} + 99.99 \times (1+5\%)^{1/12} = \$1355.49.$$

Problem 2: forward rate

1. (a) Curve of $z(T) = 5\% + T \times 0.5\%$:

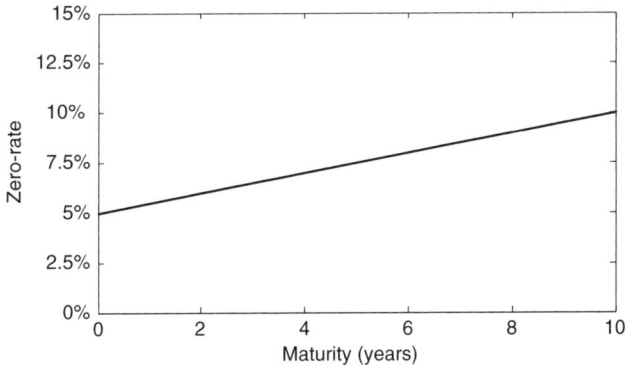

(b) First method: invest (borrow) €1 for 3 years at the zero-rate $z(3) = 6.5\%$; after compounding we get $1.065^3 = €1.208$.

Second method: invest (borrow) €1 for the first year at the zero-rate $z(1) = 5.5\%$ and get €1.055 then invest (borrow) €1.055 for the following 2 years at the forward rate $z(1, 2) = 6.5\%$; after compounding we get $1.055 \times 1.065^2 = €1.197$.

These two methods are equivalent ways of investing or borrowing euros over 3 years but yield different results. Thus there is an arbitrage opportunity: invest €1 through the first method and borrow €1 through the second method to collect $1.208 - 1.197 = €0.011$.

(c) From the previous calculation, we need the following to be sure that there are no arbitrage opportunities:

$$1.065^3 = 1.055 \times (1 + z(1, 2))^2$$

which yields: $z(1, 2) = 7\%$.

Generally:
$$(1 + z(\tau + 1))^{\tau+1} = 1.055 \times (1 + z(1, \tau))^{\tau}$$

Solving for the forward rate $z(1, \tau)$:

$$z(1, \tau) = \left[\frac{(1 + z(\tau + 1))^{\tau+1}}{1.055}\right]^{\frac{1}{\tau}} - 1 = \frac{(1.05 + 0.005\tau)^{1+\frac{1}{\tau}}}{1.055^{\frac{1}{\tau}}} - 1$$

[Graph: Rate vs Maturity (years), showing z(1; T) (forward) and z(T) (outright) curves from 0% to 15%, maturity 1 to 10 years]

2. Suppose that $(1 + z(T, \tau))^{\tau} > \dfrac{(1 + z(T + \tau))^{T+\tau}}{(1 + z(T))^{T}}$, i.e.: $(1 + z(T + \tau))^{T+\tau} <$ $(1 + z(T))^{T} (1 + z(T, \tau))^{\tau}$. Here direct compounding over $T + \tau$ years yields less than indirect compounding over T and then τ years. Hence, there is an arbitrage opportunity:

Transaction	$t = 0$	$t = T$	$t = T + \tau$
Borrow €1 over $T + \tau$ years at rate $z(T + \tau)$	+1	—	$-(1 + z(T + \tau))^{T+\tau}$
Invest €1 over T years at rate $z(T)$	−1	$+(1 + z(T))^{T}$	—
Invest € $(1 + z(T))^{T}$ forward between T and $T + \tau$ at rate $z(T, \tau)$	—	$-(1 + z(T))^{T}$	$+(1 + z(T))^{T} (1 + z(T, \tau))^{\tau}$
TOTAL	0	0	>0

Conversely, if $(1 + z(T, \tau))^{\tau} < \dfrac{(1 + z(T + \tau))^{T+\tau}}{(1 + z(T))^{T}}$, we again have an arbitrage by reversing transactions and signs.

We can easily verify the formula obtained in 1(c) by taking $T = 1$.

5 Portfolio theory

5.1 Summary of portfolio valuation

In Chapter 3 we made a distinction between the value and the price of an asset. Under the usual assumptions of absence of arbitrage and infinite liquidity, the arbitrage price of a portfolio of N assets is equal to the sum of asset prices p_k multiplied by their respective quantities q_k:

$$P = \sum_{k=1}^{N} p_k q_k = p_1 q_1 + p_2 q_2 + \cdots + p_N q_N$$

This valuation method for portfolios is known as '**mark-to-market**'. It is of course perfectly legitimate to think that a portfolio is worth more (or less) than its arbitrage price, but when it comes to buying or selling it the transaction should take place at that price to be fair.

We also saw that market agents usually have the right to short sell. In this case the quantities can be negative. In practitioners' jargon a positive quantity is called a **long position** and a negative quantity a **short position**.

Example. The mark-to-market value of a portfolio which is long 100 stocks of iBelieve.com quoting €1 in Frankfurt and short 200 stocks of Telepom SA quoting €20 in Paris is −€3900:

Asset	Position	Unit price	Mark-to-market value
iBelieve.com	+100 (long)	€1	€100
Telepom SA	−200 (short)	€20	−€4000
Portfolio	1 (long)	—	−€3900

Here we have a negative portfolio value, which is often a bit counterintuitive. We must emphasize that the price of −€3900 does *not* correspond to a latent loss, but simply to the amount of money that the owner of the portfolio should pay to get rid of it. This could be achieved by either finding a buyer of the portfolio, or finding a buyer of iBelieve.com and a seller of Telepom SA. Since the short position on Telepom SA is clearly driving the value of the portfolio, it makes sense for the owner to pay some money to get out of all the positions.

5.2 Risk and return

5.2.1 Risk and return of an asset

The table opposite shows the monthly rate of return of three assets: the stock of BigBrother Inc., a large multinational IT company; a Treasury bond issued by the government of a developed country; and a share in the Spec LLP hedge fund.

From Chapter 1 we know how to convert monthly returns into annual returns. A simplified calculation using the average return of the assets yields the following annualized returns: 13.73% for BigBrother Inc., 6.19% for Treasury and 28.44% for Spec LLP. However, we also see from the compounding table below that the annual return on 1 dollar invested in each asset is in fact 12.18%, 6.19% and 15.04%, respectively.

Based on these calculations an unsophisticated investor would probably decide to put his fortune into the asset that gives the highest return: Spec LLP. Many investors make investment decisions based on such analyses and forget to think over why company stocks or hedge funds give higher returns than Treasury bonds. The answer is that **these three assets do not carry the same risk**: recent economic history is full of spectacular scandals and collapses of multinational companies or hedge funds once thought never to go bankrupt; on the other hand, we must go back more than 50 years in history to find records of a developed country defaulting on its government bonds.

The intuitive perception by investors of the risk level of an asset will typically be reflected by the **volatility** of its returns: the higher the risk, the more volatile the returns. In the example above as well as in real life, we can notice that stock returns are more volatile than bond returns, which is consistent with the intuitive idea that stocks are subject to many more economic risks than bonds. This is why in finance risk is synonymous with volatility, which is universally measured as the annualized **standard deviation** of asset returns:[1]

$$\sigma_{periodic} = \sqrt{\frac{1}{N-1} \sum_{t=1}^{N} (r_t - \bar{r})^2}$$

$$\sigma_{annual} = \sigma_{periodic} \times \sqrt{\text{number of periods per year}}$$

---

[1] Readers not familiar with the theory of statistical estimation may be surprised by the $N-1$ denominator in our definition of standard deviation. Using N as denominator would, however, lead to a biased estimation of the volatility based on historical returns.

Monthly returns of three assets over 1 year

	Jan.	Feb.	Mar.	Apr.	May	Jun.	Jul.	Aug.	Sep.	Oct.	Nov.	Dec.	Average
BigBrother Inc.	−3.01%	1.31%	−2.87%	6.64%	3.03%	7.32%	−4.86%	−2.07%	10.35%	−4.13%	−2.54%	3.77%	1.08%
Treasury	0.43%	0.44%	0.52%	0.47%	0.61%	0.43%	0.45%	0.52%	0.53%	0.52%	0.55%	0.55%	0.50%
Spec LLP	−13.47%	18.30%	8.55%	−18.45%	3.56%	26.75%	−7.52%	2.79%	−8.19%	5.87%	−12.43%	19.53%	2.11%

Compounding table of the three assets

	Initial	Jan.	Feb.	Mar.	Apr.	May	Jun.	Jul.	Aug.	Sep.	Oct.	Nov.	Dec.
BigBrother Inc.	1	0.970	0.983	0.954	1.018	1.049	1.125	1.071	1.049	1.157	1.109	1.081	1.122
Treasury	1	1.004	1.009	1.014	1.019	1.025	1.029	1.034	1.039	1.045	1.050	1.056	1.062
Spec LLP	1	0.865	1.024	1.111	0.906	0.938	1.189	1.100	1.131	1.038	1.099	0.962	1.150

where $\bar{r}$ is the average periodic return. The annualized volatility for the three assets in our example is: 17.62% for BigBrother Inc., 0.20% for Treasury and 50.16% for Spec LLP. These numbers reflect the intuitive distribution of risk levels between stocks, bonds and hedge funds.

5.2.2 Risk-free asset; Sharpe ratio

When considering various assets, the asset with zero volatility is called the **risk-free asset** and its return is called the **risk-free rate** r_f. In our previous example the Treasury bond, whose volatility of 0.20% is very close to zero, would be a suitable proxy for the risk-free asset, in which case the risk-free return would be 6.19%.

The risk-free rate is the minimum return an investor should expect from other risky assets such as BigBrother Inc. or Spec LLP. The difference $r_A - r_f$ between the expected return of a given risky asset A and the risk-free rate is called the **risk premium** of A.

Investors should demand a higher risk premium when the risk is higher. As such, the return performance of an asset must be compared to the risk incurred. This is exactly what the **Sharpe ratio** does:

$$Sharpe_A = \frac{\text{premium}}{\text{risk}} = \frac{r_A - r_f}{\sigma_A}$$

The Sharpe ratio is the premium per unit of risk entailed. The ratio is higher if the risk premium is higher and the risk is lower. A Sharpe ratio of 1.0 is usually considered very good and above 1.5 is excellent.

The table below summarizes the risk–return profiles of the three assets in our example:

	Annual return	Annual risk	Risk premium	Sharpe ratio
Treasury	6.19%	'0%' (0.20%)	0	n/a
BigBrother Inc.	12.18%	17.62%	5.99%	0.34
Spec LLP	15.04%	50.16%	8.85%	0.18

5.2.3 Risk and return of a portfolio

Consider a portfolio which is long €1 500 000 worth of BigBrother Inc. stocks, €250 000 worth of Treasury bonds and €250 000 worth of shares in Spec LLP. The mark-to-market price and monthly returns of this portfolio are easily derived from the compounding table of the individual assets, as illustrated opposite:

	Initial amount	Jan.	Feb.	Mar.	Apr.	May	Jun.
BigBrother Inc.	€1 500 000	€1 454 902	€1 473 959	€1 431 651	€1 526 744	€1 572 970	€1 688 141
Treasury	€250 000	€251 075	€252 180	€253 491	€254 682	€256 236	€257 338
Spec LLC	€250 000	€216 325	€255 912	€277 793	€226 540	€234 605	€297 362
Portfolio	€2 000 000	€1 922 302	€1 982 051	€1 962 935	€2 007 966	€2 063 811	€2 242 841
Return		−3.88%	3.11%	−0.96%	2.29%	2.78%	8.67%

	Jul.	Aug.	Sep.	Oct.	Nov.	Dec.
BigBrother Inc.	€1 606 016	€1 572 757	€1 735 475	€1 663 847	€1 621 538	€1 682 648
Treasury	€258 496	€259 840	€261 217	€262 576	€264 020	€265 472
Spec LLC	€275 000	€282 673	€259 522	€274 756	€240 604	€287 594
Portfolio	€2 139 512	€2 115 270	€2 256 214	€2 201 178	€2 126 162	€2 235 713
Return	−4.61%	−1.13%	6.66%	−2.44%	−3.41%	5.15%

Annual portfolio return: 11.79%
Annualized volatility: 15.22%

However, there is a more direct way to calculate the return of a portfolio: one can take the average of the asset returns weighted by the respective asset proportions, or weights, in the portfolio. In our example the annual return of the portfolio is thus:

$$\frac{1\,500\,000}{2\,000\,000} \times 12.18\% + \frac{250\,000}{2\,000\,000} \times 6.19\% + \frac{250\,000}{2\,000\,000} \times 15.04\% = 11.79\%$$

which is consistent with the table. More generally, let P be a portfolio of N assets in *proportions* $w_1, w_2, \ldots, w_N$ (negative for short positions) such that $w_1 + w_2 + \ldots + w_N = 1$ with returns $R_1, R_2, \ldots, R_N$, respectively. The **portfolio return** R_P is then:

$$R_P = \sum_{k=1}^{N} w_k R_k = w_1 R_1 + w_2 R_2 + \cdots + w_N R_N$$

The formula for **portfolio volatility** is less straightforward: if we compute the weighted average of the annualized volatilities we get 19.51% instead of the actual figure of 15.22% in the table. This is because the asset returns are **correlated**. In the two-asset case the portfolio volatility can indeed be written:

$$\sigma_P = \sqrt{w_1^2 \sigma_1^2 + w_2^2 \sigma_2^2 + 2 w_1 w_2 \sigma_1 \sigma_2 \rho}$$

where w_1 and w_2 are the weights of assets 1 and 2 (with $w_2 = 1 - w_1$), σ_1 and σ_2 the asset volatilities, and ρ the correlation coefficient between the two assets.

This formula is derived from the formula for the variance of a sum of random variables (see Appendix A):

$$\sigma_P = \sqrt{\text{Var}(w_1 R_1 + w_2 R_2)} = \sqrt{w_1^2 \text{Var}(R_1) + w_2^2 \text{Var}(R_1) + 2 w_1 w_2 \text{Cov}(R_1, R_2)}$$

For N assets the generalized formula is:

$$\sigma_P = \sqrt{\text{Var}(R_P)}$$

$$\text{Var}(R_P) = \text{Var}\left(\sum_{k=1}^{N} w_k R_k\right) = \sum_{k=1}^{N} w_k^2 \text{Var}(R_k) + 2 \sum_{k=1}^{N} \sum_{j=k+1}^{N} w_k w_j \text{Cov}(R_k, R_j)$$

$$\text{Cov}(R_k, R_j) = \sigma_{R_k} \sigma_{R_j} \rho_{R_k, R_j}$$

In our example portfolio, the correlations have a positive impact on the risk–return profile since the Sharpe ratio is 0.37, a higher figure than that of the two risky assets BigBrother Inc. and Spec LLP. In the next section we examine in closer detail the gains provided by such investment **diversification**.

5.3 Gains of diversification; portfolio optimization

'**Diversification**' is the scholarly term for not putting all one's eggs into the same basket. The graph below shows the volatility over the period 1995–2004 of a portfolio made up of a growing number of constituent stocks of the EuroStoxx 50 index published by Dow Jones. Observe how volatility dramatically decreases and then stabilizes as the number of stocks increases:

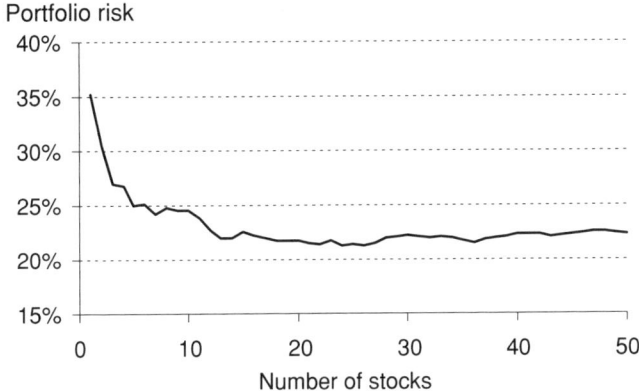

Volatility of a portfolio consisting of a growing number of stocks (1995–2004)

To understand the mechanics of diversification let us consider again the example of BigBrother Inc., Treasury and Spec LLP. The graph below shows the risk–return profile of the three assets:

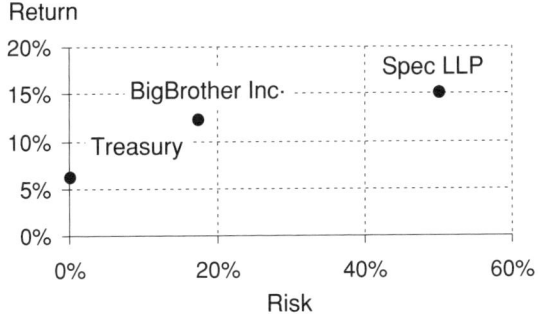

Risk and return of BigBrother Inc., Treasury and Spec LLP

The correlation between BigBrother Inc. and Spec LLP is 0.15, which is low. Does this mean that there are only minimal risk–return gains from diversification? The following table and graph show the evolution of a portfolio which is fully invested in BigBrother Inc. initially and then gradually moves towards a full investment in Spec LLP:

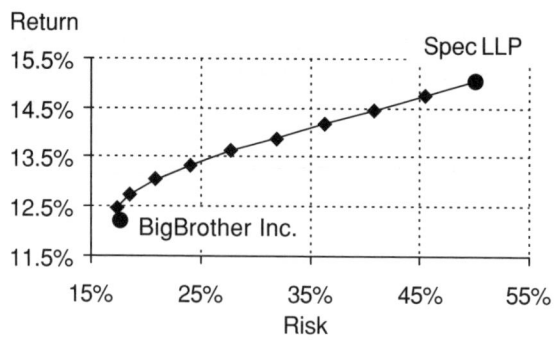

Weight Spec LLP	Risk	Return
0%	17.62%	12.18%
10%	**17.33%**	**12.47%**
20%	18.49%	12.75%
30%	20.84%	13.04%
40%	24.04%	13.32%
50%	27.80%	13.61%
60%	31.92%	13.90%
70%	36.28%	14.18%
80%	40.81%	14.47%
90%	45.44%	14.75%
100%	50.16%	15.04%

Risk and return of portfolios of BigBrother Inc. and Spec LLP

By investing 90% in BigBrother Inc. and 10% in Spec LLP, one can obtain a 0.29% improvement in return (12.47% instead of 12.18%) *and* also a 0.29% improvement in risk (17.33% instead of 17.62%) compared to the portfolio fully invested in

BigBrother Inc. Note that in general the improvement in return is not necessarily equal to the improvement in risk, if any.

Hence, there exists an **optimal portfolio** of BigBrother Inc. and Spec LLP minimizing the risk without sacrificing the return.

Naturally, these results can be generalized for the case of N assets.

5.4 Capital Asset Pricing Model

Portfolio theory can be summarized by the following two principles:

1. The more risk an asset incurs, the higher return investors can expect.
2. The more diversified a portfolio, the lower the risk.

However, these two principles are not always consistent, as illustrated by the following paradox. Let us suppose that the return of assets A and B is the same, say 10%. As such all portfolios of A and B also have a 10% return regardless of the weights. But we also know that there is an optimal portfolio P minimizing the risk. Thus, the first principle seems to be violated: the risk of A or B is higher than the risk of P, but it is mathematically impossible to get compensation by higher returns.

To resolve this paradox, the **CAPM (Capital Asset Pricing Model)** proposes a distinction between two types of risk:

- **Market risk** (or systematic risk). Common to all risky assets, and reflecting general market trends. This type of risk cannot be eliminated by diversification and must be rewarded with higher returns.
- **Specific risk** (or idiosyncratic risk). Specific to each asset, and corresponding to price fluctuations stemming from the asset's own characteristics. This type of risk can be eliminated by diversification and therefore is generally not rewarded by the market.

Example. The terrorist attack on the World Trade Center in New York on 11 September 2001 caused stock prices to collapse (inevitable market risk), a trend which particularly affected the airline industry (specific risk that could have been eliminated by investing in each one of the companies of the S&P 500 index, for instance).

Under assumptions which are beyond our scope, the conclusion of the CAPM is that the expected return r_A of any asset A is the function of only three parameters: the risk-free rate r_f, the expected market risk premium $r_M - r_f$ and the asset's sensitivity to market movements β_A. More specifically:

$$r_A = r_f + \beta_A(r_M - r_f)$$

Example. The risk-free rate is 5% and the expected market return is 8%; stock A is twice as sensitive to market movements as the reference index, i.e. when the index is up 1% the price of A is up 2%. Following the CAPM equation, the expected return of A must be:

$$r_A = 5\% + 2 \times (8\% - 5\%) = 11\%$$

Further reading

Cochrane, J.H. (2005) *Asset Pricing*, revised edn. Princeton University Press, Princeton, NJ.

Exercises

Exercise 1

'The return of my portfolio is 15% per year and its risk is 25% per year. Yoohoo.com stock has a 15% return and 30% risk. Hence, investing in Yoohoo.com would increase the risk of my portfolio without increasing its return.' Comment on this argument.

Exercise 2: zero-coupon bond portfolio

Using the following zero-rate curve, can you build a portfolio that costs nothing and yields $10 000 if all rates go up 25 basis points (i.e. a +0.25% parallel shift)? There are several suitable solutions to this problem.

Maturity	3 months	6 months	1 year	2 years	5 years
Zero-rate	3.72%	4.10%	4.44%	4.09%	3.89%

Exercise 3: risk-free rate and Sharpe ratio

Using the data for the Treasury bond given in Section 5.2, determine the risk-free rate r_f so that the Sharpe ratio equals 1.

Exercise 4: risk and return

The table below gives the price of Richky Corp. stock at the end of each month over the past year in dollars. The risk-free rate was constant at 5%.

Jan.	Feb.	Mar.	Apr.	May	Jun.	Jul.	Aug.	Sep.	Oct.	Nov.	Dec.
144	123	128	137	147	130	139	147	175	162	154	158

1. Calculate the monthly return of Richky Corp. knowing that the stock price was $134 on 31 December of the previous year and that Richky Corp. distributed a $13 dividend per share on 30 June. Assume that the dividend is reinvested in stocks.
2. What is the risk–return profile of Richky Corp. for the year?
3*. You are the Chief Financial Officer for Richky Corp. At a business meeting, Mr David Haffmann, the Production Manager, proposes a project which would

reduce annual production costs by $1.2 per share on average with a standard deviation of $0.6 per share. What do you think of this project?

Exercise 5: risk premium and CAPM

Following the CAPM, the risk-free rate is 3% and the expected market return is 7%. Calculate the risk premium and the Sharpe ratio of the following assets:

(a) Pschitzer Pharmaceuticals (stock): 15% volatility and 1.5 beta.
(b) Security (bond): 3% volatility and 0.2 beta.
(c) Gold (mutual fund): 12% volatility and −0.5 beta. Is it worth investing in this asset? Can you identify a link between the concepts of beta and correlation?

Problem 1: currency portfolio

It is recommended to use a spreadsheet to solve this exercise.

You are an investor from the euro zone and would like to invest 1 billion euros in dollars (USD), yen (JPY) or pounds (GBP). You have the following market data and forecasts:

Currency	1-year interest rate	€ exchange rate	Expected exchange rate in a year	Expected volatility for the year
USD	2.5%	$1.30	$1.40	10%
JPY	0.25%	¥130	¥120	8%
GBP	4.5%	£0.65	£0.65	6%

Correlation	USD	JPY	GBP
USD	1	0.30	0.25
JPY	0.30	1	0.50
GBP	0.25	0.50	1

1. Plot the three currencies on a risk–return graph. *Do not forget the interest!*
2. Draw the risk–return evolution of a portfolio which gradually switches from dollars to yen (i.e. 100% dollars, then 90% dollars and 10% yen, etc.). Repeat this question for a portfolio which gradually switches from yen to pounds, and then from pounds to dollars.
3. Show the risk–return profiles of all the possible portfolios made of the three currencies, considering only long positions.

4. Which portfolio would you choose to obtain an expected return around 5.25%? Is this choice optimal?

Problem 2*: portfolio optimization

Consider two assets A and B with returns R_A, R_B and volatilities σ_A, σ_B respectively, and correlation ρ. Let P be a portfolio of A and B with weights w and $1-w$ respectively.

1. Can the sign of w be negative?
2. Express the return R_P of the portfolio as a function of w, R_A and R_B.
3. Express the risk σ_P of the portfolio as a function of w, σ_A, σ_B and ρ.
4. Suppose $\rho = 1$. What is the shape of σ_P as a function of w? Is there an optimal value for w which minimizes σ_P? What if $\rho = -1$?
5. Suppose $-1 < \rho < 1$. What is the shape of σ_P as a function of w? Is there an optimal value for w which minimizes σ_P?
6. Suppose A is the risk-free asset. How does this affect σ_P? What is the optimal portfolio of A and B which minimizes σ_P?

Solutions

Exercise 1

The answer all depends on the correlation between the portfolio and Yoohoo.com. If the correlation is lower than 1 it is quite possible that adding Yoohoo.com to the portfolio will bring gains of diversification (see Problem 2).

Exercise 2: zero-coupon bond portfolio

When rates go up bond prices go down. To make a profit in this situation one must thus sell bonds before prices drop. For instance, we can take a short position in a 5-year zero-coupon with a million dollar face value. By selling this zero-coupon we collect $\frac{1\,000\,000}{(1+3.89\%)^5} = \$826\,288$ in cash. To net out this cash flow we can, for instance, buy a 1-year zero-coupon with face value $826\,288 \times (1+4.44\%) = \$862\,975$. By construction the mark-to-market price of our portfolio is zero.

Asset	Position	Unit price	Mark-to-market
5-year zero-coupon	short 1 000 000	$0.8262877	−$826 288
1-year zero-coupon	long 862 975	$0.9574875	$826 288
Portfolio	long 1	—	0

If all rates go up 25 basis points the mark-to-market of the portfolio will be:

Asset	Position	Unit price	Mark-to-market
5-year zero-coupon	short 1 000 000	$0.8164172	−$816 417
1-year zero-coupon	long 862 975	$0.9552011	$824 314
Portfolio	long 1	—	+$7897

Finally, to make exactly a $10 000 profit we should **leverage** (i.e. multiply all quantities) approximately 1.27 times (10 000/7897).

Exercise 3: risk-free rate and Sharpe ratio

Risk-free rate, so the Sharpe ratio equals 1:

$$r_f = r_{Treasury} - Sharpe \times \sigma_{Treasury} = 6.19\% - 1 \times 0.20\% = 5.99\%$$

Solutions

Exercise 4: risk and return

1. The $13 dividend per share paid on 30 June allows us to buy $\frac{13}{130} = 0.1$ extra share. Taking this into account we get the following returns:

Month	Price	Quantity	Mark-to-market	Return
Dec. N − 1	134	1	134.00	
Jan.	144	1	144.00	7.46%
Feb.	123	1	123.00	−14.6%
Mar.	128	1	128.00	4.1%
Apr.	137	1	137.00	7.0%
May	147	1	147.00	7.3%
Jun.	130	1.1	143.00	−2.7%
Jul.	139	1.1	152.90	6.9%
Aug.	147	1.1	161.70	5.8%
Sep.	175	1.1	192.50	19.0%
Oct.	162	1.1	178.20	−7.4%
Nov.	154	1.1	169.40	−4.9%
Dec.	158	1.1	173.80	2.6%

2. Using the data from the table above, the annual return of Richky Corp. is $\frac{173.80 - 134.00}{134.00} = 29.70\%$ with a monthly standard deviation of 8.76%, or $8.76\% \times \sqrt{12} = 30.36\%$ per year. With a risk-free rate of 5%, the Sharpe ratio is $\frac{29.70\% - 5\%}{30.36\%} = 0.81$, which is quite good.

3*. At a price of $158 an annual saving of $1.2 means an increase of 0.76% in the annual return. The $0.6 standard deviation means an extra risk of 0.38% per year. If the risks added up, we would get a standard deviation of 9.14% per month, i.e. 32.56% per year for an annual return of 30.46%. The Sharpe ratio would be 0.80, a slight deterioration.

However, the risks only add up if the return of David Haffmann's project is perfectly correlated with the stock price (cf. Problem 2). But in the case of zero correlation, for example, the total risk would be $\sqrt{8.76\%^2 \times 12 + 0.38\%^2 \times 12} = 30.37\%$, in which case the Sharpe ratio would improve to 0.84.

A more detailed analysis shows that the Sharpe ratio is in fact a function of the correlation between the project savings and the stock price:

$$\text{Sharpe}(\rho) = \frac{32.56\% - 5\%}{\sqrt{12 \times (8.76\%^2 + 0.38\%^2 + 2\rho \times 8.76\% \times 0.38\%)}}$$

From this relationship we obtain that the correlation must be smaller than 0.69 in order for the project to improve the risk–return profile of the company.

Exercise 5: risk premium and CAPM

(a) Pschitzer Pharmaceuticals (stock):
- Risk premium: $r_A - r_f = \beta_A(r_M - r_f) = 1.5 \times (7\% - 3\%) = 6\%$.
- Sharpe ratio: $Sharpe_A = \dfrac{r_A - r_f}{\sigma_A} = \dfrac{6\%}{15\%} = 0.4$.

(b) Security (bond):
- Risk premium: 0.8%.
- Sharpe ratio: 0.27.

(c) Gold (mutual fund):
- Risk premium: −2%.
- Sharpe ratio: −0.17.

At first sight, investing in the Gold fund seems irrational since its risk premium is negative: the expected return of this investment (1%) is inferior to the risk-free rate.

This comes from the fact that the beta is negative: when the market is up 1% the Gold fund is down 0.5%; but conversely, when the market is down 1% the fund is up 0.5%. Thus, investing in Gold allows us to reduce losses in a bear market and investors must be ready to pay for this natural protection through a lower expected return.

Clearly this protection can be very useful when optimizing a portfolio: an investor who has a long position in the market can significantly reduce her portfolio risk by investing in the Gold fund as a result of the negative correlation between the market and the fund returns. The concepts of beta and correlation are thus strongly linked. In fact one would find that:

$$\beta_A = \rho_A \dfrac{\sigma_A}{\sigma_M}$$

Therefore, the beta of an asset is nothing else but its correlation coefficient to the market normalized by the market volatility. It is also a regression coefficient.

Problem 1: currency portfolio

1. Since we already know the volatility of each currency, this question comes down to determining the expected return of the three currencies. For example, consider the yen: to invest all the capital in yen, we must first exchange 1 billion euros for 130 billion yen. As atrocious as the 0.25% Japanese interest can be, it is still better than nothing. After 1 year the capital would grow to 130 325 000 000 yen. But this amount is worth nothing for a euro zone investor: it still has to be converted at the spot euro–yen exchange rate in 1 year, which, according to expectations, would be: $\dfrac{130\,325\,000\,000}{120} = €1\,086\,041\,667$. Therefore, the expected return of an investment in yen is 8.60%.

Solutions 81

The same argument would lead to an expected return of −4.86% for the dollar and 4.50% for the pound.

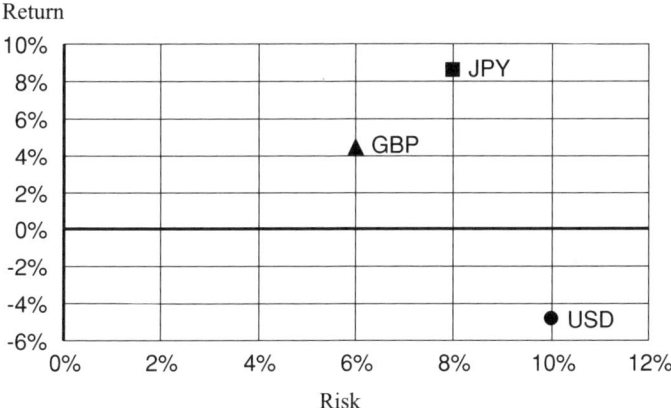

2. Evolution of the risk–return profile of a portfolio gradually switching from dollars to yen to pounds to dollars:

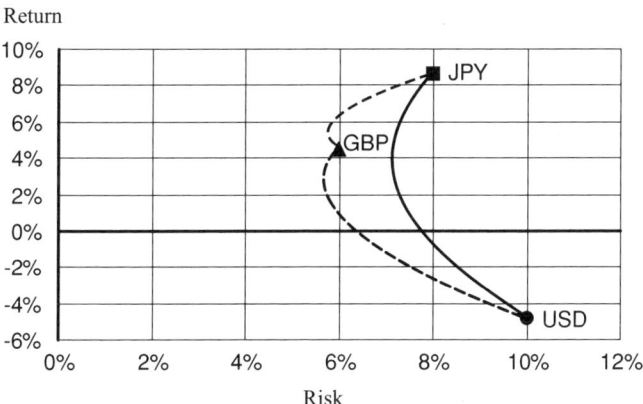

3. In this question we must determine the risk and return of all possible portfolios made up of the three currencies. Let w_{USD}, w_{JPY} and w_{GBP} denote the weights of the currencies. Since we only consider long positions, we have the following constraints:

$$\begin{cases} 0 \leq w_{USD} \leq 1, \quad 0 \leq w_{JPY} \leq 1, \quad 0 \leq w_{GBP} \leq 1 \\ w_{USD} + w_{JPY} + w_{GBP} = 1 \end{cases}$$

Under these constraints, the risk–return profile of a portfolio P = (w_{USD}, w_{JPY}, w_{GBP}) can be described by the following equations:

$$R_P = -4.82\% \times w_{USD} + 8.60\% \times w_{JPY} + 4.50\% \times w_{GBP}$$

$$\sigma_P = \sqrt{\sum_{(i,j)\in\{USD, JPY, GBP\}^2} w_i w_j \sigma_i \sigma_j \rho_{i,j}}$$

where σ_i is the risk of currency i and $\rho_{i,j}$ is the correlation coefficient between currencies i and j ($\rho_{i,j} = 1$ when $i = j$).

Following the steps below, we can use a spreadsheet to determine the risk and return of a finite number of portfolios.

1. Build a table of weights as below:

↓ w_{JPY} w_{USD} →	0%	5%	10%	...
0%	$w_{GBP} = 1 - w_{USD} - w_{JPY}$	95%	90%	...
5% ...	95%	90%	...	...

2. Build a table of portfolio returns using the table of weights above and the expected returns of each currency.
3. Build a table of portfolio volatilities using the table of weights above and the expected volatilities and correlations of the three currencies.

This methodology yields the graph below. It is interesting to note that some risk–return points are outside the frontiers of the previous graph. This means that there exists an optimal portfolio of the three currencies which has, for example, the same return as the pound with a lower risk.

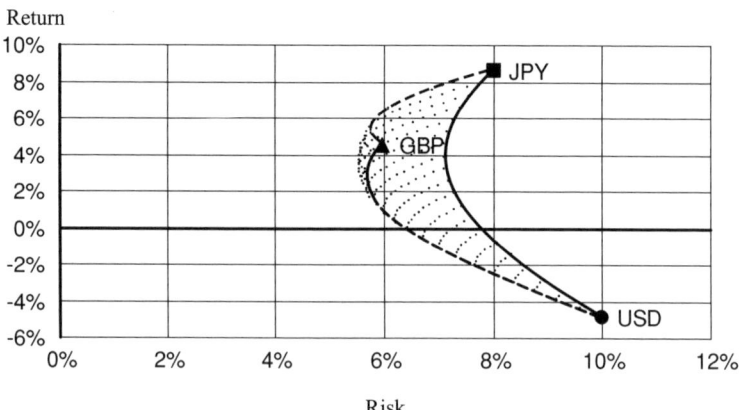

4. A mix of 25% in dollars and 75% in yen would give a 5.25% annual return for an annual risk of 7.16%. However, we know from the previous question

that there exists a better solution. Indeed, we find that a mix of 5% in dollars, 30% in yen and 65% in pounds gives a 5.27% annual return for a lower annual risk of 5.68%. Finding the optimal weights would require more sophisticated mathematics or an advanced optimization software.

Problem 2*: portfolio optimization

1. Weights can be negative in case of short positions.
2. Portfolio return as a function of w, R_A and R_B:

$$R_P = wR_A + (1-w)R_B = R_B + w(R_A - R_B)$$

3. Portfolio variance:

$$\begin{aligned}\text{Var}(R_P) &= \text{Var}(wR_A + (1-w)R_B) \\ &= w^2\sigma_A^2 + (1-w)^2\sigma_B^2 + 2w(1-w)\sigma_A\sigma_B\rho \\ &= (\sigma_A^2 + \sigma_B^2 - 2\sigma_A\sigma_B\rho)w^2 + 2\sigma_B(\sigma_A\rho - \sigma_B)w + \sigma_B^2\end{aligned}$$

Portfolio risk:

$$\sigma_P = \sqrt{\text{Var}(R_P)}$$

4. If $\rho = 1$, we have:

$$\begin{aligned}\sigma_P &= \sqrt{w^2\sigma_A^2 + (1-w)^2\sigma_B^2 + 2w(1-w)\sigma_A\sigma_B} \\ &= \sqrt{(w\sigma_A + (1-w)\sigma_B)^2} \\ &= |w\sigma_A + (1-w)\sigma_B|\end{aligned}$$

In this case, the graph of σ_P as a function of w consists of two line segments, whose minimum is reached at $w^* = -\dfrac{\sigma_B}{\sigma_A - \sigma_B}$, with $\sigma_P(w^*) = 0$. If, for example, the risk of A is higher than B we would take a short position on A and a long position on B, in proportions such that each position has the same variance. Since the assets are perfectly correlated, any profit on A would be exactly offset by a loss on B and vice versa. By construction this portfolio is riskless and must earn the risk-free rate r_f.

The case where $\rho = -1$ is similar with the benefit of only dealing with long positions.

5. In the general case, $\text{Var}(R_P)$ is parabolic with a minimum reached at:

$$w^* = -\frac{\sigma_B(\sigma_A\rho - \sigma_B)}{\sigma_A^2 + \sigma_B^2 - 2\sigma_A\sigma_B\rho}$$

In this case the minimum value $\sigma_P(w^*)$ is nonzero: if A and B are not perfectly correlated, risk cannot be entirely eliminated.

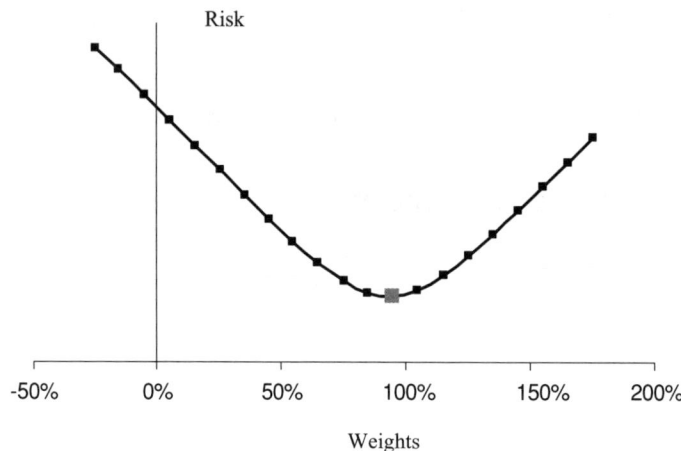

6. If A is risk-free we have $\sigma_A = 0$. $R_A = r_f$ is then a constant variable and its correlation with R_B is zero. In this case, $\sigma_P = \sqrt{(1-w)^2 \sigma_B^2} = |1-w|\sigma_B$: the risk of the portfolio is proportional to σ_B with respect to B's weight. The minimum is reached at $w = 1$, i.e. when everything is invested in the risk-free asset A. This is not very surprising.

6 Binomial model

6.1 Introduction

As we mentioned in Chapter 4, the valuation of derivatives is usually difficult and requires making several economic assumptions. Important exceptions are forward and futures contracts, whose arbitrage price can be determined with minimal assumptions.

In the case of options additional assumptions must be made about the behaviour of asset prices. The simplest and most didactic model is the **binomial model** proposed by Cox, Ross and Rubinstein in 1979, where we consider only two possible scenarios (up or down) over a specified period.

Despite its simplicity this approach leads to an efficient and robust pricing algorithm which is still very much in use on trading floors. It is only since the late 1990s that it was progressively replaced by more efficient methods to respond to the dramatic increase in trading volumes of futures and options markets (more than 300 trillion dollars in 2004 according to the Bank for International Settlements).

The binomial model is a beginner's version of the Black–Scholes model introduced in Chapter 10. Thus, we recommend a careful reading of this chapter.

6.2 Binomial trees

6.2.1 One-step binomial tree: an example

Suppose that gold currently trades at $400 per troy ounce and analysts expect it to either go up $100 or go down $50 in a month's time. The tree below summarizes this setup:

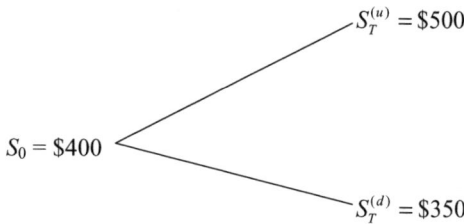

One-step binomial tree for gold prices

According to this model, the owner of a call option on gold with maturity $T = \frac{1}{12}$ and strike of \$450 faces two scenarios:

1. In the favourable case where the gold price goes up to \$500 the payoff at maturity T is:

$$c_T^{(u)} = 500 - 450 = \$50$$

2. In the unfavourable case where the price falls to \$350, the call is worth zero:

$$c_T^{(d)} = 0$$

The owner of the call option can thus choose to immediately sell his call on the market and cash in its value c_0 (a positive amount since the payoff of a plain vanilla option is always positive) or he can take the risk to wait until maturity $t = T$ and cash in a random profit. This is summarized in the tree below:

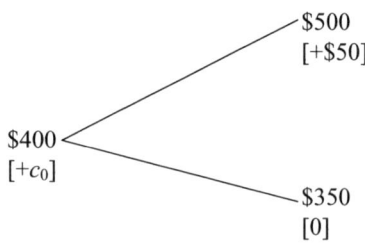

Call value at each node of the binomial tree

There is, however, a **strategy to eliminate the risk of waiting until maturity** T. If the owner of the call decides to sell a quantity Δ of gold the value of his portfolio (call and underlying) is:

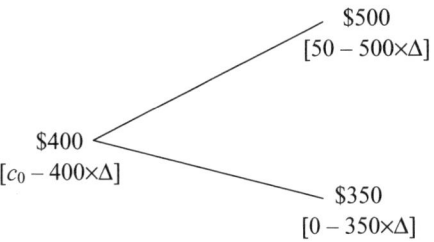

Value of a portfolio which is long one call and short Δ ounces of gold

By choosing Δ such that the two portfolio values at maturity T are the same, the owner of the call eliminates the risk he was facing before. In our example, if he chooses Δ such that: $50 - 500\Delta = -350\Delta$, i.e. $\Delta = \frac{1}{3}$, his 'long call–short 1/3 underlying' portfolio will always be worth –$116.67 at maturity,[1] *regardless of the price of gold.*

This portfolio is thus risk-free and its return between $t = 0$ and $t = T$ must be equal to the risk-free rate r_f, under penalty of arbitrage. Equivalently, since the portfolio value at maturity is a constant, we can calculate its present value:

$$PV = -\frac{166.67}{(1+r_f)^T}$$

But the arbitrage price of the portfolio at time $t = 0$ is also:

$$c_0 - 400\Delta = c_0 - \frac{1}{3} \times 400 = c_0 - 133.33$$

Equating the two results yields **the value of the call at time $t = 0$**:

$$c_0 = 133.33 - \frac{116.67}{(1+r_f)^T}$$

With a 5% risk-free rate and $T = 1/12$ we obtain: $c_0 = \$17.13$.

6.2.2 One-step binomial tree: general case

More generally, consider a derivative security whose value D_t is a function of time t and the spot price S_t of the underlying. In a one-step binomial model over the time period $[0, T]$, the initial price S_0 of the underlying is known and we only

---

[1] Recall that a negative portfolio value does not correspond to a loss, but rather to the amount to pay to get rid of the portfolio (see Chapter 5).

envisage two outcomes $S_T^{(u)}$ and $S_T^{(d)}$ for the final underlying price:

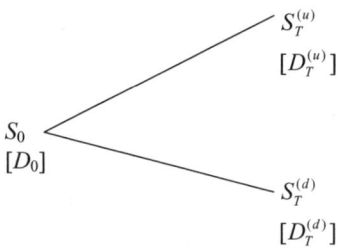

Binomial tree: general case

If we build a portfolio which is long the derivative and short a quantity Δ of the underlying, its value at any point in time t is $P_t = D_t - \Delta S_t$. Choosing Δ such that $P_T^{(u)} = P_T^{(d)}$ we get a risk-free portfolio whose value at maturity T does not depend[2] on S_T. Thus, P_T is a certain cash flow whose present value at time $t = 0$ is: $P_0 = \dfrac{P_T}{(1+r_f)^T}$, where r_f is the risk-free rate for maturity T. Furthermore, we have $P_0 = D_0 - \Delta S_0$. Equating both results yields the value D_0 of the derivative at time $t = 0$:

$$D_0 = \Delta \times S_0 + \frac{D_T^{(?)} - \Delta \times S_T^{(?)}}{(1+r_f)^T}$$

$$\Delta = \frac{D_T^{(u)} - D_T^{(d)}}{S_T^{(u)} - S_T^{(d)}}$$

where $S_T^{(?)}$ and $D_T^{(?)}$ can be taken in either outcome (*u*)p or (*d*)own.

The interpretation of the quantity Δ is straightforward: it is the ratio of the change in value of the derivative to the change in the underlying price: $\Delta = \dfrac{\delta D_T}{\delta S_T}$.

6.2.3 Multiple-step binomial model

The binomial model is easily generalized to multiple steps. We illustrate here how this is done using our example of gold. The current spot price is still at \$400 per troy ounce and the tree below shows the analysts' expected evolution for the

---

[2] Precisely, the value at maturity of the portfolio does not depend on the realization of either outcome $[S_T = S_T^{(u)}]$ or $[S_T = S_T^{(d)}]$.

following 2 months:

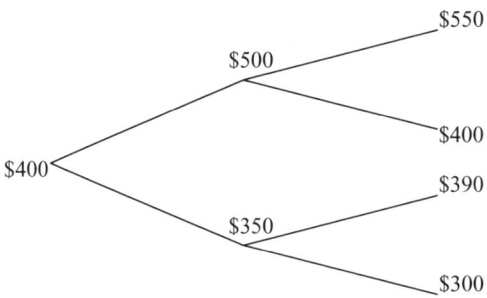

Binomial tree for gold prices over two periods

Moreover, analysts believe that the risk-free rate will remain at 4% over each period.

With this information we can calculate the value p_0 of a put on gold struck at $450 in 2 months. To do so we iterate the binomial model going backwards.

- **Step $t = 2$ months:** the value of the put is the payoff $\max(0, K - S_2) = \max(0, 450 - S_2)$. We now have the following tree:

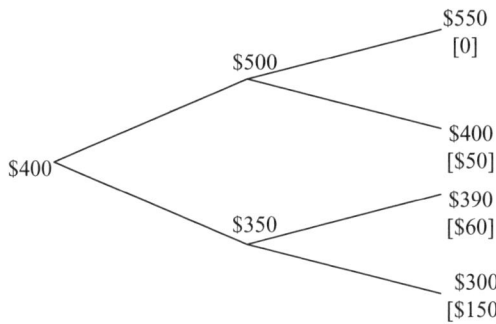

Value of the put at step $t = 2$ months

- **Step $t = 1$ month:** we use the one-step model twice for each of the 'up' and 'down' scenarios.

'Up' scenario: $\Delta^{(u)} = \dfrac{0 - 50}{550 - 400} = -\dfrac{1}{3}$;

$$p_1^{(u)} = -\dfrac{1}{3} \times 500 + \dfrac{0 - (-\tfrac{1}{3}) \times 550}{(1 + 4\%)^{1/12}} = \$16.07$$

'Down' scenario: $\Delta^{(d)} = \dfrac{60 - 150}{390 - 300} = -1$;

$$p_1^{(d)} = -350 + \dfrac{150 - (-1) \times 300}{(1 + 4\%)^{1/12}} = \$98.53$$

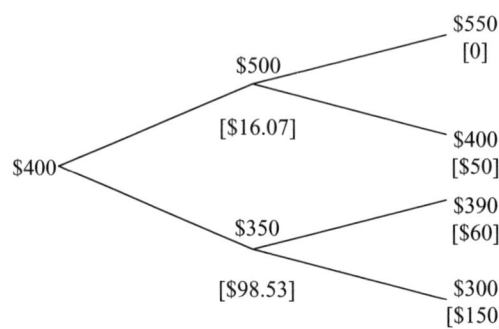

Value of the put at steps $t = 1$ month and $t = 2$ months

- **Step $t = 0$:** we use the one-step model one more time and get:

$$\Delta = \frac{16.07 - 98.53}{500 - 350} = -0.55$$

$$p_0 = -0.55 \times 400 + \frac{16.07 - (-0.55) \times 500}{(1 + 4\%)^{1/12}} = \$70.12$$

- **Conclusion**: the value of a 2-month put on gold struck at $450 is $70.12. In comparison the price of a forward contract with the same characteristics is $-\$48.53$, and $21.59 for a call.

References and further reading

Cox, J.C., Ross, S.A. and Rubinstein, M. (1979) 'Option pricing: a simplified approach'. *Journal of Financial Economics*, **7**: 229–263.

Hull, J.C. (2005) *Options, Futures and Other Derivatives*, 6th edn. Prentice Hall, Englewood Cliffs, NJ.

Shreve, S.S. (2003) *Stochastic Calculus for Finance I: The Binomial Asset Pricing Model*. Springer, Berlin.

Exercises

Exercise 1: two-step binomial tree

Wurtz AG stock currently trades at €120 in Frankfurt. Analysts expect the following price evolution for the coming 2 years:

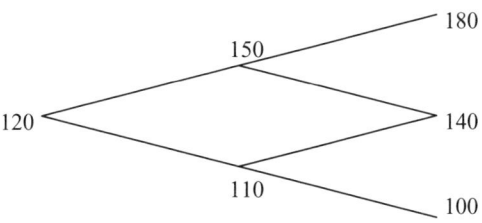

Analysts also predict that no dividend will be paid and that the risk-free rate will remain at 5% for all steps.

1. Calculate the value of a 2-year European call on Wurtz AG struck at €130.
2. Calculate the value of a 2-year European put on Wurtz AG struck at €130.

Exercise 2: 'at-the-money-forward' options

The price of a 1 kg gold bar is $10 000. Analysts predict that the price may rise or fall by 10% every 6 months and that the risk-free rate will remain at 5% per annum for all maturities.

1. Sketch a binomial tree modelling the evolution of the gold bar for the next year.
2. Calculate the 1-year forward price F of the gold bar.
3. Calculate the value of a 1-year European call on the gold bar with strike F.
4. Calculate the value of a 1-year European put on the gold bar with strike F.
5. Compare the values of the two options.

Exercise 3*: binomial model and forward contracts

Consider a one-step binomial model.

1. Show that the binomial model is consistent with the arbitrage price formula for forward contracts in Chapter 4. (In other words, apply a one-step binomial model on a forward contract with strike K and maturity T for an underlying which pays no cash flows and compare your result with the arbitrage price given in Chapter 4.)
2. Show that if $K > S_T^{(u)} > S_T^{(d)}$, the value of a put is equal to the arbitrage price of a forward contract with the same characteristics. What happens if $K < S_T^{(d)} < S_T^{(u)}$?

Exercise 4: American option

Compute the value of an *American* put with strike $50 and a 2-year maturity using a two-step binomial tree. The underlying asset pays no cash flows, its price can rise or fall by 20% each year, and the risk-free rate is constant at 5% in each annual period. *Hint:* American puts can be exercised at each node of the tree with a payoff of $K - S_t$. A rational investor will thus exercise early if the value of holding the call is below $K - S_t$.

Exercise 5

In a spreadsheet, build a 12-step binomial tree to calculate the value of a European call with a strike price of 100 and a maturity of 1 year. Assume that the 1-month annualized interest rate is 10% at every period, and that the underlying asset pays no cash flows and has a price of 100, which can go up or down by 2% every month. *Hint:* In this setup the middle branches of the binomial tree can be recombined.

Exercise 6: call on bond

We consider a world where the zero-rate curve is always flat at a rate r which can vary periodically. At present, $r = 5\%$ for all maturities. Analysts make the following scenarios for r over the next 2 years:

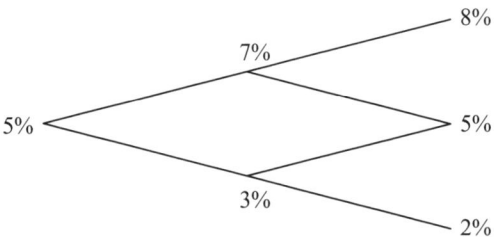

1. Calculate the corresponding evolution of the price of a 5-year zero-coupon bond at each node of the tree. *Keep in mind that the maturity of the zero-coupon will shorten at each step.*
2. Calculate the value of a 2-year European call struck at 90 on this zero-coupon.

Problem 1: Barrier option

A 'knock-out barrier option' is a call or put option which can be exercised at maturity only if the price of the underlying never hit or breached a pre-agreed barrier price H throughout the life of the option. Symmetrically, a 'knock-in barrier option' can only be exercised at maturity if the price of the underlying has hit or breached the barrier price H.

Exercises

1. Do you think barrier options should be:
   (a) more expensive than plain vanilla options of the same characteristics?
   (b) less expensive than plain vanilla options of the same characteristics?
   (c) more expensive in some cases and less expensive in other cases?
2. In this question we consider calls with strike 100 and 1-month maturity. The underlying spot price is 90.
   (a) What is the value of a knock-out call with barrier $H = 95$? Same question for a knock-in call with barrier $H = 95$?
   (b) What difference do you see between a knock-out call with barrier $H = 80$ and a knock-out call with barrier $H' = 110$?
   (c) Suppose that the value of the plain vanilla call is 2 and the value of a knock-out call with barrier $H = 80$ is 1. Can you find the value of another barrier option?
   (d) With a three-step binomial tree calculate the value of a knock-out call with barrier $H = 80$. Assume that the price of the underlying can increase or decrease by 15 at each step and the interest rate is zero.

Problem 2*: risk-neutral probability

In this problem we consider the one-step binomial model over period $[0, T]$. Let $\omega^{(u)}$ denote the 'up' scenario and $\omega^{(d)}$ the 'down' scenario with respective probabilities $p^{(u)}$ and $p^{(d)}$. The underlying asset pays no cash flows and has a price of S_t at any point in time t. D_t is the value of a derivative on this asset at time t, r is the annual risk-free rate and $r^{[T]} = (1+r)^T - 1$ is the compound rate for period $[0, T]$. Furthermore, we suppose that: $S_T^{(u)} = S_0(1+u)$ and $S_T^{(d)} = S_0(1+d)$, where u and d are parameters such that: $u > r^{[T]} > d > -1$.

1. In this question only $S_0 = 100$, $T = 1$, $r = 5\%$, $u = 6\%$, $d = -4\%$. Calculate the value of a call struck at 100. Does this value depend on probabilities $p^{(u)}$ and $p^{(d)}$?
2. Show that the value of the derivative at time $t = 0$ can be written: $D_0 = \frac{1}{(1+r)^T}\left[pD_T^{(u)} + (1-p)D_T^{(d)}\right]$, where p is a function of $r^{[T]}$, u and d.
3. Show that $0 < p < 1$ and then that if we let $p^{(u)} = p$ and $p^{(d)} = 1 - p$ the value D_0 is equal to the expected present value of the payoff D_T.
4. Suppose that $p^{(u)} = p$ and $p^{(d)} = 1 - p$.
   (a) Express the return of the underlying as a function of S_0 and S_T.
   (b) Calculate the expected return $E(R_T)$ of the underlying.
   (c) Why is p called the 'risk-neutral probability'?

Solutions

Exercise 1: two-step binomial tree

1. Value of a European call on a Wurtz AG stock:

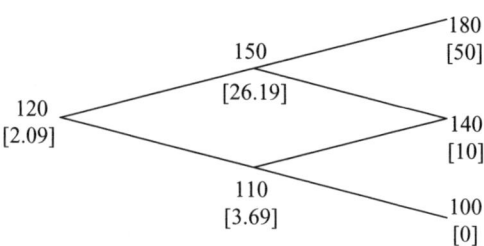

- Step $t = 1$:

  'Up' scenario: $\Delta_1^{(u)} = \dfrac{50 - 10}{180 - 140} = 1$, $c_1^{(u)} = 150 - \dfrac{130}{1 + 5\%} = €26.19$.

  'Down' scenario: $\Delta_1^{(d)} = \dfrac{10 - 0}{140 - 100} = 0.25$, $c_1^{(d)} = 0.25 \times 110 + \dfrac{0 - 0.25 \times 100}{1.05} = €3.69$.

- Step $t = 0$: $\Delta_0 = \dfrac{26.19 - 3.69}{150 - 110} = 0.5625$, $c_0 = 0.5625 \times 120 + \dfrac{26.19 - 0.5625 \times 150}{1.05} = €12.09$.

2. Value of a European put on Wurtz AG:

$$p_0 = €8.28$$

(This value can be calculated either with a binomial tree or using put–call parity.)

Exercise 2: 'at-the-money-forward' options

1. Binomial tree for the evolution of the price of the gold bar:

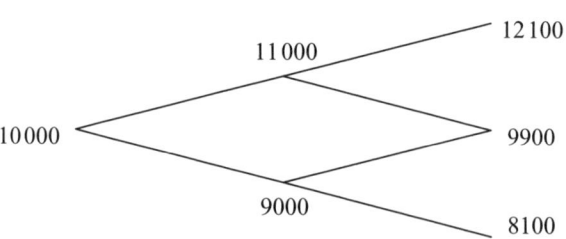

Solutions

2. 1-year forward price of the gold bar:
$$F = 10\,000 \times (1+5\%) = \$10\,500$$

3. Value of a 1-year European call on the gold bar with strike F:

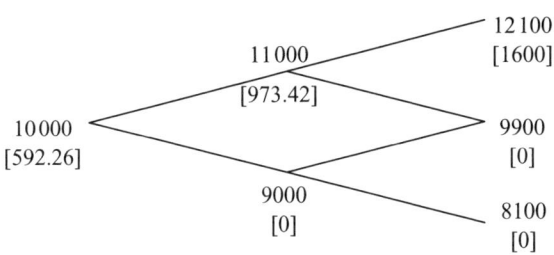

- Step $t = 0.5$: $\Delta_{0.5}^{(u)} = \dfrac{1\,600 - 0}{12\,100 - 9900} \approx 0.7272$; $c_{0.5}^{(u)} \approx 0.7272 \times 11\,000$
$$+ \dfrac{0 - 0.7272 \times 9900}{(1+5\%)^{0.5}} \approx \$973.42.$$

- Step $t \approx 0$: $\Delta_0 \approx \dfrac{973.52 - 0}{11\,000 - 9000} \approx 0.4868$; $c_0 \approx 0.4867 \times 10\,000$
$$+ \dfrac{0 - 0.4868 \times 9000}{(1+5\%)^{0.5}} \approx \$592.26.$$

4. Value of a 1-year European call on the gold bar with strike F:
$$p_0 = \$592.26$$

5. $c_0 = p_0$. According to put–call parity: $c_0 - p_0 = FC_0$. Since the strike price is here equal to the forward price F, the value of the forward contract is $FC_0 = 0$.

Exercise 3*: binomial model and forward contracts

1. The payoff of a forward contract is:
$$FC_T = S_T - K$$

Therefore:
$$\Delta = \dfrac{\left(S_T^{(u)} - K\right) - \left(S_T^{(d)} - K\right)}{\left(S_T^{(u)} - S_T^{(d)}\right)} = 1$$

Thus:
$$FC_0 = \Delta S_0 - \dfrac{\left(S_T^{(d)} - K\right) - \Delta S_T^{(u)}}{(1+r)^T} = S_0 - \dfrac{K}{(1+r)^T}$$

This result agrees with the arbitrage price formula in Chapter 4.

2. If $K > S_T^{(u)} > S_T^{(d)}$ then:

$$p_T^{(u)} = \max(K - S_T^{(u)}, 0) = K - S_T^{(u)}$$
$$p_T^{(d)} = \max(K - S_T^{(u)}, 0) = K - S_T^{(d)}$$

In other words the payoff of the put in both scenarios ('up' and 'down') is the same as a short forward contract. Thus, we know from question 1 that $p_0 = -FC_0$.

If $K < S_T^{(u)} < S_T^{(d)}$ then $p_T^{(u)} = p_T^{(d)} = 0$, thus $p_0 = 0$.

These results can easily be generalized to call options and often simplify calculations in multi-step binomial trees.

Exercise 4: American option

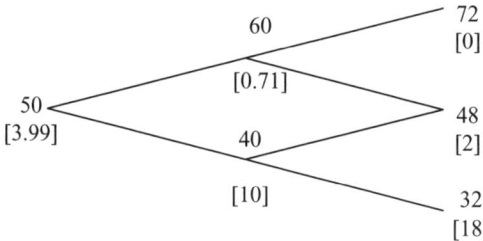

- Step $t = 1$:

    'Up' scenario: $\Delta_1^{(u)} = \dfrac{0 - 2}{72 - 48} = -0.0833$,

    $p_1^{(u)} = -0.0833 \times 60 + \dfrac{0 + 0.0833 \times 72}{1 + 5\%} = \$0.71$. With an underlying price at $60 it would be foolish to exercise the option early, thus $P_1^{US(u)} = \$0.71$.

    'Down' scenario: $\Delta_1^{(d)} = \dfrac{2 - 18}{48 - 32} = -1$,

    $p_1^{(d)} = -40 + \frac{50}{1+5\%} = \$7.62$. With an underlying price at $40 an early exercise allows us to cash in $10 which is better, thus $P_1^{US(d)} = \$10$.

- Step $t = 0$: $\Delta_0 = \dfrac{0.71 - 10}{60 - 40} = -0.4645$, $p_0 = -0.4645 \times 50 + \dfrac{10 + 0.4645 \times 40}{1 + 5\%}$
  $= \$3.99$. With an underlying price at $50 it would be foolish to exercise the option early, thus $P_0^{US} = \$3.99$.

Exercise 5

The tree below displays the results for this spreadsheet-based exercise. There are 12 periods and 13 columns. The monthly interest rate to be used in the calculations is $1.10^{1/12} - 1 = 0.8\%$.

```
                                                                                                    124.34
                                                                                            121.90  [25.13]
                                                                                    119.51  [23.48]  119.46
                                                                            117.17  [21.86]  117.12  [20.25]
                                                                    114.87  [20.29]  114.82  [18.70]  114.78
                                                            112.62  [18.76]  112.57  [17.18]  112.53  [15.57]
                                                    110.41  [17.27]  110.36  [15.70]  110.32  [14.10]  110.28
                                            108.24  [15.82]  108.20  [14.26]  108.16  [12.67]  108.11  [11.07]
                                    106.12  [14.41]  106.08  [12.86]  106.04  [11.29]  105.99  [9.69]   105.95
                            104.04  [13.04]  104.00  [11.51]  103.96  [9.95]   103.92  [8.35]   103.87  [6.74]
                    102.00  [11.73]  101.96  [10.21]  101.92  [8.67]   101.88  [7.09]   101.84  [5.47]   101.80
            100.00  [10.48]  99.96   [8.99]   99.92   [7.48]   99.88   [5.93]   99.84   [4.35]   99.80   [2.66]
    [9.29]  98.00   [7.84]   97.96   [6.38]   97.92   [4.90]   97.88   [3.40]   97.84   [1.84]   97.80
    [6.79]  96.04   [5.39]   96.00   [4.00]   95.96   [2.62]   95.92   [1.28]   95.89   [0.00]
            [4.51]  94.12   [3.23]   94.08   [2.00]   94.04   [0.89]   94.01   [0.00]   93.97
                    [2.58]  92.24   [1.52]   92.20   [0.62]   92.16   [0.00]   92.13   [0.00]
                            [1.14]  90.39   [0.43]   90.36   [0.00]   90.32   [0.00]   90.28
                                    [0.30]  88.58   [0.00]   88.55   [0.00]   88.51   [0.00]
                                            [0.00]  86.81   [0.00]   86.78   [0.00]   86.74
                                                    [0.00]  85.08   [0.00]   85.04   [0.00]
                                                            [0.00]  83.37   [0.00]   83.34
                                                                    [0.00]  81.71   [0.00]
                                                                            [0.00]  80.07
                                                                                    [0.00]
```

Exercise 6: call on bond

1. The price of a T-year zero-coupon bond is given as (Chapter 3):

$$P = \frac{100}{(1+z(T))^T}$$

Applying this formula at each node of the tree yields the zero-coupon prices:

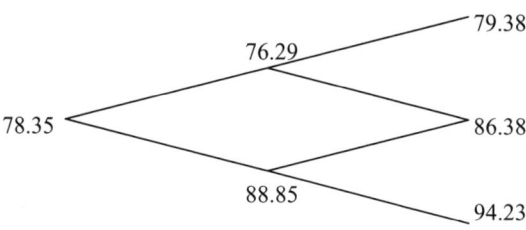

For instance, the terminal node in the middle is calculated as follows:

$$P_2^{(ud)} = \frac{100}{(1+5\%)^3} = 86.38$$

(Recall that in 2 years' time the maturity of the zero-coupon bond is $5 - 2 = 3$ years.)

2. The subtlety in this question lies in the discount rate to be used at each node: in other examples from this chapter the risk-free rate was always the same while here the risk-free rate varies. Taking this into account we find the following call values:

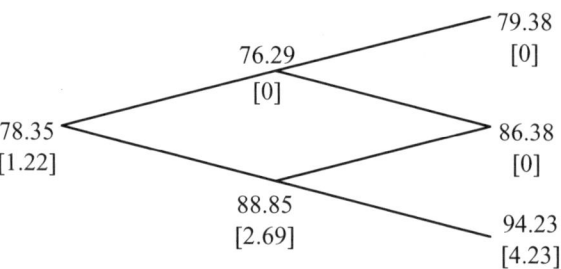

- Step $t = 1$:

$$\Delta_1^{(d)} = \frac{0 - 4.23}{86.38 - 94.23} = 0.5389$$

$$c_1^{(d)} = 0.5389 \times 88.85 + \frac{0 - 0.5389 \times 86.38}{1 + 3\%} = 2.69$$

- Step $t = 0$:

$$\Delta_0 = \frac{0 - 2.69}{76.29 - 88.85} = 0.2142$$

$$c_0 = 0.2142 \times 78.35 + \frac{0 - 0.2142 \times 76.29}{1 + 5\%} = 1.22$$

Solutions

Problem 1: Barrier options

1. Compared to plain vanilla options, barrier options must satisfy additional conditions in order to be exercised. The chances of receiving the vanilla option payoff are thus lower when there are barriers, which entails that the value of barrier options must be lower than that of plain vanilla ones.

2. (a) Consider the payoff of each barrier call:

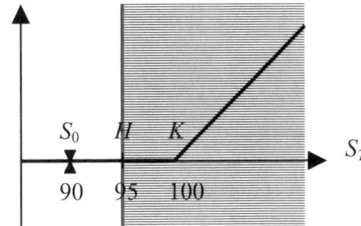 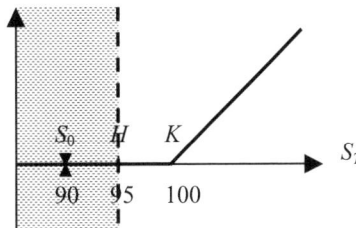

Payoff of a knock-out call with strike $K = 100$ **and barrier** $H = 95$

Payoff of a knock-in call with strike $K = 100$ **and barrier** $H = 95$

Clearly, the knock-out call has no value: starting from 90, if the underlying price exceeds the strike of 100 at maturity it must go through the 95 barrier during the life of the option, in which case it becomes worthless. Symmetrically, the knock-in call has the same value as the plain vanilla call: for the underlying price to exceed the strike it must go through the barrier during the life of the option, which 'switches the option on'.

(b) The knock-out call with barrier $H = 80$ will lose its value if the underlying price goes down from 90 to 80 or less. However, since the strike is 100, when the underlying price reaches 80 it is less likely to jump above 100 within a month. Thus, the owner of this barrier call will probably not mind losing the call when the barrier is hit.

On the other hand, if the knock-out barrier is $H = 110$, breaching the barrier is extremely frustrating since the intrinsic value[3] of the call drops from 9.99 to 0 as soon as the underlying price rises from 109.99 to 110. This is why this type of barrier call is often referred to as a '**kick-out barrier call**'.

---

[3] The intrinsic value of an option is the profit one would get by exercising the option immediately (supposing that it is possible to exercise the option before its maturity, like American options).

(c) A portfolio which is long a knock-in call and a knock-out call with the same characteristics (underlying, strike, maturity, barrier H) has the same payoff as a plain vanilla call. Thus, if the plain vanilla call is worth 2 and the knock-out call is worth 1, the knock-in call is also worth 1.

(d) Note that the value of a barrier option is **path-dependent**: at each node of the tree we must determine whether the underlying previously breached the barrier or not. This is best accomplished by using a nonrecombining binomial tree and eliminating branches where the underlying price was ever below 80:

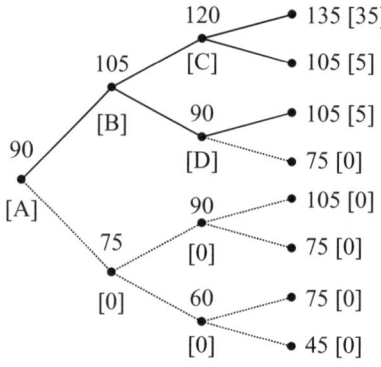

- Step $t = 2$, nodes C and D:

$$\Delta_D = 1$$
$$D = 120 - 100 = 20$$
$$\Delta_C = \frac{5 - 0}{135 - 105} = 0.1667$$
$$C = 0.1667 \times 90 + (0 - 0.1667 \times 75) = 2.5$$

- Step $t = 1$, node B:

$$\Delta_B = \frac{20 - 2.5}{120 - 90} = 0.5833$$
$$B = 0.5833 \times 105 + (20 - 0.5833 \times 120) = 11.25$$

- Step $t = 0$, node A:

$$\Delta_A = \frac{11.25 - 0}{105 - 75} = 0.375$$
$$A = 0.375 \times 90 + (0 - 0.375 \times 75) = 5.625$$

Problem 2*: risk-neutral probability

1. Value of the call:

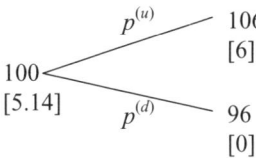

Calculation details:

$$\Delta = \frac{6-0}{106-96} = 0.6$$

$$c_0 = 0.6 \times 100 + \frac{0 - 0.6 \times 96}{1 + 5\%} = 5.14$$

This value clearly does not depend on probabilities $p^{(u)}$ and $p^{(d)}$.

2. We have:

$$D_0 = \Delta \left(S_0 - \frac{S_T^{(d)}}{(1+r)^T} \right) + \frac{D_T^{(d)}}{(1+r)^T}$$

$$= \frac{D_T^{(u)} - D_T^{(d)}}{S_T^{(u)} - S_T^{(d)}} \left(S_0 - \frac{S_T^{(d)}}{(1+r)^T} \right) + \frac{D_T^{(d)}}{(1+r)^T}$$

$$= \frac{D_T^{(u)} - D_T^{(d)}}{S_0 (u - d)} \left(S_0 - \frac{S_0 (1 + d)}{(1+r)^T} \right) + \frac{D_T^{(d)}}{(1+r)^T}$$

$$= \frac{1}{(1+r)^T} \left[\frac{(1+r)^T \left(D_T^{(u)} - D_T^{(d)} \right)}{u - d} - \frac{(1+d) \left(D_T^{(u)} - D_T^{(d)} \right)}{u - d} + D_T^{(d)} \right]$$

$$= \frac{1}{(1+r)^T} \left[\frac{(1+r)^T - 1 - d}{u - d} D_T^{(u)} + \frac{u - (1+r)^T + 1}{u - d} D_T^{(d)} \right]$$

$$= \frac{1}{(1+r)^T} \left[\frac{r^{[T]} - d}{u - d} D_T^{(u)} + \frac{u - r^{[T]}}{u - d} D_T^{(d)} \right]$$

Choosing $p = \frac{r^{[T]} - d}{u - d}$ we can verify that $1 - p = \frac{u - r^{[T]}}{u - d}$, which proves the requested formula.

3. Since $u > r^{[T]} > d > -1$, we have $u - d > r^{[T]} - d > 0$. Therefore $0 < p < 1$. It is thus legitimate to choose $p^{(u)} = p$ and $p^{(d)} = 1 - p$ for probabilities. Substituting this choice in the expression for D_0 derived in question 2 we

obtain:

$$D_0 = \frac{1}{(1+r)^T}\left[p^{(u)}D_T^{(u)} + p^{(d)}D_T^{(d)}\right]$$
$$= \frac{1}{(1+r)^T}E(D_T)$$
$$= E\left(\frac{D_T}{(1+r)^T}\right)$$

as r is a constant.

4. (a) Return of the underlying as a function of S_0 and S_T:
$$R_T = \frac{S_T - S_0}{S_0}$$

(b) Expected return of the underlying:
$$E(R_T) = E\left(\frac{S_T - S_0}{S_0}\right)$$
$$= p\frac{S_0(1+u) - S_0}{S_0} + (1-p)\frac{S_0(1+d) - S_0}{S_0}$$
$$= pu + (1-p)d$$
$$= r^{[T]}$$

(c) $r^{[T]}$ is the risk-free rate for the period $[0, T]$. This is the return an investor will obtain over the period on an investment which is not subject to any source of uncertainty. The underlying asset, however, is a risky investment since its return will either be $u > r^{[T]}$ or $d < r^{[T]}$ according to the state of nature $w^{(u)}$ or $w^{(d)}$ that is drawn. Clearly, a rational investor would only invest in S if he expects a higher return than the risk-free rate (see Chapter 5).

Nevertheless, the value D_0 of the derivative does not depend on the probabilities $p^{(u)}$ and $p^{(d)}$. To express D_0 as the expected value of the discounted payoff D_T we must pick a special probability measure: $p^{(u)} = p$ and $p^{(d)} = 1 - p$. This choice implies an interesting property: it makes the expected return of the underlying S equal to the risk-free rate (and not greater). This property can be interpreted as though we were dealing with a myopic investor who would be neutral to the risk of S and expect the same return as the risk-free rate from all assets. Hence the name 'risk-neutral probability' to qualify p.

7 Lognormal model

7.1 Lognormal model

7.1.1 Fair value

The binomial model presented in Chapter 6 envisages only two outcomes for the final price of the underlying. The main advantage of this approach is its simplicity; however, it is not very realistic. To make the model more convincing, we must develop it into multiple steps.

An alternative approach can be worked out exploiting probabilities. If we suppose that the final underlying price S_T follows a given probability distribution (uniform, normal, lognormal, or whatever), then the **fair value** D_0 of a European derivative security with payoff $D_T = f(T, S_T)$ can be represented as the expectation of the discounted payoff:

$$D_0 = \mathrm{E}\left(\frac{f(T, S_T)}{(1+r)^T}\right)$$

where r is the annual discount rate.

To properly operate in this framework we thus need to make two assumptions:

1. An assumption on the probability distribution of S_T.
2. An assumption on the discount rate r.

7.1.2 Probability distribution of S_T

The probability distribution of S_T must be chosen carefully so as to properly describe the underlying asset. As a fundamental example, the following three properties are generally considered desirable when the underlying asset is a stock.

1. $S_T > 0$: the value of a stock should always be positive.
2. $(D_T = S_T) \Rightarrow \left(D_0 = \dfrac{F_0}{(1+r)^T}\right)$: the model should be **forward-neutral**,[1] i.e. it should correctly price a forward contract delivering one unit of the underlying at maturity T (otherwise there would be an arbitrage).
3. There exists a unique reference price S^* such that for all $x > 0$, $P\left(\left[\frac{S_T}{S^*} = x\right]\right) = P\left(\left[\frac{S_T}{S^*} = \frac{1}{x}\right]\right)$: the 'probability'[2] of the stock price doubling its reference price should be equal to the probability of the stock price halving, and this should hold generally for any x-fold factor.

These three properties are verified by the lognormal distribution with mean $\ln F_0 - \frac{1}{2}\sigma^2 T$ and standard deviation $\sigma\sqrt{T}$, where F_0 is the forward price of the underlying for maturity T and σ is a volatility parameter. (See Chapter 4 for the concept of forward price and Chapter 5 for the concept of volatility.)

The two graphs below show the difference between a normal and a lognormal distribution for two volatility levels: high (40%) and low (10%).

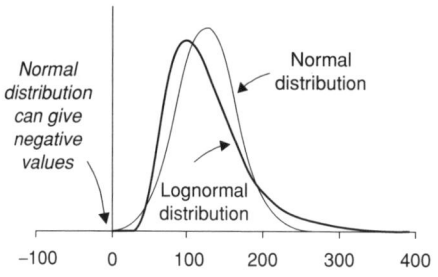
Normal and lognormal distribution
$S_0 = 100$, $F_0 = 125$, $\sigma = 40\%$, $T = 1$

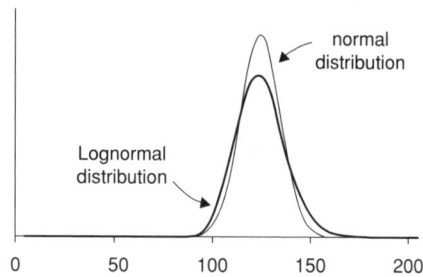
Normal and lognormal distribution
$S_0 = 100$, $F_0 = 125$, $\sigma = 10\%$, $T = 1$

7.1.3 Discount rate

How to choose an appropriate discount rate r is less obvious than it might seem. If the payoff of the derivative were a fixed cash flow C, arbitrage considerations would lead to the risk-free zero-coupon rate $z(T)$ for maturity T. However, when the payoff is subject to uncertainty, portfolio theory suggests that this risk should be rewarded by a higher return than the risk-free rate.

---

[1] The concept of forward-neutrality is close to the concept of risk-neutrality introduced in Chapter 6, Problem 2.
[2] The misleading notation $P([X = x])$ actually corresponds to a probability density function $f_X(x)$ (cf. Appendix A).

Closed-form formulas

We will see in Chapter 10 that the risk can in theory be entirely eliminated through a dynamic strategy known as *delta-hedging* introduced in Chapter 8. Thus choosing the risk-free rate $z(T)$ for r is in fact appropriate and we will do so in this chapter while inviting the reader to hold his or her breath for the detailed justification of this choice.

Note that a corollary of choosing the risk-free rate is that the property of forward-neutrality for modelling S_T becomes:

$$(D_T = S_T) \Rightarrow (D_0 = S_0)$$

under the additional assumption that the underlying asset does not pay any cash flow.

7.2 Closed-form formulas

The lognormal model is enough to find closed-form formulas for the value of European calls and puts as a function of the following parameters:

- Option characteristics: underlying S, strike K and maturity T.
- Forward price of the underlying at maturity: F_0.
- Risk-free zero-coupon rate for maturity T: $r = z(T)$.
- Volatility of the underlying: σ.

Classical integration techniques then yield the following formulas (see this chapter's problem for their derivation):

$$c_0 = \frac{1}{(1+r)^T} \left[F_0 N(d_1) - K N(d_2) \right]$$

$$p_0 = \frac{1}{(1+r)^T} \left[K N(-d_2) - F_0 N(-d_1) \right]$$

where $N(\cdot)$ is the standard normal cumulative distribution (see Appendix A) and d_1, d_2 are the coefficients:

$$d_1 = \frac{\ln \frac{F_0}{K} + \frac{1}{2}\sigma^2 T}{\sigma \sqrt{T}}$$

$$d_2 = \frac{\ln \frac{F_0}{K} - \frac{1}{2}\sigma^2 T}{\sigma \sqrt{T}}$$

Example. Standard & Logs Ltd. shares trade at 290 pence in London, pay no dividends and have a 40% volatility. The 3-month interest rate is 4%. Using the closed-form formula we calculate that the value of a 3-month call struck at 300 pence is roughly 20 pence.

- 3-month forward price of Standard & Logs Ltd.:
$$F_0 = 290 \times (1 + 4\%)^{0.25} = 292.86$$

- Coefficients d_1 and d_2:

$$d_1 = \frac{\ln \frac{292.86}{300} + \frac{1}{2} \times (0.4^2) \times 0.25}{0.4 \times \sqrt{0.25}} = -0.0205$$

$$d_2 = \frac{\ln \frac{292.86}{300} - \frac{1}{2} \times (0.4^2) \times 0.25}{0.4 \times \sqrt{0.25}} = -0.2205$$

- Using a scientific calculator or a normal distribution table we find $N(d_1) = 0.4918$ and $N(d_2) = 0.4127$, so the value of the call is:

$$c_0 = \frac{1}{(1+4\%)^{0.25}} \left[292.86 \times 0.4918 - 300 \times 0.4127 \right] = 20.01$$

The following two graphs compare the value of a call and a put respectively to their payoff. The grey area (the difference between the value and the payoff) corresponds to the **time value** of each option, which decays as we approach the maturity.

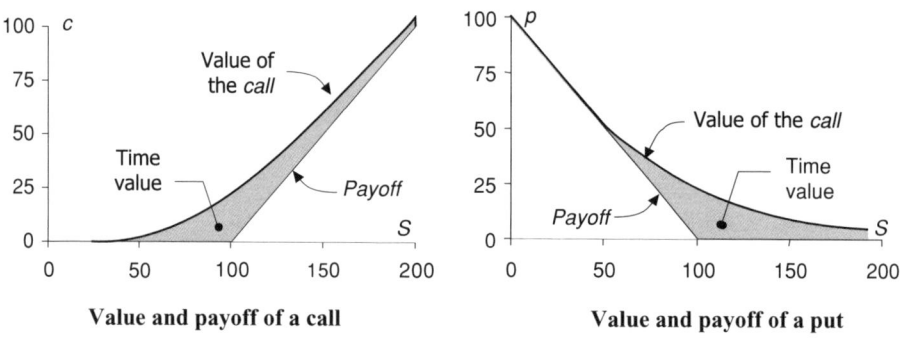

Value and payoff of a call   **Value and payoff of a put**

7.3 Monte-Carlo method

Apart from plain vanilla options and a few classic exotic options, finding closed-form formulas is usually difficult. Hence, it is often necessary to resort to numerical methods, such as the Monte-Carlo method.

This method consists of simulating a very large number of values for S_T according to its probability distribution and calculating the derivative payoff in each simulation. The value of the derivative is then approximately equal to the average simulated payoff:

$$D_0 \approx \frac{1}{(1+r)^T} \times \frac{1}{N} \sum_{i=1}^{N} f(T, s_i)$$

where N is the number of simulations and $s_1, s_2, \ldots, s_N$ are the simulated values of S_T.

The Central Limit Theorem (Appendix A) tells us that for an infinite number of simulations the Monte-Carlo method converges to the fair value of the option. The only disadvantage is that the convergence is relatively slow (the error is of order $1/\sqrt{N}$); but thanks to the ever-increasing speed of microprocessors this has become a minor issue.

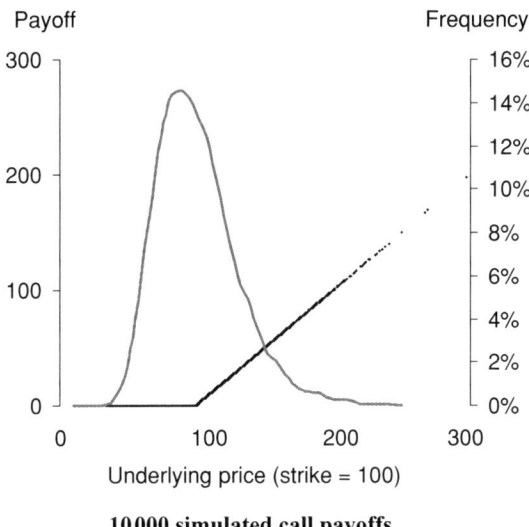

10 000 simulated call payoffs

In practice...

Monte-Carlo simulations are very easy to implement in a spreadsheet, even without using macros.

In Excel, the following functions and formulas will be useful:

- RAND() generates a uniformly distributed random number between 0 and 1.
- NORMSINV(RAND()) generates a normally distributed random number with zero mean and unit standard deviation (see Exercise 11 for proof).

- $F * \text{EXP}(-0.5 * sigma^2 * T + sigma * \text{SQRT}(T) * \text{NORMSINV}(\text{RAND}()))$ simulates a value for S_T, where F, *sigma*, T refer to the cells containing the forward price F_0, volatility and maturity.

Further reading

Glasserman, P. (2003) *Monte Carlo Methods in Financial Engineering*. Springer, New York.
Jaeckel, P. (2002) *Monte Carlo Methods in Finance*. John Wiley & Sons, Chichester.

Exercises

Exercise 1: closed-form formulas

Calculate the value today of a European call and a European put with strike of $50 and maturity of 6 months. The underlying asset is a stock with a price of $50, which pays no dividend and has a 30% volatility. The risk-free rate is 10% per annum.

Exercise 2: plain vanilla pricer

In a spreadsheet, build a pricer which calculates the value of European calls and puts using the closed-form formulas leaving the following parameters open: strike K, maturity T, underlying forward price F, risk-free rate r and volatility σ. Then prepare the following graphs:

1. Value of a 1-year call with strike 100 as a function of F, using $r = 5\%$ and $\sigma = 20\%$. Also draw the discounted forward payoff on the same graph, i.e. $\frac{\max(0, F - K)}{(1+r)^T}$.
2. Value of a 1-year and 2-year puts with strike 100 as a function of $1\% \leq \sigma \leq 100\%$, using $F = 100$ and $r = 10\%$.
3. Value of a 2-year call as time passes for strikes $K = 90$, $K = 100$, $K = 110$, using $F = 100$, $r = 5\%$, $\sigma = 40\%$.

Exercise 3

'The lognormal model builds on the assumption that the log of the final underlying price S_T follows a normal distribution centred on the log of the forward price F_0.'
Comment on this statement.

Exercise 4

Analyse the pros and cons of using a uniform and a normal distribution for modelling the final underlying price S_T of a stock.

Exercise 5: Monte-Carlo pricer

In a spreadsheet, build a pricer which calculates the price of the following derivative payoffs using the Monte-Carlo method with 5000 simulations. Then prepare the graph of the value and discounted forward payoff of the derivative as a function of the forward price F. *Hint:* Use the same random sample while changing the forward price F.

1. 'Ballena call': $D_T = 100 \times \max\left(0, \dfrac{S_T - 100}{S_T}\right)$.
2. 'Kick-out put': $D_T = \max(0, 100 - S_T)$ if $S_T > 50$, 0 otherwise.
3. 'Call spread': long call struck at 100, short call struck at 125.

Exercise 6: intrinsic value

1. Calculate the value of a 3-year European put with strike of €100 on a stock trading at €60 with a 10% volatility. The price of the 3-year zero-coupon is €80. The stock does not pay any dividend.
2. Compare your results with the intrinsic value of the put, i.e. the difference between the strike and the underlying price. Is there an arbitrage opportunity?

Exercise 7: at-the-money-forward call

In the lognormal model, we consider an 'at-the-money-forward European call': a plain vanilla call whose strike K is equal to the underlying forward price F_0.

1. What does the closed-form formula become in this case?
2. Show that the value of the call is approximately: $c_0 \approx \dfrac{40\% \times F_0 \times \sigma\sqrt{T}}{(1+r)^T}$.

   Hint: Prove and use the approximation: $N(x) \underset{x \to 0}{\overset{(1)}{\approx}} \dfrac{1}{2} + \dfrac{x}{\sqrt{2\pi}}$.
3. Compare this approximation with your results in Exercise 1.

Exercise 8*: digital option

The payoff of a digital option with strike K and maturity T is:

$$D_T = \begin{cases} 1 & \text{if } S_T > K \\ 0 & \text{otherwise} \end{cases}$$

1. Draw the payoff function of a digital option with strike 100.
2. Draw the payoff function of a call spread 100–101, i.e. a portfolio which is long a call struck at 100 and short a call struck at 101. Compare with the previous graph and find a lower boundary for the value of the digital option when $F_0 = K = 100$, $\sigma = 25\%$, $r = 0\%$ and $T = 1$.
3. Show that for all $h > 0$:

$$F_0 \dfrac{N(d_0) - N(d_h)}{h} - K\dfrac{N(d'_0) - N(d'_h)}{h} + N(d'_h) \leq D_0(1+r)^T$$

$$\leq N(d'_{-h}) + K\dfrac{N(d'_0) - N(d'_{-h})}{h} - F_0\dfrac{N(d_0) - N(d_{-h})}{h}$$

where, for any real number x:

$$d_x = \frac{\ln\left(\frac{F_0}{K+x}\right) + \frac{1}{2}\sigma^2 T}{\sigma\sqrt{T}}, \quad d'_x = \frac{\ln\left(\frac{F_0}{K+x}\right) - \frac{1}{2}\sigma^2 T}{\sigma\sqrt{T}}$$

4. Show that for all x:

$$F_0 N'(d_x) = K N'(d'_x)$$

where N' is the density of the standard normal distribution.
5. Using these elements, find a closed-form formula for digital options.

Exercise 9*: lognormal distribution

Let X be a normally distributed random variable with mean μ and standard deviation σ, and let $Y = e^X$.

1. Show that Y follows a lognormal distribution.
2. Show that the expected value of Y is: $E(Y) = \exp(\mu + \frac{1}{2}\sigma^2)$.
3. What is the expected value of Y^2? From this, calculate the variance of Y.
4. Using these elements, show that the lognormal distribution for the final underlying price S_T in Section 7.1.2 satisfies the three desired properties for stock prices.

Exercise 10: quadratic option

The payoff of a quadratic option with strike K and maturity T is:

$$D_T = (S_T - K)^2$$

1. Draw the payoff function of a quadratic option with strike 100.
2. Give the closed-form formula for quadratic options. *Hint:* Use the results of the previous exercise.
3. Calculate the value of a 1-year quadratic option with strike £100 on a share trading at £105 that does not pay dividends. Volatility is 25% per year and the risk-free rate is 10% per annum.

Exercise 11*: uniform and normal distribution

Let X be a random variable with uniform distribution over the interval [0, 1], and let $Y = N^{-1}(X)$, where $N(\cdot)$ is the cumulative distribution function of a standard normal variable. Show that Y follows a standard normal distribution.

Problem*: closed-form formulas for European calls and puts

The aim of this problem is to come up with closed-form formulas for European calls and puts using the lognormal model.

1. Show that if Y is lognormally distributed with parameters (μ, σ) there exists a normally distributed variable X such that:
$$Y = \exp(\mu + \sigma X)$$

2. Show that:
$$c_0 = \frac{1}{(1+r)^T \sqrt{2\pi}} \int_{-d_2}^{+\infty} \left[\exp\left(\sigma\sqrt{T}x + \ln F_0 - \tfrac{1}{2}\sigma^2 T\right) - K \right] e^{-\frac{x^2}{2}} dx$$

3. Derive the closed-form formula for the call using the change of variable $y = \sigma\sqrt{T} - x$.
4. Derive the formula for the put using put–call parity. *Assume that the underlying does not pay dividends.*

Solutions

Exercise 1: closed-form formulas

- Forward price:

$$F_0 = 50 \times (1 + 10\%)^{0.5} = \$52.44$$

- Coefficients d_1 and d_2:

$$d_1 = \frac{\ln \frac{52.44}{50} + 0.5 \times (0.3^2) \times 0.5}{0.3 \times \sqrt{0.5}} = 0.3307$$

$$d_2 = \frac{\ln \frac{52.44}{50} - 0.5 \times (0.3^2) \times 0.5}{0.3 \times \sqrt{0.5}} = 0.1186$$

- Value of the call and the put:

$$c_0 = \frac{52.44 \times N(0.3307) - 50 \times N(0.1186)}{(1 + 10\%)^{0.5}} = \$5.39$$

$$p_0 = \frac{50 \times N(-0.1186) - 52.44 \times N(-0.3307)}{(1 + 10\%)^{0.5}} = \$3.07$$

We can verify that $c_0 - p_0 = 5.39 - 3.07 = 2.32 = 50 - \frac{50}{(1+10\%)^{0.5}} = FC_0$ (put–call parity).

Exercise 2: plain vanilla pricer

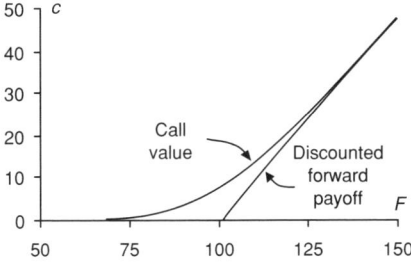

1. Value of a 1-year call as a function of F

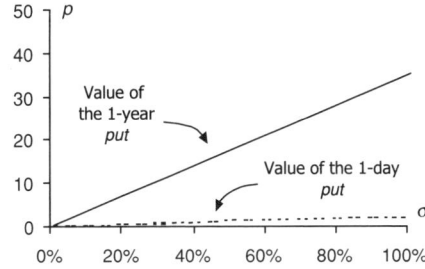

2. Value of a put as a function of volatility σ (1-year and 1-day maturities)

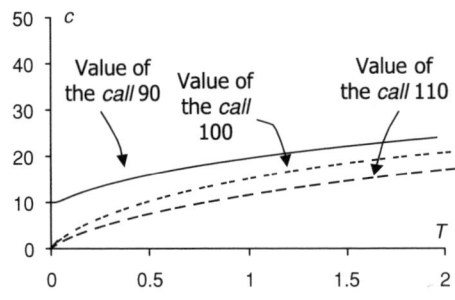

**3. Value of a call as time passes
(90, 100 and 110 strikes)**

Exercise 3

This statement is not entirely true. By definition, a random variable X is lognormally distributed with parameters (μ, σ) if the variable $Y = \ln(X)$ is normally distributed with parameters (μ, σ). In the lognormal model, the final price of the underlying S_T is lognormally distributed with parameters $(\ln F_0 - \frac{1}{2}\sigma^2 T, \sigma\sqrt{T})$, which means that $\ln(S_T)$ has a normal distribution, centred on $\ln F_0 - \frac{1}{2}\sigma^2 T$ and not around $\ln F_0$ as the statement asserts. The term $-\frac{1}{2}\sigma^2 T$ is indeed necessary so that the distribution of S_T is centred on the forward price (see Exercise 9).

Exercise 4

As an example, consider the stock of Caffè Bianco SpA, currently trading at €100 in Milan. A uniform distribution on the interval [€0, €200] would give a zero probability for the stock to have a negative value (which is desirable) or to have a value greater than €200 (a more cumbersome restriction but not necessarily unrealistic). However, the problem with the uniform distribution is that it assigns the same probability to Caffè Bianco SpA staying at its current level of €100, increasing moderately to €105 or plummeting to €20 – which is counter-intuitive.

The normal distribution is more realistic: the probability that the stock price deviates from its starting level decreases exponentially with the size of the deviation. Thus, a normal distribution would be perfectly satisfactory, with only two exceptions: it gives a non-zero probability to Caffè Bianco SpA's having a negative value and it assigns the same probability to the stock price going up or down 100%. With stocks, however, doubling the price has a different meaning than losing all value, which is a bankruptcy.

Exercise 5: Monte-Carlo pricer

The screen capture below shows our solution for the 'Ballena call'. Note that we used the Table function in Excel to automatically calculate the price and discounted forward payoff for various forward prices.

Solutions

	A	B	C	D	E	F	G	H
1		Forward	110					
2		Maturity	2	years				
3		Risk-free rate	6.00%					
4		Volatility	30%					
5				=AVERAGE(D10:D5				
6		Price	12.15	009)/(1+C3)^C2				
7		Disc. Fwd Payoff	8.09					
8								
9	Simulation	Uniform	S_T	Payoff		Forward	Price	Disc. Fwd Payoff
10	1	0.885956609	167.64	40.35		110	12.15	8.09
11	2	0.011100996	60.40	0.00		50	0.39	0.00
12	3	Cells generated with RAND() then Copy / Paste Special... Values	17	=$C$1*EXP($C$4*SQRT($C$2)*NORMSINV(B10)-0.5*$C$4^2*$C$2)	65	=100*MAX(1-100/C10,0)	39	60	1.16	0.00
13	4		19		84		81	70	2.48	0.00
14	5		91		39		25.59	80	4.30	0.00
15	6		49		59		0.00	90	6.60	0.00
16	7		84		60		0.00	100	9.27	0.00
17	8		73		93		46.50	110	12.15	8.09
18	9		92		74		0.00	120	15.13	14.83
19	10	0.156409396	65.51	0.00		130	18.14	20.54
20	11	0.308008368	81.26	0.00		140	21.14	25.43
21	12	0.161508195	66.10	0.00		150	24.06	29.67
22	13	0.383307603	88.64	0.00		160	26.90	33.37
23	14	0.675298416	121.92	17.98		170	29.63	36.65
24	15	0.317074791	82.15	0.00		180	32.23	39.56
25	16	0.202852292	70.65	0.00		190	34.69	42.16
26	17	0.423689874	92.65	0.00		200	37.00	44.50
27	18	0.269583157	77.47	0.00				
28	19	0.787513608	141.03	29.09				
29	20	0.382469661	88.56	0.00				
5002	4993	0.643433402	117.50	14.90				
5003	4994	0.370767142	87.40	0.00				
5004	4995	0.515425176	102.20	2.15				
5005	4996	0.20197664	70.56	0.00				
5006	4997	0.82391307	149.19	32.97				
5007	4998	0.861587123	159.47	37.29				
5008	4999	0.858459816	158.52	36.92				
5009	5000	0.145181732	64.19	0.00				
5010								

Using this spreadsheet, we obtained the following graphs:

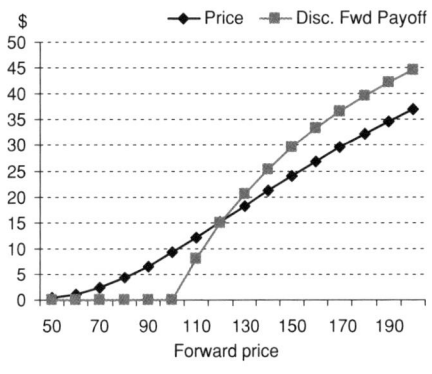

1. 'Ballena call'

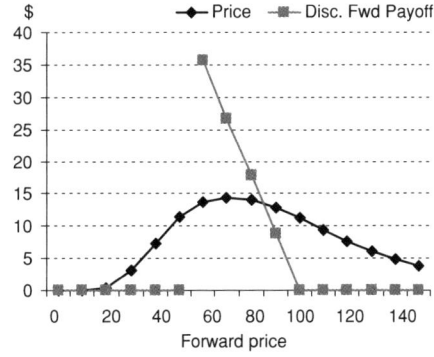

2. 'Kick-out put'

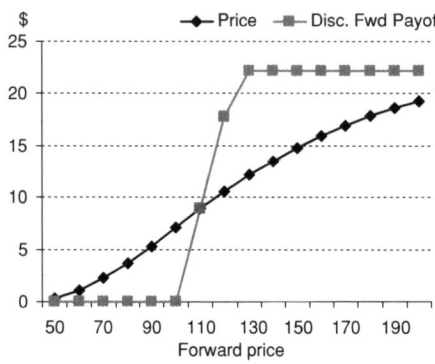

3. 'Call spread'

Exercise 6: intrinsic value

1. Value of the European put.
   - 3-year zero-coupon rate:

$$z = \left(\frac{100}{80}\right)^{\frac{1}{3}} - 1 = 7.7217\%$$

   - Forward price:

$$F_0 = 60 \times (1 + 7.7217\%)^3 = \frac{60}{0.8} = €75$$

   - Coefficients d_1 and d_2:

$$d_1 = \frac{\ln\frac{75}{100} + 0.5 \times (0.1^2) \times 3}{0.1 \times \sqrt{3}} = -1.5743$$

$$d_2 = \frac{\ln\frac{75}{100} - 0.5 \times (0.1^2) \times 3}{0.1 \times \sqrt{3}} = -1.7475$$

   - Put value:

$$p_0 = \frac{100 \times N(1.7475) - 75 \times N(1.5743)}{(1 + 7.7217\%)^3} = €20.24$$

2. Intrinsic value of the put: $100 - 60 = €40$. The put is thus worth about half its intrinsic value, which might seem surprising. However, this is not an arbitrage opportunity: the put is European and cannot be exercised before maturity.

Exercise 7: at-the-money-forward call

1. An at-the-money-forward call has strike $K = F_0$, hence the coefficients d_1 and d_2 are:

$$d_1 = \frac{\ln \frac{F_0}{F_0} + \frac{\sigma^2}{2} T}{\sigma \sqrt{T}} = \frac{\sigma \sqrt{T}}{2}$$

$$d_2 = d_1 - \sigma \sqrt{T} = -\frac{\sigma \sqrt{T}}{2} = -d_1$$

According to the closed-form formula of the lognormal model, the value of the call is:

$$c_0 = \frac{1}{(1+r)^T} \left[F_0 N(d_1) - F_0 N(d_2) \right]$$

$$= \frac{F_0}{(1+r)^T} \left[N(d_1) - N(-d_1) \right]$$

$$= \frac{F_0}{(1+r)^T} (2N(d_1) - 1)$$

since $N(-x) = 1 - N(x)$. (Note that if the underlying does not pay dividends, then $\frac{F_0}{(1+r)^T} = S_0$.)

2. Using a Taylor expansion for $N(x)$ around 0 we have:

$$N(x) \underset{x \to 0}{\approx} N(0) + N'(0)(x - 0)$$

$$\underset{x \to 0}{\approx} \frac{1}{2} + \frac{x}{\sqrt{2\pi}}$$

since $N'(x) = \frac{1}{\sqrt{2\pi}} e^{-\frac{x^2}{2}}$. Moreover, $d_1 = \frac{\sigma \sqrt{T}}{2}$ is close to 0 for reasonable values of σ (typically σ is below 50%) and T (typically T is shorter than 2 years). Thus:

$$c_0 = \frac{F_0}{(1+r)^T} \left[2N(d_1) - 1 \right]$$

$$\approx \frac{F_0}{(1+r)^T} \left[2\left(\frac{1}{2} + \frac{d_1}{\sqrt{2\pi}}\right) - 1 \right]$$

$$\approx \frac{2}{\sqrt{2\pi}} \times \frac{F_0 \times \sigma \sqrt{T}}{(1+r)^T}$$

Noting that $\frac{2}{\sqrt{2\pi}} \approx 0.4$ we obtain the required formula. (Note that if the underlying does not pay dividends we have $c_0 \approx 40\% \times S_0 \times \sigma \sqrt{T}$).

3. According to this approximation, the value of a 6-month European call on a zero-dividend stock struck at $50 equal to the current stock price (thus close to the forward price) using a volatility of 30% is:

$$c_0 \approx 40\% \times 50 \times 30\%\sqrt{0.5} \approx \$4.24$$

This value is not too far from the $5.39 price calculated in Exercise 1.

Exercise 8*: digital option

1. Payoff of a digital option with strike 100:

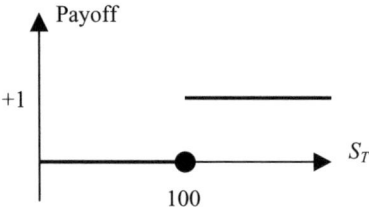

2. Payoff of a call spread 100–101:

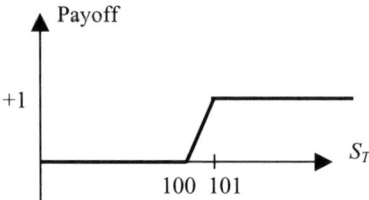

Comparing the two graphs we can see that the payoff of the call spread is dominated by the digital option. Thus the digital option is worth at least as much as the call spread.

3. Generalizing the results of the previous question the payoff of a digital option with strike K is always between a call spread K—$(K+h)$ and a call spread $(K-h)$—K, normalized by h. Using the closed-form formulas, we find that the value of a call spread K—$(K+h)$ at $t=0$ is:

$$\begin{aligned} \text{call spread}_0 &= \frac{1}{(1+r)^T}\left[F_0 N(d_0) - K N(d'_0)\right] - \frac{1}{(1+r)^T} \\ &\quad \times \left[F_0 N(d_h) - (K+h) N(d'_h)\right] \\ &= \frac{1}{(1+r)^T}\left[h N(d'_h) + F_0\left(N(d_h) - N(d_0)\right) - K\left(N(d'_h) - N(d'_0)\right)\right] \end{aligned}$$

Similarly, we can calculate the value of a call spread $(K-h)$–K at $t=0$, which yields the required inequality.

4. The density function of the standard normal distribution is:
$$N'(u) = \frac{1}{\sqrt{2\pi}} e^{-\frac{u^2}{2}}$$

Hence:

$$F_0 N'(d_0) = \frac{F_0}{\sqrt{2\pi}} \exp\left(-\frac{\left(\ln\left(\frac{F_0}{K}\right) + \frac{1}{2}\sigma^2 T\right)^2}{2\sigma^2 T}\right)$$

$$= \frac{F_0}{\sqrt{2\pi}} \exp\left(-\frac{\left(\ln\left(\frac{F_0}{K}\right) - \frac{1}{2}\sigma^2 T\right)^2 + 2\ln\left(\frac{F_0}{K}\right)\sigma^2 T}{2\sigma^2 T}\right)$$

$$= \frac{F_0}{\sqrt{2\pi}} \frac{K}{F_0} \exp\left(-\frac{\left(\ln\left(\frac{F_0}{K}\right) - \frac{1}{2}\sigma^2 T\right)^2}{2\sigma^2 T}\right)$$

$$= K N'(d'_0)$$

5. As $h \to 0$ the limit of the expression found in question 3 is:
$$F_0 N'(d_0) - K N'(d'_0) + N(d'_0) \le d_0(1+r)^T \le N(d'_0) + F_0 N'(d_0) - K N'(d'_0)$$

And from question 4:
$$F_0 N'(d_0) - K N'(d'_0) = 0$$

Thus $D_0(1+r)^T$ is bounded by the same quantity, whence:
$$d_0 = \frac{N(d'_0)}{(1+r)^T}$$

Exercise 9*: lognormal distribution

1. Y is lognormally distributed since $\ln(Y) = X$ is normally distributed.
2. Using the transfer theorem:
$$E(Y) = E(e^X) = \frac{1}{\sqrt{2\pi}} \int_{-\infty}^{+\infty} e^x e^{-\frac{(x-\mu)^2}{2\sigma^2}} dx$$

Writing $e^x e^{-\frac{(x-\mu)^2}{2\sigma^2}} = e^{-\frac{(x-\mu)^2 - 2\sigma^2 x}{2\sigma^2}}$ and noting that:
$$(x-\mu)^2 - 2\sigma^2 x = x^2 - 2(\mu + \sigma^2)x + \mu^2$$
$$= (x - \mu - \sigma^2)^2 - \sigma^2(2\mu + \sigma^2)$$

we obtain:

$$E(Y) = e^{\mu + \frac{1}{2}\sigma^2} \int_{-\infty}^{+\infty} \frac{e^{-\frac{(x-\mu-\sigma^2)^2}{2\sigma^2}}}{\sigma\sqrt{2\pi}} dx$$

Identifying the integral of the density function of a normal distribution with mean $\mu + \sigma^2$ and standard deviation σ, whose value is 1 by definition, we obtain the desired result.

3. From the definition of Y: $E(Y^2) = E(e^{2X})$. Since the variable $X' = 2X$ is normally distributed with mean $\mu' = 2\mu$ and standard deviation $\sigma' = 2\sigma$, we have:

$$E(Y^2) = e^{2\mu + 2\sigma^2}$$

Thus:

$$\text{Var}(Y) = E(Y^2) - [E(Y)]^2 = e^{2\mu + 2\sigma^2} - e^{2\mu + \sigma^2} = e^{2\mu + \sigma^2}\left(e^{\sigma^2} - 1\right)$$

4. Let X be a normally distributed random variable with mean $\ln F_0 - \frac{1}{2}\sigma^2 T$ and standard deviation $\sigma\sqrt{T}$. Choosing $S_T = e^X$ we verify the three properties:
   - $S_T = e^X > 0$ (positivity);
   - $E(S_T) = \exp\left(\ln F_0 - \frac{1}{2}\sigma^2 T + \frac{1}{2}\sigma^2 T\right) = F_0$ (forward-neutrality);
   - for all $x > 0$:

$$P\left(\left[\frac{S_T}{S^*} = x\right]\right) = P\left(\left[\ln\left(\frac{S_T}{S^*}\right) = \ln x\right]\right)$$
$$= P\left(\left[X - \ln(S^*) = \ln x\right]\right)$$
$$= P\left(\left[X^* = \frac{\ln(S^*) - \ln(F_0) + \frac{1}{2}\sigma^2 T + \ln x}{\sigma\sqrt{T}}\right]\right)$$

where $X^* = \dfrac{X - \ln(F_0) + \frac{1}{2}\sigma^2 T}{\sigma\sqrt{T}}$ has a standard normal distribution.

Selecting $S^* = F_0 e^{-\frac{1}{2}\sigma^2 T}$ we obtain as a result of the symmetry of the density function of the standard normal distribution:

$$P\left(\left[\frac{S_T}{S^*} = x\right]\right) = P\left(\left[X^* = \frac{\ln x}{\sigma\sqrt{T}}\right]\right) = P\left(\left[X^* = -\frac{\ln x}{\sigma\sqrt{T}}\right]\right)$$
$$= P\left(\left[\frac{S_T}{S^*} = \frac{1}{x}\right]\right)$$

Exercise 10: quadratic option

1. Payoff of a quadratic option with strike 100:

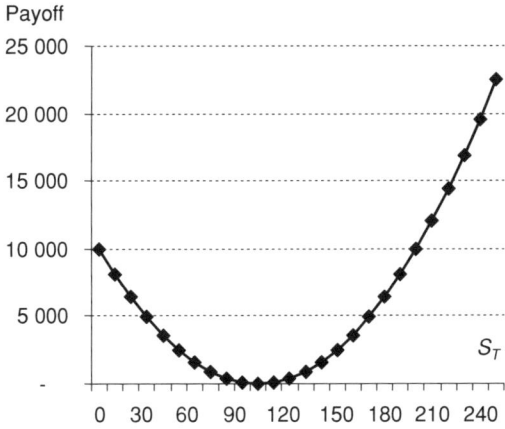

2. Expanding the square:
$$D_T = S_T^2 - 2K S_T + K^2$$
Discounting both sides of this equation and then taking expectations we find that the value of the quadratic option at $t = 0$ can be written:
$$d_0 = \frac{E(D_T)}{(1+r)^T} = \frac{1}{(1+r)^T} \left[E(S_T^2) + 2K\, E(S_T) + K^2 \right]$$
From the forward-neutrality property:
$$E(S_T) = F_0$$
And from the previous exercise:
$$E(S_T^2) = \exp\left(2\ln F_0 - \sigma^2 T + 2\sigma^2 T\right) = F_0^2 e^{\sigma^2 T}$$
It then follows that:
$$D_0 = \frac{1}{(1+r)^T} \left[F_0^2 e^{\sigma^2 T} - 2K F_0 + K^2 \right]$$

3. Value of the 1-year quadratic option with strike £100.
   - Forward price:
   $$F_0 = 105 \times (1 + 10\%) = £115.50$$
   - Option value:
   $$D_0 = \frac{1}{1 + 10\%} \left[115.5^2 \times e^{0.25^2} - 2 \times 100 \times 115.5 + 100^2 \right] \approx £1000$$

Thus, the quadratic option's value is significantly larger than a naïve calculation would have us believe: $(115.5 - 100)^2 / 1.1 = 218.41$!

Exercise 11*: uniform and normal distribution

Let us show that the cumulative distribution function of Y is the same as that of the standard normal distribution. Let $U(z) = z$ denote the cumulative distribution function of the uniform distribution for the interval $[0, 1]$. For all x we have:

$$P([Y \leq x]) = P\left([N^{-1}(X) \leq x]\right) = P\left([N\left(N^{-1}(X)\right) \leq N(x)]\right)$$
$$= P([X \leq N(x)]) = U(N(x)) = N(x)$$

Problem*: closed-form formula for the European call and put

1. Y is lognormally distributed with parameters (μ, σ) if $\ln Y$ is normally distributed with parameters (μ, σ). Therefore $X = \dfrac{\ln Y - \mu}{\sigma}$ is normally distributed and we have:

$$Y = \exp(\mu + \sigma X)$$

2. Following the lognormal model, the fair value of a call with payoff $D_T = \max(0, S_T - K)$ is:

$$C_0 = \frac{E\left[\max(0, S_T - K)\right]}{(1+r)^T}$$

From the previous question and the transfer theorem:

$$C_0 = \frac{1}{(1+r)^T \sqrt{2\pi}} \int_{-\infty}^{+\infty} \max\left[0, \exp\left(\sigma\sqrt{T}x + \ln F_0 - \frac{1}{2}\sigma^2 T\right) - K\right] e^{-\frac{x^2}{2}} dx$$

But $\max\left[0, \exp\left(\sigma\sqrt{T}x + \ln F_0 - \frac{1}{2}\sigma^2 T\right) - K\right] = 0$ if and only if:

$$\exp\left(\sigma\sqrt{T}x + \ln F_0 - \frac{1}{2}\sigma^2 T\right) \leq K$$

i.e.:

$$x \leq \frac{\ln K - \ln F_0 + \frac{1}{2}\sigma^2 T}{\sigma\sqrt{T}}$$

Identifying the expression on the right-hand side as the coefficient $-d_2$ yields the desired expression.

3. Splitting the integral in two and observing that $\int_{-d_2}^{+\infty} e^{-\frac{x^2}{2}} dx = \int_{-\infty}^{d_2} e^{-\frac{x^2}{2}} dx$ we obtain:

$$C_0 = \frac{1}{(1+r)^T}\left[\int_{-d_2}^{+\infty} \frac{1}{\sqrt{2\pi}} \exp\left(\sigma\sqrt{T}x + \ln F_0 - \frac{1}{2}\sigma^2 T - \frac{x^2}{2}\right) dx - KN(d_2)\right]$$

Solutions

With the change of variable $y = \sigma\sqrt{T} - x$ we have:

$$c_0 = \frac{1}{(1+r)^T}\left[\int_{-\infty}^{\sigma\sqrt{T}+d_2} \frac{1}{\sqrt{2\pi}} \exp\left(-\sigma\sqrt{T}y + \ln F_0 + \frac{1}{2}\sigma^2 T - \frac{(y-\sigma\sqrt{T})^2}{2}\right)dy - KN(d_2)\right]$$

Expanding the quadratic component and simplifying yields:

$$c_0 = \frac{1}{(1+r)^T}\left[\int_{-\infty}^{\sigma\sqrt{T}+d_2} \frac{1}{\sqrt{2\pi}} \exp(\ln F_0)\exp\left(-\frac{y^2}{2}\right)dy - KN(d_2)\right]$$

Finally, using the fact that $d_1 = d_2 + \sigma\sqrt{T}$, we obtain the closed-form formula for the call.

4. Put–call parity tells us that:

$$c_0 - p_0 = S_0 - \frac{K}{(1+r)^T}$$

Assuming the underlying does not pay dividends we have:

$$S_0 = \frac{F_0}{(1+r)^T}$$

Thus:

$$p_0 = c_0 - \frac{1}{(1+r)^T}[F_0 - K]$$

$$= \frac{1}{(1+r)^T}\left[F_0(N(d_1) - 1) - K(N(d_2) - 1)\right]$$

Noting that $N(-x) = 1 - N(x)$ yields the closed-form formula for the put.

8 Dynamic hedging

This chapter deals with practical aspects of option trading.[1] However, we also recommend a careful reading for those who are more specifically interested in the option pricing theory.

8.1 Introduction

The reason why calls or puts became popular derivatives is relatively straightforward: they allow buyers to bet on the direction of asset prices while limiting losses to the option premium. Such payoff asymmetry appears clearly when looking at the graphs of the final **P&L** (**profit and loss**):

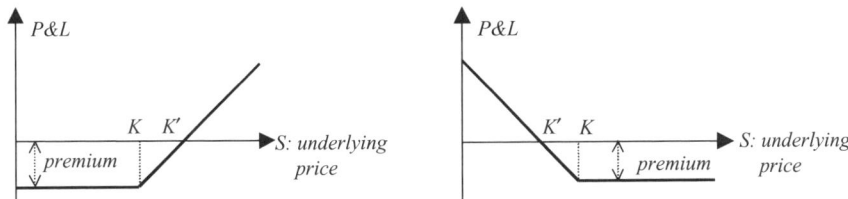

P&L of a long call at maturity   **P&L of a long put at maturity**

On these two graphs, K denotes the strike price and K' is the **break-even** point. The strike price is the price level the underlying must reach for the option to pay some amount. The break-even K' is the price level the underlying must reach for the option position to become profitable, i.e. have a positive P&L. The difference between K and K' is roughly equal to the option premium.[2]

---

[1] For the most part, the concepts introduced in this chapter are in fact applicable to derivatives in general. We decided to use the term 'option' for didactic reasons.
[2] More precisely, since the option premium is paid at $t=0$ and not at maturity T, the difference between K and K' is equal to the option premium compounded at the zero-rate r between $t=0$ and $t=T$.

The reason why counterparties (typically banks) issue options to investors may seem less evident. Flipping the graphs above we can see that option sellers seem to face a higher risk:

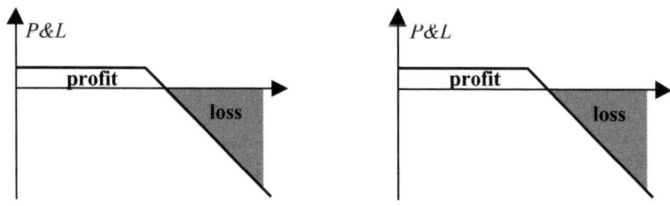

P&L of a short call at maturity   **P&L of a short put at maturity**

How do option sellers manage their risks into a profitable business? In the following sections we introduce the vocabulary and techniques used by practitioners to achieve this.

8.2 Delta-hedging

The most commonly used strategy on option trading desks is called **delta-hedging**. The legendary option pricing model of Black, Scholes and Merton introduced in Chapter 10 is also based on this strategy.

An option's **delta** is the change in the option's value due to a unit change in the underlying price. Mathematically it is simply the first derivative with respect to the underlying price:

$$\delta = \frac{\partial f}{\partial S}$$

where f is the option's value and S is the underlying price.

Example. The value of a European call on Dull Inc. stock is $12 and its delta is 0.5. The current stock price is $100 in New York. If Dull Inc.'s price goes up to $101 the option value will be approximately: $12 + 0.5 \times (101 - 100) = \$12.50$.

Hedging the delta of an option position means taking an opposite position in the underlying with a quantity δ, thereby building a **delta-neutral** portfolio. Such a portfolio is thus immune to small changes in the underlying price.

Example. To delta-hedge a *short* position on 1000 calls on Dull Inc., one must take a *long* position of $0.5 \times 1000 = +500$ stocks (i.e. buy 500 stocks). Using our results from the previous example, we verify that the portfolio is now

delta-neutral: if Dull Inc.'s price goes up $1 the change in portfolio value is:
$$-1000 \times (12.5 - 12) + 500 \times (101 - 100) = 0$$

Delta-hedging is a trading strategy which continuously maintains a delta-neutral portfolio throughout the life of the option. This is achieved by constantly buying and selling the underlying.[3] In theory, this strategy is sufficient for option traders to entirely eliminate their risk from price movements and replicate the option payoff with a profit. It goes without saying that reversing operations and signs, an option trader can implement the same strategy to eliminate the risk when buying the option.

Delta-hedging is an example of a **dynamic trading strategy**, in contrast with static strategies which are only executed when issuing the option. For instance, a static strategy to cover a short position on 1000 calls on Dull Inc. (current price $100) struck at $125 could be immediately to buy 1000 stocks on the market for $100 000 and wait until maturity. Thus, if the buyer of the call exercises the option, the option seller is able to deliver the 1000 stocks against $125 000. However, if the buyer does not exercise the option, the option seller will remain long the 1000 stocks. With a final stock price at $80 for instance, the option seller would incur a loss of $20 000. Delta-hedging eliminates this risk.

8.3 Other risk parameters: the Greek letters

8.3.1 The Greek letters

Option buyers and sellers are exposed to many more risks than delta. The other classical risk parameters are known to practitioners as 'sensitivities' or 'Greeks': convexity (Γ, gamma); time decay (θ, theta); volatility risk ($\mathcal{V}$, vega[4]); interest rate risk (ρ, rho).

The closed-form formulas of the Greeks for European calls and puts on an underlying asset that does not pay any cash flow are given in Appendix C.

We must emphasize that each Greek letter is a first-order, *ceteris paribus* approximation. For instance a daily theta of –2¢ means that the option will approximately lose 2¢ in value after 1 day provided all other parameters ($S, \sigma, r \ldots$) are unchanged.

---

[3] In reality continuous rebalancing of the delta-neutral portfolio is impossible as it would incur infinite transaction costs. An example of how delta-hedging would be carried out in practice on a monthly basis is given in Exercise 4.

[4] Hellenist readers will probably be surprised by this unknown letter in the Greek alphabet. It was indeed invented by market practitioners. Rumour has it that it comes from the TV serial *Star Trek*.

δ or Δ (delta)	Γ (gamma)	θ (theta)	$\mathcal{V}$ (vega)	ρ (rho)
$\dfrac{\partial f}{\partial S}$	$\dfrac{\partial^2 f}{\partial S^2} = \dfrac{\partial \Delta}{\partial S}$	$\dfrac{\partial f}{\partial t}$	$\dfrac{\partial f}{\partial \sigma}$	$\dfrac{\partial f}{\partial r}$
Change in option value when the underlying price S_t increases by +1	Change in option's delta when the underlying price S_t increases by +1	Change in option value due to the passage of time (generally converted into 1 day)	Change in option value when the volatility σ increases by +1 point (+1%)	Change in option when the interest rate r increases by 100 basis points (i.e. +1%)

Example: call on Dull Inc., zero-dividend, $t = 0$, $S_0 = \$100$, $c_0 = \$12$, strike $K = \$100$, maturity $T = 1$ year, volatility $\sigma = 24\%$, interest rate $r = 5\%$

$\delta = 0.62$	$\Gamma = 0.02$	$\theta = -2¢$ per day	$v = 37¢$ per volatility point	$\rho = 50¢$ per interest rate point
'If the stock price is up \$1 the option value will be up 62¢'	'If the stock price is up \$1 the option's delta will increase from 0.62 to 0.64'	'By the end of the day the option value will be down 2¢'	'If volatility goes up from 24% to 25%, the option value will be up 37¢'	'If interest rates go up 50 basis points the option value will be up 25¢'

Note that **Greek letters can be generalized to portfolios of options on the same underlying**: the delta of a portfolio which is long 1000 calls with delta δ_1 and short 500 calls with delta δ_2 is $\delta_P = 1000\delta_1 - 500\delta_2$.

Example. For $\delta_1 = 0.5$ and $\delta_2 = 0.4$ this gives $\delta_P = 1000 \times 0.5 - 500 \times 0.4 = 300$. In other words, if the underlying price goes up \$1 this portfolio gains \$300 in value.

8.3.2 Gamma

Because gamma is a second-order derivative, its interpretation tends to be less straightforward to beginners than are the other Greeks.

The first interpretation of gamma is purely analytical through a second-order Taylor expansion:

$$f(S') - f(S) \approx \left(\frac{\partial f}{\partial S}\right)(S' - S) + \frac{1}{2}\left(\frac{\partial^2 f}{\partial S^2}\right)(S' - S)^2$$

Other risk parameters: the Greek letters

In short:

$$\Delta f \approx \delta \times (\Delta S) + \frac{1}{2}\Gamma \times (\Delta S)^2$$

When the change in underlying price ΔS is small, the second term in $(\Delta S)^2$ is negligible and one can rely on the approximation $\Delta f \approx \delta \times (\Delta S)$. For large movements, however, the second term can be significant, especially if the Γ coefficient is high as illustrated in the two graphs below. Therefore, **the gamma measures the delta-hedging error**: when gamma is high, the delta-hedge should be rebalanced more frequently.

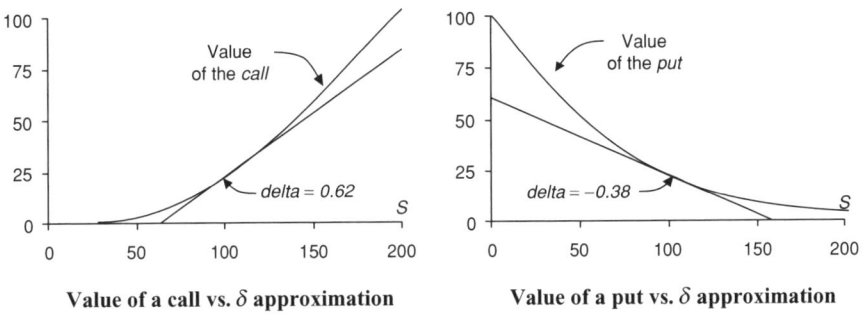

Value of a call vs. δ approximation   **Value of a put vs. δ approximation**

The second interpretation is of more fundamental nature and shows why option traders tend to be more comfortable with a 'long gamma' position, meaning that their option portfolio has positive gamma.

To understand this point, consider the two graphs below which show the P&L of a delta-hedged call and a delta-hedged put as a function of the underlying price (i.e. the change in value of a portfolio which is long the option and short δ units of the underlying asset).

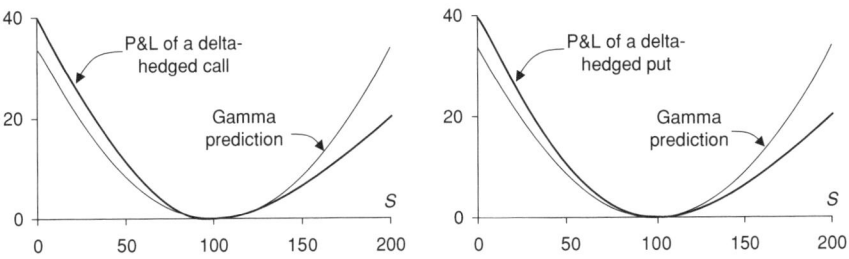

P&L and gamma P&L of a delta-hedged call   P&L and gamma P&L of a delta-hedged put

We can make three observations:

1. The two graphs are identical. Thus, we could have displayed a single graph but we wanted to emphasize that **delta-hedged calls and puts are the same** (see Exercise 10).
2. The P&L is positive. Thus, **a delta-hedged long call or put will always generate profits as the underlying price moves away from its initial price**. Unsurprisingly, there is a downside to this otherwise engaging statement, which we investigate in the following section.
3. The P&L prediction using Γ is quite accurate. Thus, the gamma is a good measure for the P&L of a delta-hedged option position caused by movements in the underlying price. In particular, a positive gamma means profits and a negative gamma means losses. The larger the gamma and the movement, the larger the profit or loss.

8.3.3 Theta vs. gamma

The daily theta of an option measures the P&L after 1 day if all other parameters – in particular the underlying price S – remain unchanged. For plain vanilla options, theta is negative: as time passes and we approach maturity, the option loses time value.

There is an **inverse relationship between theta and gamma**:

$$\Theta \approx -\frac{1}{2}\Gamma\sigma^2 S_t^2$$

Example. The gamma of an option is 0.0671831, the volatility is 25% and the underlying price is $20. According to the previous formula, theta is approximately $-\frac{1}{2} \times 0.0671831 \times 0.25^2 \times 20^2 = -\$0.839789$ per annum, i.e. $\frac{-83.9789}{365} = -0.2301¢$ per day.

The meaning of this relationship for an option trader following a delta-hedging strategy is crucial: as time passes, the profits on a long gamma position will be counterbalanced by losses on the theta as illustrated opposite, and conversely for a short gamma position. Therefore, the trader will want to be long gamma when she expects large moves in the underlying price and short gamma when she expects gains on theta to more than compensate losses on gamma.

Example. The underlying asset trades at $20, the daily theta of a delta-hedged call on that asset is −$0.0222 and the gamma is 0.01265. In order to have a positive P&L at the end of the day the underlying price has to move up or down by more than $\Delta S = \sqrt{-2\frac{\Theta}{\Gamma}} = \sqrt{-2\frac{-0.0222}{0.01265}} = \$1.87$. Thus, the two break-even points are at $S = \$18.13$ and $S = \$21.87$.

Other risk parameters: the Greek letters

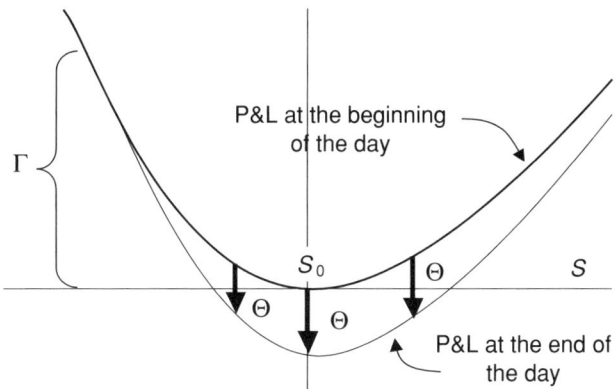

Effect of theta on the P&L of a delta-hedged call or put

In the following paragraphs we give an 'intuitive' justification for the inverse relationship between theta and gamma. A more rigorous and complete proof can be found in Chapter 10, Exercise 8.

Consider a delta-neutral portfolio made up of a long option and a short position on the underlying asset in quantity δ, where δ denotes the delta of the option. We denote by S the current price at time t of the underlying, $f(t, S)$ the option value and $V(t, S) = f(t, S) - \delta S$ the mark-to-market value of the portfolio. A second-order Taylor expansion yields an expression of the portfolio P&L:

$$P\&L = \Delta V = V(t + \Delta t, S + \Delta S) - V(t, s)$$
$$\approx \frac{\partial f}{\partial t} \Delta t + \frac{\partial f}{\partial S}(\Delta S) + \frac{1}{2}\frac{\partial^2 f}{\partial S^2}(\Delta S)^2 - \delta \times (\Delta S)$$

Identifying each partial derivative with the associated Greek letter:

$$P\&L \approx \Theta \times \Delta t + \delta \times (\Delta S) + \tfrac{1}{2}\Gamma \times (\Delta S)^2 - \delta \times (\Delta S)$$

After simplifying the offsetting terms in (ΔS):

$$P\&L \approx \Theta \times \Delta t + \tfrac{1}{2}\Gamma \times (\Delta S)^2$$

We now use an economic argument: in a fair game, the expected P&L of a delta-neutral portfolio should be zero. Thus, taking expectations of both sides of the previous equation:

$$\Theta \times \Delta t + \tfrac{1}{2}\Gamma \times \mathrm{E}\left[(\Delta S)^2\right] \approx \mathrm{E}(\Delta V) = 0$$

Writing $(\Delta S)^2 = S^2 \times \left(\frac{\Delta S}{S}\right)^2$ and noting that $\left(\frac{\Delta S}{S}\right)$ is the return of the underlying between times t and $t + \Delta t$, we see that $\mathrm{E}\left[(\Delta S)^2\right]$ is the 'squared volatility' (i.e.

variance) of the underlying between times t and $t + \Delta t$ multiplied by S^2:

$$E\left[(\Delta S)^2\right] = E\left[\left(\frac{\Delta S}{S}\right)^2\right] \times S^2 = (\sigma^2 \Delta t) \times S^2$$

(Recall that volatility σ is given on an annual basis. The volatility for the period $[t, t + \Delta t]$ is $\sigma\sqrt{\Delta t}$.) After substituting in the expected P&L equation:

$$\Theta \times \Delta t + \tfrac{1}{2}\Gamma S^2 \sigma^2 \Delta t \approx 0$$

Dividing both sides by Δt then yields the relationship between theta and gamma.

Further reading

Hull, J.C. (2005) *Options, Futures and Other Derivatives*, 6th edn. Prentice Hall, Englewood Cliffs, NJ.

Exercises

Exercise 1

'Delta-hedging eliminates the volatility risk of the underlying by constructing a portfolio which is insensitive to movements in the underlying price.' Comment on this statement.

Exercise 2: Greek letters

The table below gives the Greek letters of a portfolio of options on Swinger Corp.'s stock. The current price of Swinger Corp. in New York is $80, its annual volatility is 40% and the company does not pay any dividend. The risk-free rate is 3%.

δ	Γ	θ/day	ν	ρ
1 500 000	−10 000	14 222	−500 000	300 000

1. Can you predict the profit or loss of the portfolio if the stock price of Swinger Corp. goes down 1%? 10%?
2. Can you predict the profit or loss of the portfolio at the end of the day if nothing happens on the markets?
3. After a press release, the trading volume of Swinger Corp.'s stock doubles but the stock price remains around $80. Do you think this situation is favourable, unfavourable or indifferent for you?
4. There are market rumours that the Federal Reserve is about to raise its rate by 25 basis points to 3.25%. Estimate your gain or loss in such a scenario.

Exercise 3: delta-hedge, break-even

You just sold 1 million puts on Plumet SA's stock which is currently trading at €20 in Paris. The delta of the put is –0.3.

1. You want to delta-hedge your position. What do you do?
2. The theta of the put is −€0.002301 per day and the gamma is 0.0671831. Estimate your P&L if the price of Plumet SA drops by €0.50 in one day. By €5.
3. What is the break-even of your P&L on the downside? On the upside? *The break-even is the stock price level for which the P&L is nil.*

Exercise 4: delta-hedging

The table below shows the evolution of the share price of Range Ltd. for the past year, and the value and delta of a call on this share maturing at the end of the period. Compute the monthly and cumulative P&L of a delta-hedging strategy on a long position of 10 000 calls bought at the beginning of the period.

Time (month)	0	1	2	3	4	5	6
Share price (£)	100	90	105	90	85	95	100
Value of the call (£)	12.36	6.84	14.27	5.83	3.56	6.83	8.67
Delta	0.57	0.42	0.63	0.40	0.30	0.46	0.55
Time (month)	7	8	9	10	11	12	
Share price (£)	110	115	125	120	115	110	
Value of the call (£)	14.33	17.45	25.73	20.55	15.28	10.00	
Delta	0.72	0.81	0.94	0.94	0.95	1.00	

Exercise 5: Greeks for the underlying and for the forward contract

Determine the Greeks for:

(a) the underlying asset S;
(b) a forward contract on S with delivery price K and maturity T. *Assume that S does not pay any cash flow.*

Exercise 6: gamma-hedging

1. Calculate the quantities x and y to make the portfolio below delta-neutral and gamma-neutral:

Security	Quantity	Unit value	Delta	Gamma
Option 1	−1	12.36	0.57	0.013076
Option 2	x	5.71	0.33	0.012153
Underlying	y	100	1	0

2*. Determine x and y as a general function of the respective values of the securities V_1, V_2, S, their deltas δ_1, δ_2, 1, and their gammas Γ_1, Γ_2, 0.

Exercise 7*: delta of the call and the put

We consider the closed-form formulas for the European call and European put given in Chapter 7.

1. Show that: $F_0 N'(d_1) = K N'(d_2)$. *Hint*: $d_2 = d_1 - \sigma\sqrt{T}$.

2. Show that: $\delta_{call} = \frac{\partial c}{\partial S} = N(d_1)$, $\delta_{put} = \frac{\partial p}{\partial S} = -N(-d_1)$ and that $\delta_{call} - \delta_{put} = 1$. *Assume that the underlying does not pay any cash flow.*

Exercise 8: call and put have the same gamma

Using put–call parity, show that a European call has the same gamma as a European put with the same characteristics (underlying, strike, maturity). *Assume that the underlying does not pay any cash flow.*

Solutions

Exercise 1

Delta-hedging only hedges against small changes in the underlying price. In case of large changes the delta-hedger is still exposed to some risk measured by the gamma. In practice, the hedger is also exposed to changes in other parameters such as the volatility σ or the short-term interest rate r.

Exercise 2: Greek letters

1. The current price of Swinger Corp.'s stock is \$80 so a 1% decrease is worth 80¢. Since the delta is 1 500 000, the portfolio's loss will be approximately:

$$P\&L \approx \delta \times \Delta S = 1\,500\,000 \times (-0.8) = -\$1\,200\,000$$

   In case of a 10% drop worth \$8, the first-order approximation in delta would be inaccurate and we have to take gamma into account:

$$\begin{aligned} P\&L &\approx \delta \times \Delta S + \tfrac{1}{2}\Gamma(\Delta S)^2 \\ &\approx 1\,500\,000 \times (-8) - \tfrac{1}{2} \times 10\,000 \times (-8)^2 \\ &\approx -\$12\,320\,000 \end{aligned}$$

2. The theta of this portfolio is positive: if all other parameters remain constant the value of the portfolio will increase by \$14 222 by the end of the day.
3. A high volume of trading orders on Swinger Corp. indicates that there is a transfer of risk between market agents. Usually, a high trading volume is associated with large price movements but in this example the price remains stable. Nevertheless, we have good reasons to believe that the volatility risk of our options portfolio is higher, which is unfavourable as the vega is negative (−\$500 000 per volatility point).
4. Interest rate risk is measured by the rho of \$300 000, which is our approximate P&L if the interest rate increases by one point (100 basis points). Therefore, if the interest rate increases by a quarter of a point the P&L is \$75 000.

Exercise 3: delta-hedge, break-even

1. A delta of −0.3 means that the value of the put decreases by €0.3 when the stock price of Plumet SA goes up €1. Since we have a *short* position of 1 million puts, if the share price increases by €1 we gain €300 000, and conversely if the share price decreases by €1 we lose €300 000. Thus, to hedge this delta risk we need to sell 300 000 stocks of Plumet SA.

2. A theta of −€0.002301 per day on a short position of 1 million means that we gain €2301 per day if nothing happens (in particular, the underlying price must remain constant). Having delta-hedged the position, only the gamma will have an impact on our P&L as the stock price of Plumet SA drops by €0.50:

$$\text{Gamma P\&L} = \tfrac{1}{2}\Gamma(\Delta S)^2$$
$$= -1\,000\,000 \times \tfrac{1}{2} \times 0.0671831 \times (0.50)^2$$
$$\approx -8398$$

Thus, taking theta into consideration, our total P&L at the end of the day will be a loss of $(8398 - 2301) = €6097$. In case the price drops by €5 (10 times more), the loss in gamma will be 100 times higher due to the quadratic nature of the gamma P&L, and our total loss will be $(839\,800 - 2301) = €838\,000$.

3. We break even when the loss in gamma is exactly offset by the profit in theta. This will happen when the change in the underlying price ΔS satisfies:

$$\tfrac{1}{2}\Gamma(\Delta S)^2 = -\Theta$$

i.e.:

$$\tfrac{1}{2} \times 0.0671831 \times (\Delta S)^2 = 0.002301$$

This equation has two solutions with opposite signs:

$$\Delta S = \pm\sqrt{\frac{2 \times 0.002301}{0.0671831}} = \pm €0.2617$$

In other words, we break even when the stock price of Plumet SA decreases from €20 to $(20 - 0.2617) = €19.7383$ or increases to $(20 + 0.2617) = €20.2617$.

Exercise 4: delta-hedging

The evolution of the cumulative P&L is given in the table overleaf:

Notes:

(a) Underlying position: number of shares held at the beginning of the month. Equals column (f) of the previous month.
(b) Underlying P&L (£): profit or loss on the share position. Equals the underlying position multiplied by the change in the share price.
(c) Call P&L (£): profit or loss on the call position (long 10 000). Equal to 10 000 times the change in call value.
(d) Total monthly P&L (£): (b) + (c).
(e) Cumulative P&L (£): sum of column (d) up to present.
(f) Final underlying position: number of shares held at the end of the month. Equals the delta multiplied by the call position (10 000).

Time (month)	Share price (£)	Value of the call (£)	Delta	Call position	(a) Underlying position (shares)	(b) Underlying P&L (£)	(c) Call P&L (£)	(d) Total monthly P&L (£)	(e) Cumulative P&L (£)	(f) Final underlying position (shares)
0	100	12.36	0.57	10 000	—	—	—	—	—	−5,700
1	90	6.84	0.42	10 000	−5,700	57,000	−55,200	**1,800**	**1,800**	−4,200
2	105	14.27	0.63	10 000	−4,200	−63,000	74,300	**11,300**	**13,100**	−6,300
3	90	5.83	0.40	10 000	−6,300	94,500	−84,400	**10,100**	**23,200**	−4,000
4	85	3.56	0.30	10 000	−4,000	20,000	−22,700	**−2,700**	**20,500**	−3,000
5	95	6.83	0.46	10 000	−3,000	−30,000	32,700	**2,700**	**23,200**	−4,600
6	110	14.33	0.72	10 000	−4,600	−69,000	75,000	**6,000**	**29,200**	−7,200
7	115	17.45	0.81	10 000	−7,200	−36,000	31,200	**−4,800**	**24,400**	−8,100
8	125	25.73	0.94	10 000	−8,100	−81,000	82,800	**1,800**	**26,200**	−9,400
9	120	20.55	0.94	10 000	−9,400	47,000	−51,800	**−4,800**	**21,400**	−9,400
10	115	15.28	0.95	10 000	−9,400	47,000	−52,700	**−5,700**	**15,700**	−9,500
11	110	10	1	10 000	−9,500	47,500	−52,800	**−5,300**	**10,400**	−10,000

Solutions

Exercise 5: Greeks for the underlying and for the forward contract

The Greeks for the underlying and for the forward contract are obtained by calculating the first or second-order derivative of their price with respect to the corresponding variable. The results are given in the table below:

Payoff	δ	θ	Γ	V	ρ
a) $f(t, S_t) = S_t$	1	0	0	0	0
b) $f(t, S_t) = S_t - \dfrac{K}{(1+r)^{T-t}}$	1	$-\dfrac{K\ln(1+r)}{(1+r)^{T-t}}$	0	0	$-\dfrac{Kt}{(1+r)^{T-t+1}}$

Exercise 6: gamma-hedging

1. The delta and gamma of the portfolio are given as functions of x and y as:

$$\delta = -0.57 + 0.33x + y$$
$$\Gamma = -0.013076 + 0.012153x$$

The condition $\Gamma = 0$ yields:

$$x = \frac{0.013076}{0.012153} \approx 1.076$$

Substituting x by its value in the first equation and using the condition $\delta = 0$ yields:

$$y = 0.57 - 0.33 \times 1.076 \approx 0.215$$

Hence, to construct a delta and gamma-neutral portfolio, we need to sell 1 unit of option 1, buy 1.076 units of option 2 and 0.215 units of the underlying.

2*. Generally:

$$x = \frac{\Gamma_1}{\Gamma_2} \text{ and } y = \delta_1 - \frac{\Gamma_1}{\Gamma_2}\delta_2$$

Exercise 7*: delta of the call and the put

1. This question is answered in Chapter 7, Exercise 8, question 4.
2. If the underlying does not pay any cash flow, its forward price F is given as:

$$F = S(1+r)^T$$

Thus, the closed-form formula for the call becomes:

$$c = SN(d_1) - \frac{K}{(1+r)^T} N(d_2)$$

Differentiating with respect to S yields:

$$\delta_{call} = N(d_1) + S\frac{\partial d_1}{\partial S} N'(d_1) - \frac{K}{(1+r)^T} \frac{\partial d_2}{\partial S} N'(d_2)$$

Since $d_2 = d_1 - \sigma\sqrt{T}$, d_1 and d_2 have the same derivative with respect to S and:

$$\delta_{call} = N(d_1) + \left(\frac{\partial d_1}{\partial S}\right)\left[SN'(d_1) - \frac{K}{(1+r)^T} N'(d_2)\right]$$

Factoring the expression in brackets by $\frac{1}{(1+r)^T}$ we recognize the two sides of the equation found in question 1:

$$\delta_{call} = N(d_1) + \left(\frac{\partial d_1}{\partial S}\right) \frac{1}{(1+r)^T} \left[FN'(d_1) - KN'(d_2)\right]$$

Whence:

$$\delta_{call} = N(d_1)$$

Finally, put–call parity ensures that $\delta_{call} - \delta_{put} = 1$, and from $N(x) = 1 - N(-x)$ we obtain:

$$\delta_{put} = -N(-d_1)$$

Exercise 8: call and put have the same gamma

When the underlying does not pay any cash flow, put–call parity says that:

$$c - p = S - \frac{K}{(1+r)^T}$$

Taking the second derivative of both sides of this equation with respect to S yields:

$$\frac{\partial^2 c}{\partial S^2} - \frac{\partial^2 p}{\partial S^2} = 0$$

Thus, call and put indeed have the same gamma.

9 Models for asset prices in continuous time

9.1 Continuously compounded interest rate

We say[1] that the annual interest rate $r_{[m]}$ is **fractioned m times** when payments are split over the year into m equal fractions. Starting with capital K, the table of cash flows and compounding of capital for the first year is as follows:

Interest payments at rate $r_{[m]}$ fractioned m times

t (years)	0	$\frac{1}{m}$	$\frac{2}{m}$	...	$\frac{m}{m} = 1$
Cash flow	—	$\frac{r_{[m]}}{m} \times K_0$	$\frac{r_{[m]}}{m} \times K_{\frac{1}{m}}$	...	$\frac{r_{[m]}}{m} \times K_{\frac{m-1}{m}}$
Capital	K	$K_{\frac{1}{m}} = K\left(1 + \frac{r_{[m]}}{m}\right)$	$K_{\frac{2}{m}} = K\left(1 + \frac{r_{[m]}}{m}\right)^2$	...	$K_1 = K\left(1 + \frac{r_{[m]}}{m}\right)^m$

Thus, the equivalent annual compound rate for $r_{[m]}$ is:

$$r = \left(1 + \frac{r_{[m]}}{m}\right)^m - 1$$

Note that $r_{[m]} < r$: **a fractioned rate underestimates its equivalent compound rate**.

Example. A 2-year US Treasury bond with face value $100 and face coupon[2] 10% pays $5 every 6 months. The 10% face coupon is in fact fractioned twice,

---

[1] We use here a nonstandard terminology for didactic reasons. In practice fractioned rates are simply called 'semi-annual' or 'quarterly', which is often confusing since these rates are annualized.

[2] The face coupon, also called nominal coupon, is the coupon rate which is advertised at issuance and used to determine the actual coupon payments according to market conventions. In practice, most government bonds detach an annual coupon equal to the face coupon, a major exception being US government bonds which detach a semi-annual coupon equal to half the face coupon.

and the equivalent compound rate is:

$$r = \left(1 + \frac{10\%}{2}\right)^2 - 1 = 10.25\%$$

The annual rate $r_{[c]}$ is said to be **continuous** or **continuously compounded** when it is fractioned an infinite number of times. The equivalent annual compound rate is then (see Chapter 1, Exercise 7):

$$r = \lim_{m \to +\infty} \left(1 + \frac{r_{[c]}}{m}\right)^m - 1 = e^{r_{[c]}} - 1$$

Hence, after 1 year the capital amounts to: $K_1 = Ke^{r_{[c]}}$, and generally after T years: $K_T = Ke^{r_{[c]} \times T}$.

Continuously compounded rates are easy to convert into a given period τ, as summarized below:

Annual rate \ Converted rate	Annualized: r	Compounded over period τ: $r^{[\tau]}$	Continuously compounded over period τ: $r_{[c]}^{[\tau]}$
Gross rate r	r	$r^{[\tau]} = (1+r)^\tau - 1$	$r_{[c]}^{[\tau]} = \tau \ln(1+r)$
Fractioned m times $r_{[m]}$	$r = \left(1 + \frac{r_{[m]}}{m}\right)^m$	$r^{[\tau]} = \left(1 + \frac{r_{[m]}}{m}\right)^{m\tau} - 1$	$r_{[c]}^{[\tau]} = \tau \ln\left(1 + \frac{r_{[m]}}{m}\right)$
Continuously compounded $r_{[c]}$	$r = e^{r_{[c]}} - 1$	$r^{[\tau]} = e^{r_{[c]} \times \tau} - 1$	$r_{[c]}^{[\tau]} = r_{[c]} \times \tau$

Continuous rates are almost never encountered in practice, albeit frequently used in financial theory. However, switching between theory and practice is easily performed through the conversion formulas.

9.2 Introduction to models for the behaviour of asset prices in continuous time

As we explained in earlier chapters, finance is exclusively concerned with future gains, as opposed to accounting which is mostly interested in past profits or losses. That said, past information is often too precious to be completely disregarded.

For example, the study of the historical time series of stock prices, which is the core focus of econometrics, leads to a satisfying mathematical model for the future behaviour of asset prices. As a means of introduction, consider the graph below of the daily prices of the S&P 500 index and their moving average over 50 days.[3]

---

[3] Each point of the moving average curve is calculated as the average price of the S&P 500 over the preceding 50 days.

Introduction to models for the behaviour of asset prices in continuous time

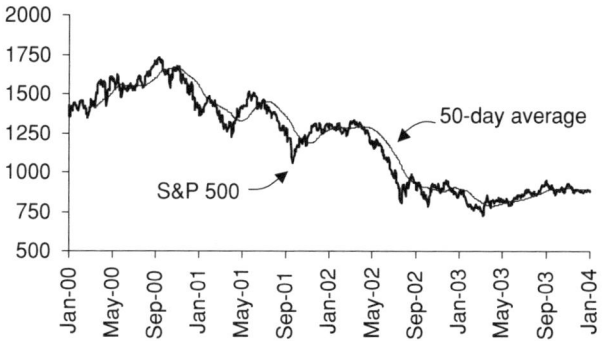

Daily historical prices of the S&P 500 index (2000–2003)

The empirical analysis of this graph reveals two components:

1. A **general upward or downward trend** (in markets' parlance: bull or bear), whose cycles are best observed on the moving average curve.
2. **Random variations** around the trend, which add up positively or negatively to the latter.

Following this analysis and denoting by X_t the asset price at time t, m_t the market trend and Z_t the random variation, we can decompose the daily change in asset price as:

$$X_{t+1 \text{ day}} - X_t = (m_{t+1 \text{ day}} - m_t) + (Z_{t+1 \text{ day}} - Z_t)$$

More generally, over an infinitesimal time interval dt:

$$X_{t+dt} - X_t = (m_{t+dt} - m_t) + (Z_{t+dt} - Z_t)$$

i.e.:

$$dX_t = dm_t + dZ_t$$

From this basic decomposition, we can derive a sensible model for the future behaviour of X_t:

- The general trend $m(t) = m_t$ is a reasonably smooth, differentiable function of time. Denoting its first-order derivative $\mu_t = \frac{dm_t}{dt}$, we can write: $dm_t = \mu_t dt$. Hence:

$$dX_t = \mu_t dt + dZ_t$$

- On the other hand, the random variations $Z(t) = Z_t$ constitute a fairly irregular, nondifferentiable function of time. Thus, we cannot express dZ_t with a derivative, and we must instead model it as a random variable. The classic distribution used here is the normal distribution.

To verify that this approach is sensible, we can simulate random series on a computer and compare the results with real-life examples. For instance, with $dt = 1$ day, $X_0 = 100$, $\mu_t = 3$, $dZ_t \sim N(0, 5)$, we obtain a graph which comes across as a very plausible evolution for the daily price of an asset:

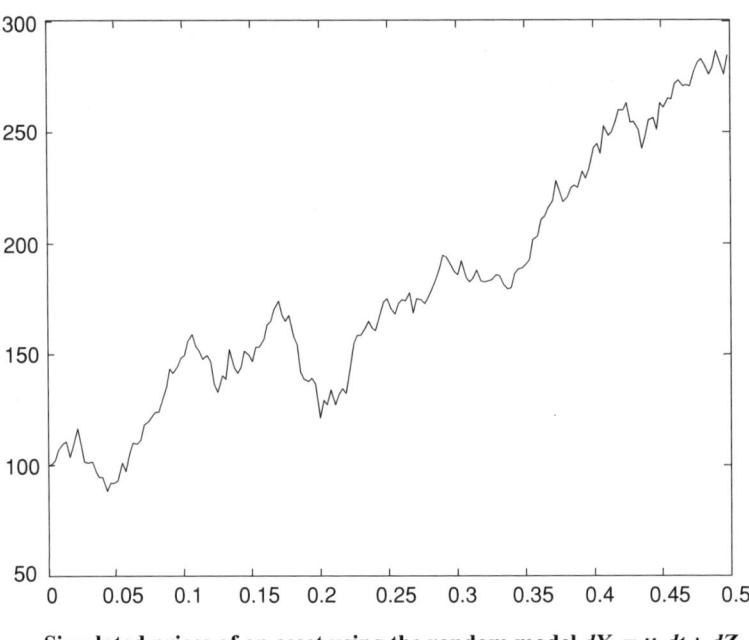

Simulated prices of an asset using the random model $dX_t = \mu_t dt + dZ_t$

In the following paragraphs, we introduce in further detail the various random processes, also called **stochastic processes**, which are commonly used in finance to model the behaviour of asset prices in continuous time. This is the first step of the Black–Scholes model for option valuation in continuous time introduced in Chapter 10.

9.3 Introduction to stochastic processes

The complete and rigorous study of stochastic processes in continuous time constitutes an entire field of mathematics and statistics and could easily fill several books. Our aim here is more practical: to introduce the concepts and vocabulary which are necessary for a satisfactory understanding of the results presented in Chapter 10. Readers who need to refresh their background in probability and statistics will find a brief review in Appendix A.

In the following paragraphs, we have the usual representation of uncertainty as a universe Ω of all possible states of nature ω, which can happen in the future with a given probability.

9.3.1 Some definitions

- A **stochastic process** is a sequence $(X_t)_{t\geq 0}$ of random variables indexed by time t in $[0, \infty)$.
- The process $(X_t)_{t\geq 0}$ follows a particular **path** in each state of nature ω which is given by the function $t \mapsto X_t(\omega)$.
- The process $(X_t)_{t\geq 0}$ is said to be **continuous** if every path $t \mapsto X_t(\omega)$ is a continuous function of time for all states of nature ω in Ω.

9.3.2 Standard Brownian motion

A **standard Brownian motion**, also called **standard Wiener process**, is a *continuous* stochastic process $(W_t)_{t\geq 0}$ which satisfies:

1. $W_0 = 0$.
2. For all $0 \leq t < t'$, the increment variable $D = W_{t'} - W_t$ follows a normal distribution with zero mean and standard deviation $\sqrt{t' - t}$.
3. For all $0 \leq t_1 < t_2 \leq t_3 < t_4$, the increment variables $D = W_{t_2} - W_{t_1}$ and $\Delta = W_{t_4} - W_{t_3}$ are independent.[4]

Using properties 2 and 3 we can represent the infinitesimal increment $dW_t = W_{t+dt} - W_t$ as a random variable following a normal distribution with zero mean and standard deviation $\sqrt{dt}$, and we can write: $dW_t \equiv \tilde{e}_t \sqrt{dt}$, where $(\tilde{e}_t)_{t\geq 0}$ is a sequence of independent standard normals.

Example. A simulation using computer-generated random numbers gave the following Brownian paths for $0 \leq t \leq 1$ and steps $dt = 0.05$ and 0.01:

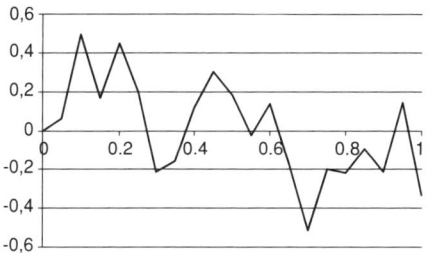 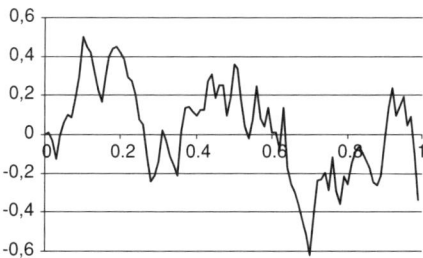

Brownian path simulated with step $dt = 0.05$ Brownian path simulated with step $dt = 0.01$

---

[4] This is a simplified version of the independence property of Brownian motions. The correct version is: any finite sequence of increments $(W_{t_2} - W_{t_1})$, $(W_{t_4} - W_{t_3})$,... such that $0 \leq t_1 < t_2 \leq t_3 < t_4 \leq \ldots$ is independent.

Brownian motions have some remarkable properties:

- Brownian paths tend to exhibit alternate cycles above or below the time axis. In fact it can be shown that the expected number of times a Brownian motion will hit the axis is infinite. This is because the increments are centred around 0, in other words the process has no general upward or downward trend.
- Brownian paths are continuous at every point in time but nowhere differentiable. A heuristic proof of this property can be found in Exercise 5.

9.3.3 Generalized Brownian motion

A **generalized Brownian motion** or Wiener process $(X_t)_{t \geq 0}$ is defined as:

$$dX_t = a\,dt + b\,dW_t$$

where a and b are constants and $(W_t)_{t \geq 0}$ is a standard Brownian motion.

This definition is often difficult to grasp the first time, and it usually helps to consider both components $a\,dt$ and $b\,dW_t$ separately, as illustrated in the graph below:

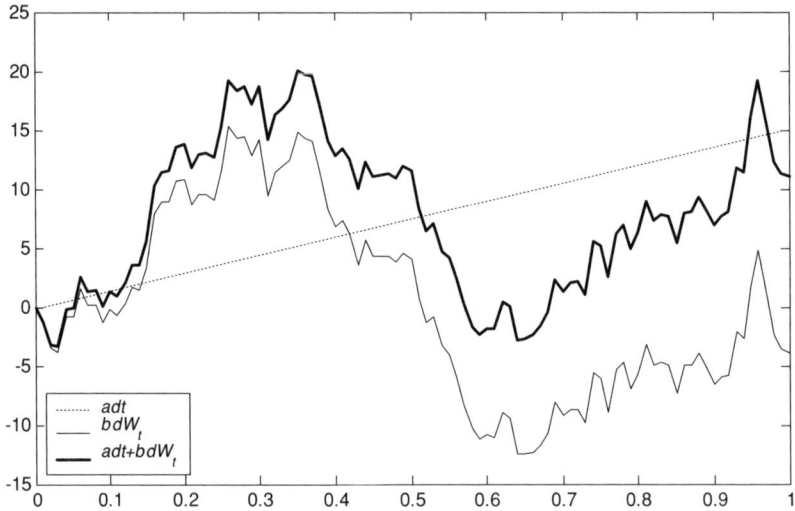

Path of a generalized Brownian motion simulated with parameters $a = 15$, $b = 20$ and $dt = 0.01$

- $a\,dt$ corresponds to a general, deterministic upward or downward trend of the process called **drift**. Omitting the random component $b\,dW_t$ we would have $dX_t = a\,dt$, i.e. $\dfrac{dX_t}{dt} = a$, and by integration we would obtain the line $X_t = at + X_0$.

- $b\,dW_t$ corresponds to a random variation around the general trend whose amplitude is controlled by the time interval dt (remember that dW_t can be represented as a standard normal with zero mean and standard deviation $\sqrt{dt}$).

Integrating[5] both sides of the relationship $dX_t = a\,dt + b\,dW_t$, we obtain a useful analytical expression for $(X_t)_{t\geq 0}$:

$$X_t = X_0 + at + bW_t$$

9.3.4 Geometric Brownian motion

A **geometric Brownian motion** or Wiener process $(X_t)_{t\geq 0}$ is defined as:

$$dX_t = (aX_t)dt + (bX_t)dW_t$$

The financial interpretation of this definition becomes apparent when we divide both sides by X_t and write:

$$\frac{X_{t+dt} - X_t}{X_t} = a\,dt + b\,dW_t$$

For a price process $(X_t)_{t\geq 0}$, the quantity $\dfrac{X_{t+dt} - X_t}{X_t}$ is the rate of return over an infinitesimal time interval dt.

A geometric Brownian motion is thus particularly suited to model the behaviour of asset prices through their returns. This is the preferred approach in finance.

The derivation of an explicit expression for $(X_t)_{t\geq 0}$ requires further knowledge in stochastic calculus and will be carried out in exercises.

9.4 Introduction to stochastic calculus

An **Ito process** $(X_t)_{t\geq 0}$ is an even more general form of the processes seen thus far, and is defined as:

$$dX_t = a(t, X_t)dt + b(t, X_t)dW_t$$

where a and b are now two 'sufficiently smooth' *functions* of two variables.[6]

---

[5] Here we must emphasize that stochastic integration follows different rules than classical integration. However, in this case, we simply wrote that the sum of infinitesimal increments dX_t is equal to the total process X_t.

[6] By 'sufficiently smooth' we mean that each function is differentiable with respect to the time variable t and twice differentiable with respect to the state variable X.

This type of stochastic process is named after the mathematician Kiyosi Ito who is responsible for the unappetizing yet revolutionary formulas below. Note that if a and b are constant $(X_t)_{t\geq 0}$ is a generalized Brownian motion, and if $a(t, X_t) = \alpha X_t$ and $b(t, X_t) = \beta X_t$ then $(X_t)_{t\geq 0}$ is a geometric Brownian motion.

The Ito–Doeblin Theorem.[7] Let $(X_t)_{t\geq 0}$ be an Ito process and f a 'sufficiently smooth' function of time and X. The stochastic process $(Y_t)_{t\geq 0}$ defined as $Y_t = f(t, X_t)$ is then an Ito process which satisfies:

$$dY_t = df(t, X_t) = \left[\frac{\partial f}{\partial t}(t, X_t) + a(t, X_t)\frac{\partial f}{\partial X}(t, X_t) + \frac{1}{2}b^2(t, X_t)\frac{\partial^2 f}{\partial X^2}(t, X_t)\right]dt$$
$$+ \left[b(t, X_t)\frac{\partial f}{\partial X}(t, X_t)\right]dW_t$$

In abridged format, omitting evaluations at point (t, X_t):

$$dY_t = df = \left(\frac{\partial f}{\partial t} + a\frac{\partial f}{\partial X} + \frac{1}{2}b^2\frac{\partial^2 f}{\partial X^2}\right)dt + \left(b\frac{\partial f}{\partial X}\right)dW_t$$

Example. If (X_t) is a generalized Brownian motion and $Y_t = X_t^2$, we can apply the Ito–Doeblin theorem on $f(t, X) = X^2$ and obtain:

$$dY_t = df = \left(\frac{\partial f}{\partial t} + a\frac{\partial f}{\partial X} + \frac{1}{2}b^2\frac{\partial^2 f}{\partial X^2}\right)dt + \left(b\frac{\partial f}{\partial X}\right)dW_t$$
$$= \left(0 + 2X_t a + \frac{1}{2} \times 2 \times b^2\right)dt + (2X_t b)\,dW_t$$
$$= (2aX_t + b^2)dt + (2bX_t)dW_t$$

References and further reading

Hull, J.C. (2005) *Options, Futures and Other Derivatives*, 6th edn. Prentice Hall, Englewood Cliffs, NJ.

Jarrow, R. and Protter, P. (2004) 'A short history of stochastic integration and mathematical finance the early years, 1880–1970'. In *The Herman Rubin Festschrift*, IMS Lecture Notes, **45**: 75–91.

Shreve, S.S. (2004) *Stochastic Calculus Models for Finance II: Continuous-Time Models*. Springer, New York.

---

[7] Until recently, academic literature referred to this theorem as 'Ito's lemma'. Recent discoveries (see Jarrow and Protter, 2004) show that earlier work by Wolfgang Doeblin reached similar results which remained unknown for 50 years as his notes were sealed in a safe of the Académie des Sciences in Paris after his tragic death during the course of World War II.

Exercises

Exercise 1: conversion of interest rates

Fill the gaps in the table of equivalent interest rates below:

Annual gross rate	Fractioned twice	Fractioned 12 times	Continuously compounded
10%			
	10%		
		10%	
			10%

Exercise 2: continuous compounding

Let R be the risk-free interest rate and K_t the amount of capital and interest after t years, starting with initial capital K.

1. Suppose that interest is paid annually. Determine K_t as a function of R and t.
2. Suppose that interest is fractioned m times. Determine K_t as a function of R and t.
3. Suppose that interest is paid continuously.
   (a) Determine K_t as a function of R and t.
   (b) Use a financial argument to show that K_t must satisfy the differential equation: $dK_t = RK_t \, dt$, and verify your previous result. *Hint:* The solutions to the differential equation $f' = af$ have the form $f(x) = f(0)\exp(ax) + c$, where a and c are constants.

Exercise 3: some econometrics

Look up the historical prices at market close of a stock or equity index over a 1-year period and use a spreadsheet to answer the following questions:

1. Calculate the mean and standard deviation.
2. Draw a distribution histogram with nine intervals and compare it with a normal distribution.
3. Calculate the series of daily returns and repeat the questions above.

Exercise 4[†]: simulation of Brownian motions

In a spreadsheet, simulate 100 normally distributed variables (see Chapter 7) and answer the following questions.

[†] Exercises 4, 5 and 6 should be solved in that order.

1. Draw the path of a standard Brownian motion with time interval $\Delta t = 0.1$, then $\Delta t = 0.01$.
2. Draw the path of a generalized Brownian motion with initial value $X_0 = 100$ and parameters $a = 30$, $b = 5$.
3. Draw the path of a geometric Brownian motion with initial value $X_0 = 100$ and parameters $a = 10\%$, $b = 40\%$.

Exercise 5[†]: trading simulation

In a spreadsheet, simulate the daily prices S_t of an asset over a year on a 252 trading days basis using the model: $dS_t = \mu S_t \, dt + \sigma S_t \, dW_t$, with $S_0 = 100$, $\mu = 10\%$ and $\sigma = 40\%$. Then use the closed-form formulas in Appendix C with a risk-free rate $r = 5\%$ and calculate for each day:

- The value of a European call with strike 100 and initial maturity 1 year.
- The delta of the call.
- The gamma of the call.
- The theta of the call.

Draw the graph of the evolution of each quantity through time for two simulations and comment on your results.

Exercise 6[†]: delta-hedging simulation

Using your spreadsheet from the previous exercise, implement a delta-hedging strategy for a short call position with strike 100 and 1-year maturity. Indicate for each day:

- The position in the underlying asset at the beginning of the day.
- The quantity of underlying to buy or sell.
- The position in the underlying asset after executing the previous transaction.
- The daily and cumulative P&L.

Comment on your results.

Exercise 7: the Ito–Doeblin theorem

Let (X_t) be a geometric Brownian motion with parameters (μ, σ), and initial value $X_0 = 1$.

1. What is the stochastic process followed by $Y_t = \ln X_t$? *Hint:* Use the Ito–Doeblin theorem.
2. What is the stochastic process followed by $Z_t = X_t^n$ (where n is a positive integer)?
3. What is the stochastic process followed by $H_t = \dfrac{1}{X_t}$?

Exercise 8: standard Brownian motion

Let $(W_t)_{t\geq 0}$ be a standard Brownian motion. *The following questions are independent.*

1. Show that for any time $T > 0$, W_T is normally distributed and give its parameters.
2. Let $0 < t < t'$. Determine whether the random variables W_t and $W_{t'}$ are independent. *Hint:* Calculate the covariance.
3. Let $H_t = \exp(\sigma W_t)$, $h_t = E(H_t)$ and $G_t = H_t h_t^{-1}$. Express h_t as a function of σ and t. Using the Ito–Doeblin theorem, show that G_t is a geometric Brownian motion and calculate its parameters.

Exercise 9: continuity and nondifferentiability of Brownian motions

Let $(W_t)_{t\geq 0}$ be a standard Brownian motion, $t > 0$, $h > 0$, $D_t = W_{t+h} - W_t$, $\delta_t = \frac{D_t}{h}$.

1. What is the distribution of D_t and δ_t?
2. Calculate the variance of D_t, and its limit when h goes to 0. Interpret your results.
3. Calculate the variance of δ_t, and its limit when h goes to 0. Interpret your results.

Exercise 10*: positivity of geometric Brownian motions

Let $(X_t)_{t\geq 0}$ be a geometric Brownian motion with parameters (a, b), and initial value $X_0 = 1$. Let $t > 0$ be fixed, and $R_n = \dfrac{X_{t+\frac{1}{n}} - X_t}{X_t}$ for a positive integer n.

1. Explain why, for large n, the distribution of R_n can be approximated by a normal distribution. Find the mean and standard deviation of this distribution.
2. Let p_n be the probability that $R_n < -1$. Find the limit of p_n when n goes to infinity and interpret your result.

Problem 1: stock price modelling

In this problem, we consider two continuous time models for the stock price of Winner AG, which currently trades at €100 in Frankfurt. Using historical data we can estimate the average annual return of Winner AG at 12%. This return is significantly higher than the risk-free rate of 3% because of a high volatility risk of 40% per annum.

1. In this question we model Winner AG's stock price process with a generalized Brownian motion with parameters (m, s), and initial value $X_0 = 100$.
   (a) Determine the expectation and variance of X_t as a function of m, s and t. What values would you propose for parameters m and s?
   (b) Calculate the probability of the stock price to be above €120 in 1 year, then 2 years.
   (c) Can Winner AG's stock price lose all value in this model?
2. In this question we model Winner AG's stock price process with a generalized Brownian motion $(G_t)_{t \geq 0}$ which satisfies: $dG_t = \mu G_t \, dt + \sigma G_t \, dW_t$, and initial value $G_0 = 100$.
   (a) Using the Ito–Doeblin theorem, show that $L_t = \ln(G_t)$ follows a generalized Brownian motion and derive the following explicit formula:

   $$G_t = G_0 \exp\left(\mu t - \frac{1}{2}\sigma^2 t + \sigma W_t\right)$$

   (b) Determine the expectation and variance of G_t as a function of μ, σ and t. What values would you propose for parameters μ and σ?
   (c) Calculate the probability of the stock price to be above €120 in 1 year, then 2 years.
   (d) Can Winner AG's stock price lose all value in this model?

Problem 2*: the Ito–Doeblin theorem

The aim of this problem is to obtain an intuitive derivation of the Ito–Doeblin theorem in the simplified case where $(Y_t)_{t \geq 0}$ is only a function of $(X_t)_{t \geq 0}$, which follows a generalized Brownian motion with parameters (a, b), i.e.: $Y_t = f(X_t)$. To solve this problem you need to be familiar with the notion of negligible quantities $y = o(x)$.

1. Let x and x' be two real numbers, $\Delta x = x' - x$, $\Delta f = f(x') - f(x)$. Show that:

   $$\Delta f = f'(x)\Delta x + \frac{1}{2}f''(x)(\Delta x)^2 + o((\Delta x)^2)$$

2. Let G be a random variable following a standard normal distribution. Calculate the expectation and variance of G^2.
3. Let $t < t'$, $\Delta t = t' - t$, $\Delta X = X_{t'} - X_t$, $\Delta Y = Y_{t'} - Y_t$.
   (a) Explain the equations:

   $$\Delta X = a\Delta t + b\sqrt{\Delta t}\, G$$
   $$(\Delta X)^2 = b^2 \Delta t G^2 + o(\Delta t)$$

   (b) Explain the equation:

   $$\Delta t G^2 = \Delta t$$

(c) Explain the equation:
$$\Delta Y = \left(af'(X_t) + \tfrac{1}{2}b^2 f''(X_t)\right)\Delta t + o(\Delta t) + bf'(X_t)\sqrt{\Delta t}\, G$$
4. How does the previous equation change when Δt is infinitesimal?

Problem 3*: binomial tree and Brownian motion

The aim of this problem is to show that the Brownian motion is the limit-case of a binomial tree as the number of periods n goes to infinity. *To solve this problem you need to be familiar with binomial distributions and the Central Limit Theorem.*

Consider a binomial tree over the period $[0, T]$ with n steps of length τ for the price S_t of an asset. The branches of the tree recombine at each intermediary node and have the pattern:

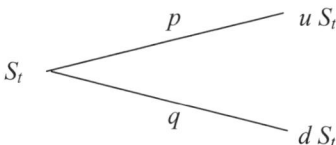

where $u = \exp(\sigma \sqrt{\tau})$, $d = \exp(-\sigma \sqrt{\tau})$, $p = q = \tfrac{1}{2}$, and $\sigma > 0$ is an arbitrary parameter.

1. (a) How many nodes are there in the tree?
   (b) How many paths are there between the initial price S_0 and the final price $u^i d^j S_0$ (where i, j are nonnegative integers)?
   (c) What is the distribution of S_T?
2. Let I_T be the (random) number of 'up' branches followed by the underlying between $t = 0$ and $t = T$.
   (a) Express I_T as a function of $\ln(S_T)$.
   (b) Show that I_T has a binomial distribution and determine the distribution parameters.
3. Using the Central Limit Theorem, show that $\ln(S_T)$ converges to a normal distribution as n goes to infinity and give its parameters.
4. Generalizing the results, show that if $(\tilde{S}_t)_{0 \leq t \leq T}$ is the limit process as n goes to infinity, then $W_t = \dfrac{1}{\sigma} \ln \dfrac{\tilde{S}_t}{\tilde{S}_0}$ satisfies the three properties of a standard Brownian motion. What is the distribution of $\tilde{S}_T$? Assuming zero rates, is this distribution consistent with the lognormal model of Chapter 7?

Solutions

Exercise 1: conversion of interest rates

The numbers below were obtained using the conversion formulas in Section 9.1:

Annual gross rate	Fractioned twice	Fractioned 12 times	Continuously compounded
10%	9.76%	9.57%	9.53%
10.25%	10%	9.80%	9.76%
10.47%	10.21%	10%	9.96%
10.52%	10.25%	10.04%	10%

Exercise 2: continuous compounding

1. With annual compounding, we have:

$$K_t = K(1+R)^t, t = 1, 2, \ldots$$

2. With fractioned compounding, we have:

$$K_t = K\left(1 + \frac{R}{m}\right)^{mt}, t = \frac{1}{m}, \frac{2}{m}, \ldots$$

3. (a) With continuous compounding, we have:

$$K_t = Ke^{Rt}, t \geq 0$$

(b) Over the period $[t, t+dt]$, the return on $(K_t)_{t \geq 0}$ is $\frac{K_{t+dt} - K_t}{K_t}$. Since interest is paid continuously we can write $\frac{K_{t+dt} - K_t}{K_t} = R \times dt$, which yields the desired differential equation. Thus: $\frac{dK_t}{dt} = RK_t$, whose solutions are of the form $K_t = c + K_0 e^{Rt}$. Since $K_0 = K$ we obtain $c = 0$, which verifies the previous result.

Exercise 3: some econometrics

We chose the S&P 500 index published by Standard & Poor's for the year 2004.

1. Mean price: 909.42. Standard deviation: 20.24.

Solutions

2. The distribution of the S&P 500 index for the year 2004 is similar to a normal distribution but slightly skewed to the left.

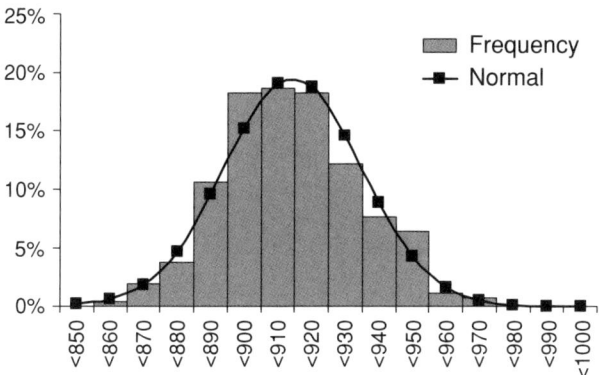

3. The series of daily returns of the S&P 500 index has a mean of 0.0156% and a standard deviation of 0.882%. Their distribution is also similar to a normal distribution but is not skewed. This is why it is better to model asset prices through their returns.

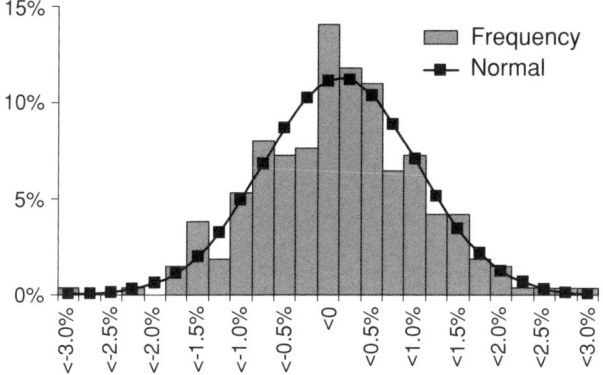

Exercise 4: simulation of Brownian motions

The screen capture overleaf shows how to obtain the desired results:

	A	B	C	D	E	F
1				**Parameters**		
2	dt	0.01				
3				a	30	10%
4				b	5	40%
5	t	Uniform	Std Normal	1) Brownian (LHS)	2) Generalized (RHS)	3) Geometric (RHS)
6	0			0	100	100
7	0.01	0.41970394	-0.20265134	-0.020265134	100.1986743	100.0189395
8	0.02	=RAND()	=NORMSINV(B6)	=D5+SQRT(dt)*C6	=E5+$E$1*dt+$E$2*SQRT(dt)*C6	=F5*(1+$F$1*dt+$F$2*SQRT(dt)*D6)
9	0.03					
10	0.04	0.98805422		0.106095058		
11	0.05	0.89181454	1.23623522	0.164943231	102.6247162	100.1369833
12	0.06	0.72189531	0.58848173	0.32495609	103.7247805	101.5387252
13	0.07	0.94521475	1.6001286	0.227703822	103.5385191	102.5650942
14	0.08	0.1653952	-0.97252268	0.242201054	103.9110053	103.6613142
15	0.09	0.55763377	0.14497232	0.304256105	104.5212805	105.026559
16	0.1	0.73255244	0.62055051	0.331873366	104.9593668	106.5258063
17	0.11	0.60879203	0.27617261	0.231524723	104.7576236	107.6188664
18	0.12	0.15781328	-1.00348643	0.100778493	104.4038925	108.160312
19	0.13	0.09552779	-1.3074623	0.072780608	104.563903	108.5833512
20	0.14	0.38974708	-0.27997885	0.211569045	105.5578452	109.6108496
21	0.15	0.9174141	1.38788437	0.101378532	105.3068927	110.1649479
22	0.16	0.13525132	-1.10190513	0.105020604	105.625103	110.7378965
23	0.17	0.51452658	0.03642072	0.073655769	105.7682788	111.1748938
24	0.18	0.37689438	-0.31364834	0.123528025	106.3176401	111.8353973
25	0.19	0.69101257	0.49872256	0.160935542	106.8046777	112.6671643
26	0.2	0.64582549	0.37407517	0.270546025	107.6527301	113.9990976
27	0.21	0.863483234	1.09610482			

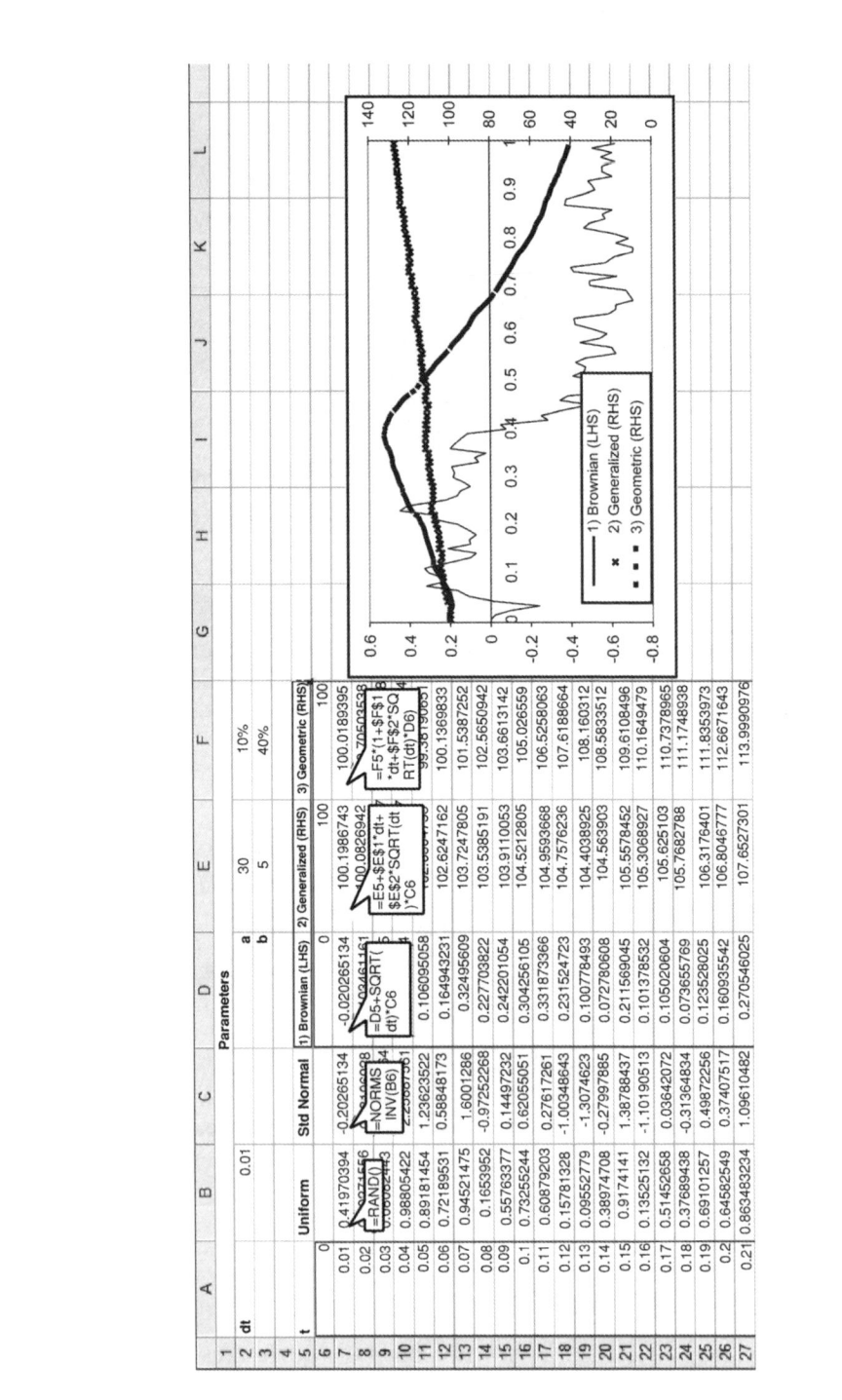

Exercise 5: trading simulation

Following the same methodology as in Exercise 4 to simulate a geometric Brownian motion, we obtained the following results.

(a) Scenario 1: 'growth'

In this simulation, the underlying asset grew from its initial price of 100 to 140 after a year. Accordingly, the call value converged to a payoff of 40, following a similar pattern. The delta, which is the number of units of the underlying to hold in order to replicate the call payoff at maturity, converged to 1, also following a similar pattern. The gamma, however, followed a reverse pattern. The gamma, which measures the uncertainty in delta, initially oscillated, and then dropped to a low level as the underlying was well above the strike. The theta followed an opposite pattern to the gamma due to the mathematical relationship between these two Greeks.

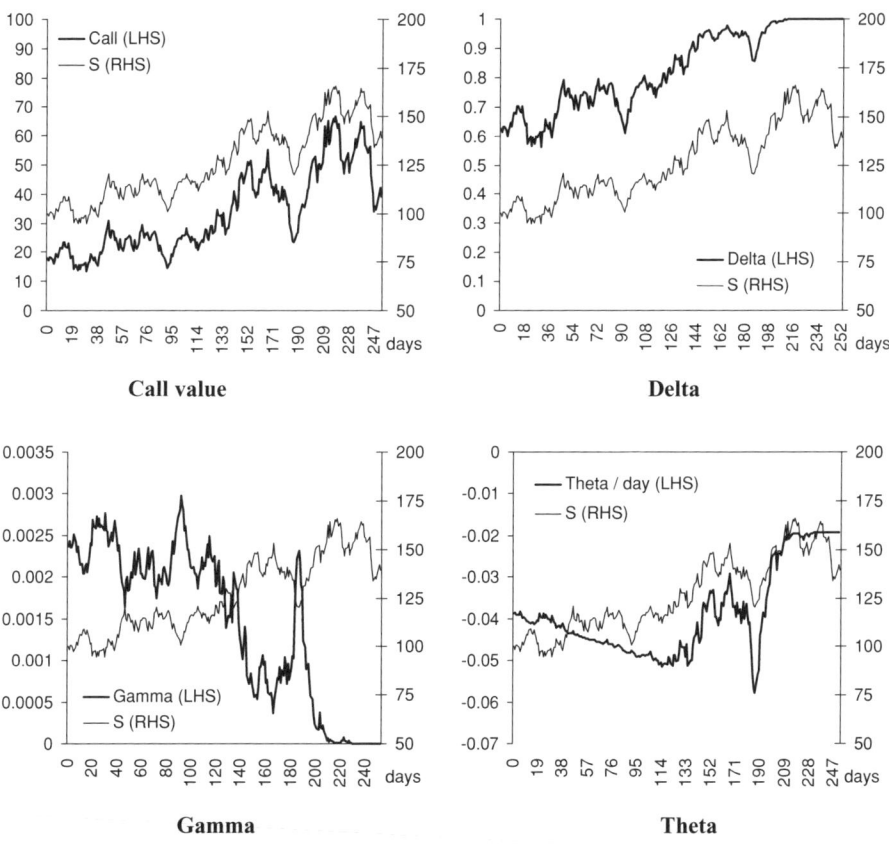

(b) Scenario 2: 'pinned at the strike'

In this simulation, the underlying asset oscillated around the strike throughout the year and finished slightly above 100. The call value followed a similar pattern and converged to a payoff close to 0. The delta also started to oscillate around its initial value of 0.6, however we notice that it experienced increasingly large swings as maturity was approaching. Accordingly, the gamma and thus theta became larger as time passed. This scenario is the option trader's nightmare: because the underlying is 'pinned at the strike', it remains unclear whether she should be long the underlying asset at maturity, and her risk parameters become wild.

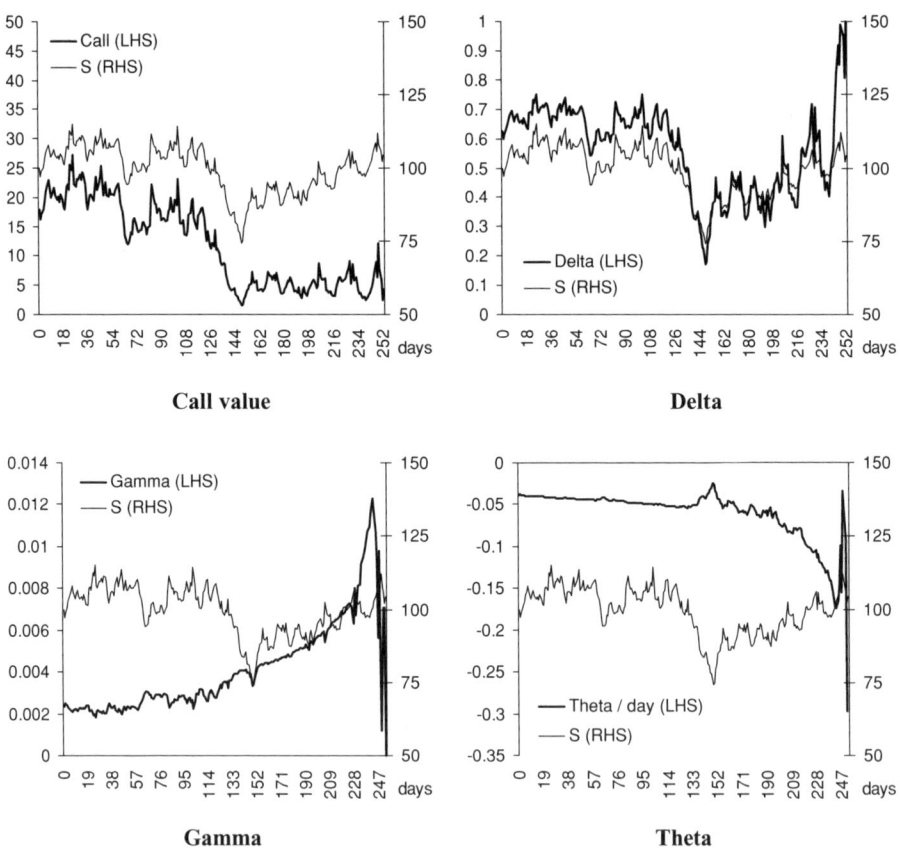

Exercise 6: delta-hedging simulation

The screen capture below shows how to obtain the desired results. We notice that the final cumulative P&L is small but nonzero: this is because delta-hedging takes place at discrete points in time rather than continuously. In fact, this residual P&L vanishes as the hedging interval goes to zero.

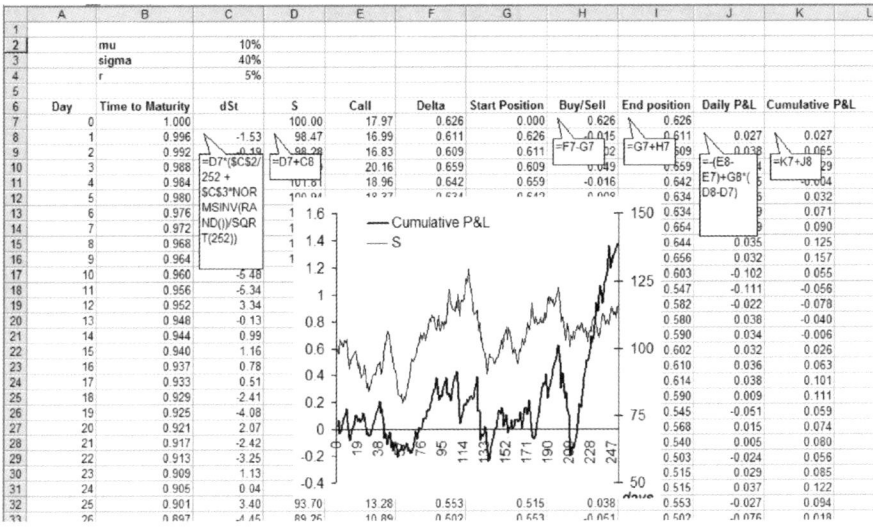

Exercise 7: the Ito–Doeblin theorem

1. Choosing $f(t, X) = \ln X$, $a(t, X_t) = \mu X_t$, $b(t, X_t) = \sigma X_t$ and applying the Ito–Doeblin theorem yields:

$$dY_t = df = \left(\frac{\partial f}{\partial t} + \mu X_t \frac{\partial f}{\partial X} + \frac{1}{2}\sigma^2 X_t^2 \frac{\partial^2 f}{\partial X^2}\right) dt + \left(\sigma X_t \frac{\partial f}{\partial X}\right) dW_t$$

$$= \left(0 + \mu X_t \frac{1}{X_t} - \frac{1}{2}\sigma^2 X_t^2 \frac{1}{X_t^2}\right) dt + \left(\sigma X_t \frac{1}{X_t}\right) dW_t$$

$$= \left(\mu - \frac{1}{2}\sigma^2\right) dt + \sigma dW_t$$

Thus, $Y_t = \ln X_t$ follows a generalized Brownian motion with parameters $(\mu - \sigma^2/2, \sigma)$.

2. Choosing $f(t, X) = X^n$, $a(t, X_t) = \sigma X_t$, $b(t, X_t) = \sigma X_t$ and applying the Ito–Doeblin theorem yields:

$$dZ_t = df = \left(\frac{\partial f}{\partial t} + \mu X_t \frac{\partial f}{\partial X} + \frac{1}{2}\sigma^2 X_t^2 \frac{\partial^2 f}{\partial X^2}\right) dt + \left(\sigma X_t \frac{\partial f}{\partial X}\right) dW_t$$

$$= \left(0 + n\mu X_t X_t^{n-1} + \frac{1}{2}n(n-1)\sigma^2 X_t^2 X_t^{n-2}\right) dt + \left(n\sigma X_t X_t^{n-1}\right) dW_t$$

$$= \left(n\mu + \frac{1}{2}n(n-1)\sigma^2\right) X_t^n dt + n\sigma X_t^n dW_t$$

$$= \left(n\mu + \frac{1}{2}n(n-1)\sigma^2\right) Z_t dt + n\sigma Z_t dW_t$$

Thus, Z follows a geometric Brownian motion with parameters $(n\mu + n(n-1)\sigma^2/2, n\sigma)$.

3. Choosing $f(t, X) = 1/X$, $a(t, X_t) = \mu X_t$, $b(t, X_t) = \sigma X_t$ and applying the Ito–Doeblin theorem yields:

$$dH_t = df = \left(\frac{\partial f}{\partial t} + \mu X_t \frac{\partial f}{\partial X} + \frac{1}{2}\sigma^2 X_t^2 \frac{\partial^2 f}{\partial X^2}\right) dt + \left(\sigma X_t \frac{\partial f}{\partial X}\right) dW_t$$

$$= \left(0 - \mu X_t \frac{1}{X_t^2} + \frac{1}{2}\sigma^2 X_t^2 \frac{2}{X_t^3}\right) dt - \left(\sigma X_t \frac{1}{X_t^2}\right) dW_t$$

$$= (-\mu + \sigma^2) \frac{1}{X_t} dt - \sigma \frac{1}{X_t} dW_t$$

$$= (-\mu + \sigma^2) H_t - \sigma H_t dW_t$$

Thus, H follows a geometric Brownian motion with parameters $(-\mu + \sigma^2, -\sigma)$. Because $(-W)$ is a standard Brownian motion, this is equivalent to saying that H follows a geometric Brownian motion with parameters $(-\mu + \sigma^2, \sigma)$.

Exercise 8: standard Brownian motion

1. Using the second property of Brownian motions, we know that $W_T = W_T - W_0$ follows a normal distribution with zero mean and standard deviation $\sqrt{T}$. Using the first property we have $W_0 = 0$. Thus W_T is normally distributed with mean zero and standard deviation $\sqrt{T}$.
2. $\text{Cov}(W_t, W_{t'}) = \text{Cov}(W_t, W_{t'} - W_t + W_t) = \text{Cov}(W_t - W_0, W_{t'} - W_t) + \text{Var}(W_t) = 0 + t$ (remember that the two increment variables $D = W_t - W_0$ and $\Delta = W_{t'} - W_t$ are independent, which implies that their covariance is zero). Thus the covariance between W_t and $W_{t'}$ is nonzero: these two variables are clearly *not* independent.
3. Using the transfer formula:

$$b_t = \text{E}\left(e^{\sigma W_t}\right) = \text{E}\left(e^{\sigma \sqrt{t}\tilde{e}}\right)$$

$$= \frac{1}{\sqrt{2\pi}} \int_{-\infty}^{+\infty} e^{\sigma \sqrt{t}x} e^{-\frac{x^2}{2}} dx$$

$$= e^{\frac{\sigma^2 t}{2}} \frac{1}{\sqrt{2\pi}} \int_{-\infty}^{+\infty} e^{-\frac{(x-\sigma\sqrt{t})^2}{2}} dx$$

$$= e^{\frac{\sigma^2 t}{2}}$$

(Remember that $\frac{1}{\sqrt{2\pi}} \int_{-\infty}^{+\infty} e^{-\frac{(x-\sigma\sqrt{t})^2}{2}} dx = 1$ since it is the integral of a density function between $-\infty$ and $+\infty$.)

Therefore: $G_t = e^{\sigma W_t - \frac{1}{2}\sigma^2 t}$. Choosing $f(t, X) = e^{\sigma X - \frac{1}{2}\sigma^2 t}$, $X_t = W_t$, $dX_t = dW_t$, $a = 0$, $b = 1$ and applying the Ito–Doeblin theorem yields:

$$dG_t = df = \left(\frac{\partial f}{\partial t} + a\frac{\partial f}{\partial X} + \frac{1}{2}b^2\frac{\partial^2 f}{\partial X^2}\right) dt + \left(b\frac{\partial f}{\partial X}\right) dW_t$$

$$= \left(-\frac{1}{2}\sigma^2 G_t + 0 + \frac{1}{2}\sigma^2 G_t\right) dt + (\sigma G_t) dW_t$$

$$= \sigma G_t dW_t$$

Thus, G follows a geometric Brownian motion with parameters $(0, \sigma)$.

Exercise 9: continuity and nondifferentiability of Brownian motions

1. Using the second property of Brownian motions, D_t follows a normal distribution with zero mean and standard deviation $\sqrt{h}$. Thus, δ_t follows a normal distribution with zero mean and standard deviation $\frac{1}{\sqrt{h}}$.
2. $\text{Var}(D_t) = h \to 0$. A random variable with zero variance is a constant, and since D_t has zero mean this result means that D_t converges to zero as the time interval h goes to 0. In other words two points of a Brownian motion taken at infinitesimally close times are also infinitesimally close: the path of a Brownian motion is thus continuous. (Note that this is an interpretation, not a proof.)
3. $\text{Var}(\delta_t) = \frac{1}{h} \to +\infty$. δ_t is the slope of the Brownian path over a time interval of length h. A slope which converges to a finite limit as h goes to zero means that the path is differentiable. In this case, however, the variance of the slope goes to infinity, which precludes convergence: the path of a Brownian motion is thus nondifferentiable. (Note that this is an interpretation, not a proof.)

Exercise 10*: positivity of geometric Brownian motions

1. For large n, $\frac{1}{n}$ is close to 0 and we have $X_{t+\frac{1}{n}} - X_t \approx dX_t = aX_t dt + bX_t dW_t$. Thus, $R_n \approx a dt + b dW_t$ which follows a normal distribution with mean $a dt$ and standard deviation $b\sqrt{dt}$. But $dt = \frac{1}{n}$, thus R_n can be approximated by a normal distribution with parameters $\frac{a}{n}$ and $\frac{b}{\sqrt{n}}$.

2. Since $-y^2 < y$ for $y < -1$, and since the exponential function is increasing, we have:

$$p_n = \frac{\sqrt{n}}{b\sqrt{2\pi}} \int_{-\infty}^{-1} \exp\left(-\frac{n(x-\frac{a}{n})^2}{2b^2}\right) dx$$

$$\leq \frac{\sqrt{n}}{b\sqrt{2\pi}} \int_{-\infty}^{-1} \exp\left(\frac{n(x-\frac{a}{n})}{2b^2}\right) dx$$

$$\leq \frac{\sqrt{n}}{b\sqrt{2\pi}} \frac{2b^2}{n} \exp\left(\frac{n(-1-\frac{a}{n})}{2b^2}\right)$$

$$\leq b\sqrt{\frac{2}{\pi n}} \exp\left(-\frac{n+a}{2b^2}\right)$$

Thus, p_n is bounded by a quantity which goes to 0 when n goes to infinity: the probability that $R_\infty < -1$ is nil. If X_t is the price of an asset, R_n is the return on that asset between t and $t + dt$, and the event $R_\infty < -100\%$ means that the asset loses more than 100% of its value, i.e. $X_{t+dt} < 0$. As a result X_t is always nonnegative, which is a useful property of geometric Brownian motions for modelling asset prices.

Problem 1: stock price modelling

1. (a) Using the analytical expression for generalized Brownian motions given in Section 9.3.3, we have:

$$X_t = 100 + mt + s W_t$$

Therefore, $E(X_t) = 100 + mt$, and $\text{Var}(X_t) = s^2 t$. Based on the numerical data, we want $E(X_1) = 100 \times (1 + 12\%) = 112$ and $\sigma(X_1) = 100 \times 40\% = 40$, whence the parameters: $m = 20$ and $s = 40$.

(b) With these values for m and s, X_t is normally distributed with parameters $(100 + 12t, 40\sqrt{t})$. We can now compute the probability that X_t is above 120 in a year's time:

$$P([X_1 > 120]) = P\left(\left[\frac{X_1 - 112}{40} > \frac{120 - 112}{40}\right]\right) = 1 - N(0.2) \approx 42\%$$

And in 2 years' time:

$$P([X_2 > 120]) = P\left(\left[\frac{X_1 - 124}{40\sqrt{2}} > \frac{120 - 124}{40\sqrt{2}}\right]\right) 1 - N(-0.0707) \approx 52\%$$

(c) The probability that X_t is below zero is:

$$P([X_t \le 0]) = P\left(\left[\frac{X_t - 100 - 12t}{40\sqrt{t}} \le \frac{-100 - 12t}{40\sqrt{t}}\right]\right)$$

$$= N\left(\frac{-100 - 12t}{40\sqrt{t}}\right) > 0$$

The model gives a nonzero probability that Winner AG loses all its value or even takes a negative value. This is a problem, as a stockholder can never lose more than her capital when investing in a stock.

2. (a) From Exercise 7 we know that L_t follows a generalized Brownian motion with parameters $(\mu - \sigma^2/2, \sigma)$; and from the analytical expression for generalized Brownian motions given in Section 9.3.3 we obtain:

$$L_t = L_0 + \left(\mu - \frac{1}{2}\sigma^2\right)t + \sigma W_t$$

Substituting L_t and L_0 with their definition:

$$\ln G_t = \ln G_0 + \left(\mu - \frac{1}{2}\sigma^2\right)t + \sigma W_t$$

Taking the exponential of both sides finally yields:

$$G_t = G_0 e^{(\mu - \frac{1}{2}\sigma^2)t + \sigma W_t}$$

(b) From Exercise 8, question 3: $E(G_t) = G_0 e^{\mu t} E\left(e^{\sigma W_t - \frac{1}{2}\sigma^2 t}\right) = 100 e^{\mu t}$.

For variance:

$$\text{Var}(G_t) = G_0^2 e^{2\mu t} \text{Var}\left(e^{\sigma W_t - \frac{1}{2}\sigma^2 t}\right)$$

$$= 100^2 e^{2\mu t} \left[E\left(e^{2\sigma W_t - \sigma^2 t}\right) - E\left(e^{\sigma W_t - \frac{1}{2}\sigma^2 t}\right)^2\right]$$

$$= 100^2 e^{2\mu t} \left[e^{\sigma^2 t} E\left(e^{2\sigma W_t - 2\sigma^2 t}\right) - 1\right]$$

$$= 100^2 e^{2\mu t} \left(e^{\sigma^2 t} - 1\right)$$

Based on the numerical data, we want $E(G_1) = 112$, i.e. $\mu = \ln(112/100) \approx 11.33\%$, and $\sigma(G_1) = 40$, i.e. $e^{\sigma^2} - 1 = \left(\frac{40}{112}\right)^2$, which yields $\sigma = \sqrt{\ln\left(1 + \left(\frac{40}{112}\right)^2\right)} \approx 34.64\%$.

(c) The probability that G_t is above 120 is:

$$P([G_t > 120]) = P\left(\left[\left(0.1133 - \frac{1}{2}0.3664^2\right)t + 0.3664 W_t > \ln\frac{120}{100}\right]\right)$$

$$= P\left(\left[\frac{W_t}{\sqrt{t}} > \frac{1}{0.3664\sqrt{t}}\left(\ln(1.2) - \left(0.1133 - \frac{1}{2}0.3664^2\right)t\right)\right]\right)$$

Thus: $P([G_1 > 120]) \approx 35\%$, and $P([G_2 > 120]) \approx 44\%$.

(d) Since $G_t = G_0 \exp\left(\mu t - \frac{1}{2}\sigma^2 t + \sigma W_t\right) > 0$, the probability that Winner AG loses all its value is nil. This is better than with the previous model.

Problem 2*: the Ito–Doeblin theorem

1. This is simply a second-order Taylor expansion around x.
2. The expectation of G^2 is easily obtained with the formula $\text{Var}(G) = E(G^2) - (E(G))^2$:

$$E(G^2) = \text{Var}(G) + (E(G))^2 = 1 + 0^2 = 1$$

For variance, we use the transfer theorem and then integration by parts:

$$\text{Var}(G^2) = E(G^4) - (E(G^2))^2$$

$$= \frac{1}{\sqrt{2\pi}} \int_{-\infty}^{+\infty} x^4 e^{-x^2/2} dx - 1$$

$$= \frac{1}{\sqrt{2\pi}}\left[-x^3 e^{-x^2/2}\right]_{-\infty}^{+\infty} + \frac{1}{\sqrt{2\pi}} \int_{-\infty}^{+\infty} 3x^2 e^{-x^2/2} dx - 1$$

$$= 0 + 3E(G^2) - 1$$

$$= 2$$

3. (a) Using the analytical formula for generalized Brownian motions in Section 9.3.3, we have:

$$\Delta X = X_{t'} - X_t = a(t' - t) + b(W_{t'} - W_t)$$

From the second property of Brownian motions, we know that $W_{t'} - W_t$ follows a normal distribution with zero mean and standard deviation $\sqrt{t' - t}$. Therefore ΔX follows a normal distribution with mean $a\Delta t$ and standard deviation $b\sqrt{\Delta t}$, which justifies the equation:

$$\Delta X = a\Delta t + b\sqrt{\Delta t}\, G$$

Squaring both sides and expanding:

$$(\Delta X)^2 = a^2(\Delta t)^2 + b^2 \Delta t G^2 + 2ab \Delta t \sqrt{\Delta t}\, G = b^2 \Delta t G^2 + o(\Delta t)$$

(b) Intuitively, G^2 is a random variable with a mean of 1 and variance of 2, which means that it typically takes values between $1 - \sqrt{2}$ and $1 + \sqrt{2}$. Consequently, $\Delta t G^2$ has a mean of Δt and typically takes values between

$\Delta t - \Delta t\sqrt{2}$ and $\Delta t + \Delta t\sqrt{2}$. For small Δt, we can thus justify the approximation $\Delta tG^2 = \Delta t$ at any desired precision level.

More specifically, given a precision level ε and confidence level θ, we can use Chebyshev's inequality to justify the approximation $\Delta tG^2 = \Delta t$:

$$P([|\Delta tG^2 - E(\Delta tG^2)| > \varepsilon]) \leq \frac{\text{Var}(\Delta tG^2)}{\varepsilon^2}$$

i.e.:

$$P([|\Delta tG^2 - \Delta t| > \varepsilon]) \leq \frac{2\Delta t^2}{\varepsilon^2}$$

Thus we can always find Δt small enough such that $\frac{2\Delta t^2}{\varepsilon^2} < 1 - \theta$ (in practice we can pick any $\Delta t < \varepsilon\sqrt{\frac{1-\theta}{2}}$), in which case the approximation $\Delta tG^2 = \Delta t$ is true with precision $\pm\varepsilon$, at a confidence level of θ. For instance, for $\varepsilon = 0.01$, $\theta = 99.9\%$, $\Delta t < 0.0003$ we have: $P([-0.01 < \Delta tG^2 - \Delta t < 0.01]) \geq 99.9\%$.

(c) From question 1 with $Y_t = f(X_t)$,:

$$\Delta Y = \Delta f = f'(X_t)\Delta X + \tfrac{1}{2}f''(X_t)(\Delta X)^2 + o((\Delta X)^2)$$

Then, from 3(a):

$$\Delta Y = f'(X_t)\left(a\Delta t + b\sqrt{\Delta t}G\right) + \tfrac{1}{2}f''(X_t)\left(b^2 \Delta tG^2 + o(\Delta t)\right)$$
$$+ o\left(b^2 \Delta tG^2 + o(\Delta t)\right)$$

And from 3(b):

$$\Delta Y = f'(X_t)\left(a\Delta t + b\sqrt{\Delta t}G\right) + \tfrac{1}{2}b^2 \Delta t f''(X_t) + o(\Delta t)$$

which is what we wanted to prove.

4. For infinitesimal Δt, we rather use the notations dt, dY_t, and write:

$$dY_t = \left(af'(X_t) + \tfrac{1}{2}b^2 f''(X_t)\right)dt + bf'(X_t)\sqrt{dt}G$$

or:

$$dY_t = \left(af'(X_t) + \tfrac{1}{2}b^2 f''(X_t)\right)dt + bf'(X_t)dW_t$$

This is the Ito–Doeblin theorem when f does not depend on t.

Problem 3*: binomial tree and Brownian motion

1. (a) The branches of the tree recombine at each intermediary node so there are $n+1$ final nodes (rather than 2^n).
   (b) In order to reach the final node $u^i d^j S_0$, the underlying must have followed i 'up' branches and j 'down' branches, with $i + j = n$. Coding each path with a sequence of n 'u' or 'd', we find that the total number of possible paths with i 'u' and $n-i$ 'd' is $\binom{n}{i} = \frac{n!}{i!(n-i)!} = \frac{(i+j)!}{i!j!}$.

(c) S_T is a discrete random variable whose $n+1$ possible values are $S_0 u^n$, $S_0 u^{n-1} d$, $S_0 u^{n-2} d^2$, ..., $S_0 d^n$, each having a probability of $\left(\frac{1}{2}\right)^n$, $n\left(\frac{1}{2}\right)^n$, $\frac{n(n-1)}{2}\left(\frac{1}{2}\right)^n$, ..., $\binom{n}{i}\left(\frac{1}{2}\right)^n$, ..., $\left(\frac{1}{2}\right)^n$ respectively.

2. (a) Since $S_T = S_0 u^{I_T} d^{n-I_T} = S_0 u^{2I_T - n}$, taking the log of both sides yields:

$$I_T = \frac{n}{2} + \frac{1}{2 \ln u} \ln \frac{S_T}{S_0} = \frac{n}{2} + \frac{1}{2\sigma \sqrt{\tau}} \ln \frac{S_T}{S_0}$$

(b) Using the result in 1(c), we can show that I_T follows a binomial distribution with parameters $(n, 1/2)$.

3. From 2(a) we can write: $\ln \frac{S_T}{S_0} = (2I_T - n) \ln u = (2I_T - n)\sigma \sqrt{\tau}$. A variable with a binomial distribution can be decomposed into a sum of independent, identically distributed binary variables: $\ln \frac{S_T}{S_0} = \left(\sum_{i=1}^{n} B_{T,i}\right) \sigma \sqrt{\tau}$, where $B_{T,i} = -1$ if the underlying goes down at step i and $+1$ if it goes up.

But $E(B_{T,i}) = 0$, $Var(B_{T,i}) = E(B_{T,i}^2) = 1$ and $\tau = T/n$. Hence:

$$\frac{1}{\sigma \sqrt{T}} \ln \frac{S_T}{S_0} = \frac{1}{\sqrt{n}} \sum_{i=1}^{n} B_{T,i}$$

According to the Central Limit Theorem $\frac{1}{\sqrt{n}} \sum_{i=1}^{n} B_{T,i}$ converges towards the distribution of a standard normal as the number of steps n goes to infinity. Equivalently, $\ln S_T$ converges towards a normal distribution with mean $\ln S_0$ and standard deviation $\sigma \sqrt{T}$.

4. Let us show that (W_t) satisfies the three properties of a Brownian motion:

- $W_0 = \frac{1}{\sigma} \ln \frac{\tilde{S}_0}{S_0} = 0$.
- Generalizing the results of question 3 for any interval $[t, t']$, the distribution of any increment $D = W_{t'} - W_t = \frac{1}{\sigma} \ln \frac{\tilde{S}_{t'}}{\tilde{S}_t}$ is normal with zero mean and standard deviation $\sqrt{t' - t}$.
- The independence between two increments stems from the independence of the 'up' and 'down' movements of the underlying asset. This property will also hold in the limit case. Note that we should actually verify that any finite sequence of increments is independent.

The distribution of $\ln \tilde{S}_T$ is normal with mean $\ln \tilde{S}_0$ and standard deviation $\sigma \sqrt{T}$, thus $\tilde{S}_T$ follows a lognormal distribution with these parameters. This distribution is *not* consistent with the lognormal model where the mean is $\ln \tilde{S}_0 - \frac{1}{2}\sigma^2 T$ when interest rates are nil. This is easily fixed by introducing a drift correction using $u = \exp(-\frac{1}{2}\sigma^2 \tau + \sigma \sqrt{\tau})$ and $d = \exp(-\frac{1}{2}\sigma^2 \tau - \sigma \sqrt{\tau})$.

10 The Black–Scholes model

10.1 The Black–Scholes partial differential equation

In Chapters 6 and 7, we saw two different approaches for option pricing: the binomial model, based on an arbitrage argument applied to a tree; and the lognormal model, based on the calculation of an expectation. The Black–Scholes model can be seen as a combination of these two approaches:[1] an arbitrage argument and lognormal distribution of asset prices set within a continuous time framework.

Black–Scholes appeared in 1973 during a time of economic turmoil and the emergence of many new financial risks. Options were an attractive investment with the potential to reduce risk, but no good or consistent pricing model existed. Black–Scholes remedied the situation and is widely viewed as having enabled the dramatic expansion of options markets. It remains the standard model for option pricing some three decades later.

Like the binomial model, Black–Scholes assumes that the underlying asset is subject to random variations with respect to its initial price level S_t between two infinitesimally close times t and $t + dt$. However, Black–Scholes considers an infinity of final levels[2] S_{t+dt} rather than only two outcomes $S_t(1 + u)$ and $S_t(1 + d)$. The final levels are distributed according to a lognormal distribution, i.e. $S_{t+dt} = S_t(1 + X)$, where X is the normally distributed return.

---

[1] The binomial model appeared after Black–Scholes.

[2] To stay in line with notations in Chapter 6, define $S_t = S_0$, $S_{t+dt} = S_T$, $u = \dfrac{S_t^{(u)} - S_0}{S_0}$ (return on the underlying asset in the 'up' scenario) and d similarly.

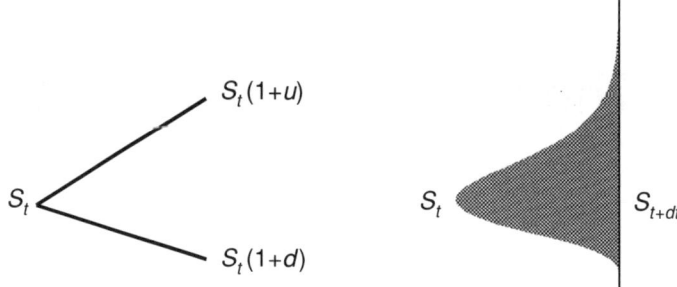

The binomial and Black–Scholes models of asset prices

The assumptions of the Black–Scholes model are:

- The price (S_t) of the underlying asset follows a geometric Brownian motion:
$$dS_t = \mu S_t\, dt + \sigma S_t\, dW_t$$
- The yield curve is flat and constant throughout time, with r being the continuous interest rate.
- The underlying asset pays no income and has no cost of carry.

Together with the traditional economic assumptions:

- There are no arbitrage opportunities on the markets.
- Transactions take place in continuous time, have no cost, and assets are infinitely liquid.
- Short-selling is allowed.

Let D_t be the value of the derivative at time t, and assume that it is only a function of time and the price of the underlying asset:
$$D_t = f(t, S_t) \quad \text{for all } t \geq 0$$

If f is 'sufficiently smooth' (i.e., continuously differentiable with respect to t and twice continuously differentiable with respect to S), then the Ito–Doeblin theorem yields:
$$dD_t = df = \left(\frac{\partial f}{\partial t} + \mu S_t \frac{\partial f}{\partial S} + \frac{1}{2}\sigma^2 S_t^2 \frac{\partial^2 f}{\partial S^2}\right) dt + \left(\sigma S_t \frac{\partial f}{\partial S}\right) dW_t$$

From a financial standpoint, this equation means that between times t and $t + dt$, the value of the derivative is exposed to a **drift** $\left(\frac{\partial f}{\partial t} + \mu S_t \frac{\partial f}{\partial S} + \frac{1}{2}\sigma^2 S_t^2 \frac{\partial^2 f}{\partial S^2}\right) dt$ (mean growth or decay over time) and to a **volatility risk** $\left(\sigma S_t \frac{\partial f}{\partial S}\right) dW_t$. Note that this risk is *proportional* to the volatility risk of the underlying $\sigma S_t dW_t$, the coefficient of proportionality being $\frac{\partial f}{\partial S}$. The diagram below shows the

The Black–Scholes partial differential equation

simultaneous drift and volatility behaviours of the underlying and the derivative:

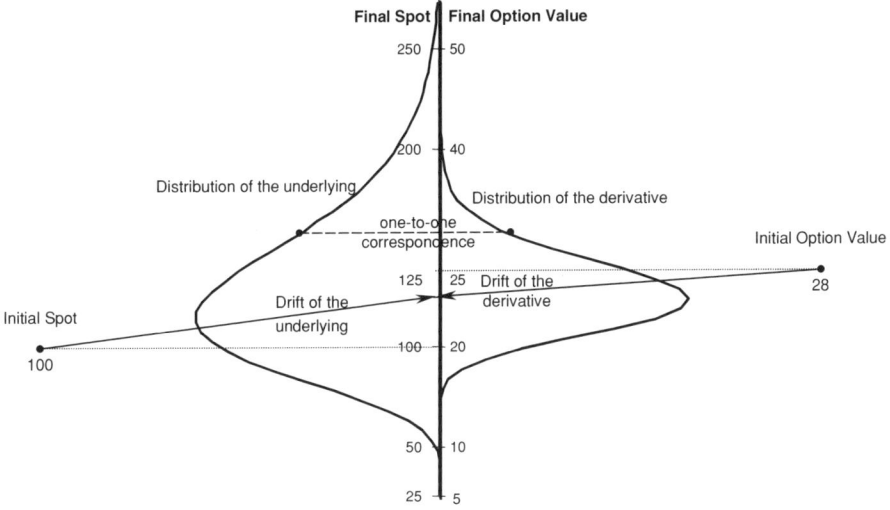

Drift and distribution of the underlying and the derivative

As with the binomial model, the holder of one unit of derivative can eliminate at any time t the volatility risk on horizon $t + dt$ by selling δ units of underlying. Define P_t as the value at time t of a portfolio long one single unit of derivative and short δ units of underlying:

$$P_t = f(t, S_t) - \delta S_t$$

At time $t + dt$, the portfolio value is:

$$P_{t+dt} = f(t + dt, S_{t+dt}) - \delta S_{t+dt}$$

and after the Ito–Doeblin theorem and the price model equation for S:

$$\begin{aligned} dP_t &= P_{t+dt} - P_t \\ &= df - \delta dS_t \\ &= \left[\left(\frac{\partial f}{\partial t} + \mu S_t \frac{\partial f}{\partial S} + \frac{1}{2}\sigma^2 S_t^2 \frac{\partial^2 f}{\partial S^2}\right) - \delta \mu S_t\right] dt + \left[\sigma S_t \frac{\partial f}{\partial S} - \delta \sigma S_t\right] dW_t \end{aligned}$$

The portfolio is riskless between t and $t + dt$ if and only if the change in value dP_t has no random component, i.e., iff the second bracket is nil:

$$\sigma S_t \frac{\partial f}{\partial S} - \delta \sigma S_t = 0$$

or:

$$\delta = \frac{\partial f}{\partial S}$$

This result is expected since we already identified that the volatility risk of the derivative is exactly proportional to that of the underlying, with coefficient (or **hedge ratio**) $\frac{\partial f}{\partial S}$.

Substituting δ with its value in our equation for dP_t yields:

$$dP_t = \left(\frac{\partial f}{\partial t} + \frac{1}{2}\sigma^2 S_t^2 \frac{\partial^2 f}{\partial S^2}\right) dt \qquad (10.1)$$

Finally, since this portfolio is riskless and there is no arbitrage, its value must grow at the risk-free continuous interest rate r:

$$dP_t = r P_t \, dt$$

Since $P_t = f(t, S_t) - \delta S_t$, we obtain another equation for dP_t:

$$dP_t = r\left(f - \delta S_t\right) dt$$
$$= \left(rf - r\frac{\partial f}{\partial S} S_t\right) dt \qquad (10.2)$$

Equations (10.1) and (10.2) both characterize in deterministic terms the change in value of the portfolio between times t and $t + dt$, therefore their drift coefficients must be equal. This yields the **Black–Scholes partial differential equation**:

$$rf = \frac{\partial f}{\partial t} + rS_t \frac{\partial f}{\partial S} + \frac{1}{2}\sigma^2 S_t^2 \frac{\partial^2 f}{\partial S^2}$$

This partial differential equation has an infinite number of solutions, which define the admissible (or tradable) derivatives of the underlying asset S. To determine an individual solution, additional constraints must be specified, such as a final condition. In the case of European options, this condition is the *payoff* at maturity, for instance:

- for a vanilla call, $f(T, S_T) = \max(0, S_T - K)$;
- for a vanilla put, $f(T, S_T) = \max(0, K - S_T)$.

The fact that the hedge ratio $\delta = \frac{\partial f}{\partial S}$ continuously changes over time must be emphasized. The strength of Black–Scholes is to rely on a **dynamic strategy** called **delta-hedging**, which we introduced in Chapter 8. In theory, this strategy allows an option trader to replicate perfectly the payoff at a cost equal to the option value without incurring any risk.

10.2 Black–Scholes formulas

For vanilla European options, there are closed-form solutions to the Black–Scholes partial differential equation. The step-by-step derivation is quite technical; we refer interested readers to Wilmott (2001).

The Black–Scholes formulas for the value at time $t = 0$ of the European call and the put maturing at $t = T$ are:

$$c_0 = S_0 N(d_1) - K e^{-rT} N(d_3)$$
$$p_0 = K e^{-rT} N(-d_2) - S_0 N(-d_1)$$

where $N(\cdot)$ is the cumulative distribution function of a standard normal, and d_1, d_3 the coefficients:

$$d_1 = \frac{\ln \frac{S_0}{K} + \left(r + \frac{\sigma^2}{2}\right) T}{\sigma \sqrt{T}}$$

$$d_2 = \frac{\ln \frac{S_0}{K} + \left(r - \frac{\sigma^2}{2}\right) T}{\sigma \sqrt{T}} = d_1 - \sigma \sqrt{T}$$

These formulas appear very similar to those obtained in Chapter 7. In fact, they are rigorously identical, since e^{-rT} is nothing else than the discount factor while $S_0 e^{rT}$ is the forward price F_0 of the underlying for maturity T. Substituting $F_0 e^{-rT}$ for S_0 in the Black–Scholes formulas, we find once more:

$$c_0 = e^{-rT} \left[F_0 N(d_1) - K N(d_2) \right]$$
$$p_0 = e^{-rT} \left[K N(-d_2) - F_0 N(-d_1) \right]$$

with:

$$d_1 = \frac{\ln \frac{F_0}{K}}{\sigma \sqrt{T}} + \frac{1}{2} \sigma \sqrt{T}, \quad d_2 = d_1 - \sigma \sqrt{T}$$

One may then question the advantage of Black–Scholes over the lognormal model. The answer almost entirely relies on the arbitrage argument: should the price of the derivative differ from its theoretical value, Black–Scholes assures us that it is possible to implement a delta-hedging strategy and make riskless profits. Naturally, this assertion is subject to the model hypotheses, and much empirical and theoretical research has been carried out to identify the shortcomings of Black–Scholes theory. Yet, the success of the Black–Scholes model is such that one can consider its assumptions reasonably reflective of market behaviour.

10.3 Volatility

Recall the model of asset prices for (S_t):

$$\frac{dS_t}{S_t} = \mu \, dt + \sigma \, dW_t$$

The drift coefficient μ is the mean continuous rate of return of the underlying.[3] The fact that this parameter does not appear in Black–Scholes formulas is striking: the value of an option does not depend on the expected return of the underlying. At first this may seem somewhat counter-intuitive, but it must be recalled that asset prices already include expectations of future growth. In other words, when the expected return μ increases, the price S_t of the underlying will usually increase as well, and this change will be reflected in the option price. **However, if the price of the underlying happens to remain unchanged, the price of the option will stay unchanged as well.**

The volatility coefficient σ is the standard deviation of the return of the underlying: $\sqrt{\mathrm{Var}\left(\dfrac{dS_t}{S_t}\right)} = \sigma\sqrt{dt}$. Volatility plays a crucial role in Black–Scholes formulas, as option prices are extremely sensitive to this parameter. For example, consider a 1-year European call struck at €110 on a stock currently trading at €100. If the volatility of the stock increases, the probability that its price in 1 year will be well above €110 (where the option is 'in-the-money', i.e., has positive payoff) is higher than before. Naturally, the probability that the stock price will be below €100 also increases, but in this case the option value is zero. The asymmetry of the payoff results in a higher option value: when volatility goes up the option is more expensive, and when volatility goes down the option is cheaper. In the jargon of option markets, the option is said to be 'long volatility'.[4]

There are two traditional techniques to determine the volatility parameter σ:

1. historical volatility;
2. implied volatility.

10.3.1 Historical volatility

Volatility can be estimated using a historical sample of prices of the underlying. Given observations $s_0, s_1, s_2, \ldots, s_n$ taken at regular time intervals of period τ, one can compute the continuous periodic returns: $u_i = \ln \dfrac{s_i}{s_{i-1}}$, and the usual mean

---

[3] $\dfrac{dS_t}{S_t} = \dfrac{S_{t+dt} - S_t}{S_t}$ is the instantaneous rate of return on (S_t). Since dW_t has zero mean (see Chapter 9) we have: $E\left(\dfrac{dS_t}{S_t}\right) = \mu dt$.

[4] Vanilla options are all long volatility, but some exotic options are short volatility: when volatility goes up, the option price is cheaper. Consider for instance a call option struck at 100 with a knock-out barrier at 90 (i.e. the call becomes worthless if the barrier is hit), when the underlying trades very close to the barrier, e.g. at 92.

and variance estimates:[5]

$$\bar{u} = \frac{1}{n}\sum_{i=1}^{n} u_i, \quad s^2 = \frac{1}{n-1}\sum_{i=1}^{n}(u_i - \bar{u})^2$$

An annualized estimate of volatility σ is then: $\bar{\sigma} = \frac{s}{\sqrt{\tau}}$.

The table below illustrates this process for the exchange rate of the euro in dollars.

Exchange rate of the euro in dollars, January 2005

Date	S_i	$u_i = \ln S_i/S_{i-1}$	Date	S_i	$u_i = \ln S_i/S_{i-1}$
31-Dec-04	1.3554		18-Jan-05	1.302	−0.360%
3-Jan-05	1.3465	−0.659%	19-Jan-05	1.301	−0.077%
4-Jan-05	1.3279	−1.391%	20-Jan-05	1.2963	−0.362%
5-Jan-05	1.3261	−0.136%	21-Jan-05	1.3039	0.585%
6-Jan-05	1.3173	−0.666%	24-Jan-05	1.306	0.161%
7-Jan-05	1.3054	−0.907%	25-Jan-05	1.2973	−0.668%
10-Jan-05	1.3074	0.153%	26-Jan-05	1.3073	0.768%
11-Jan-05	1.3107	0.252%	27-Jan-05	1.3045	−0.214%
12-Jan-05	1.3255	1.123%	28-Jan-05	1.3038	−0.054%
13-Jan-05	1.3224	−0.234%	31-Jan-05	1.3038	0.000%
14-Jan-05	1.3112	−0.851%	Mean		−0.185%
17-Jan-05	1.3067	−0.344%	Std. Dev.		0.587%

In this example, the period is 1 day: $\tau = 1/365$. A possible estimate for volatility is thus: $\bar{\sigma} = 0.587\% \times \sqrt{365} \approx 11.22\%$ per annum. However, data from the days when foreign exchange markets are closed is missing. It is common practice to adjust for this effect by using 255 trading days per year, which yields a second possible estimate: $\bar{\sigma} = 0.587\% \times \sqrt{255} \approx 9.38\%$ per annum.

The historical approach leaves several issues unresolved. How far back in time should one go? Should prices be observed every second, hour, day, or month? Is past volatility a good estimate for future volatility? Because these questions do not have definite answers, historical volatility is only used as a very rough estimate to determine the Black–Scholes value of an option. This is useful for fundamental valuation, e.g., when quoting a price for an option on a new underlying such as an emerging market equity index, provided there is enough data history. However, for actively traded underlyings with a liquid option market, one can hardly match market prices using historical volatility.

---

[5] Recall that $\frac{1}{n}\sum(u_i - \bar{u})^2$ is a biased estimation of the variance of a sample (u_i) of length n (see Chapter 5).

10.3.2 Implied volatility

The implied approach consists in finding the value of parameter σ which matches the Black–Scholes value of an option with its present market price, as illustrated in the two diagrams below. Such value for σ is called **implied volatility**.

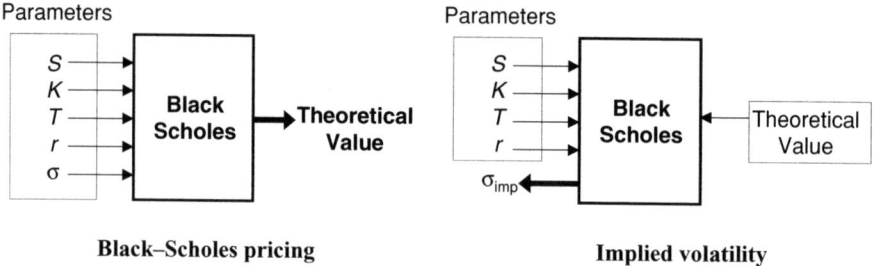

Black–Scholes pricing   Implied volatility

For example, if gold trades at $400 per troy ounce, the risk-free interest rate is at 10% per annum and a 3-month call struck at $450 quotes at $6, the implied volatility σ_{imp} is the unique solution to the equation:

$$400 \times N(d_1) - 450 \times e^{-10\% \times 0.25} \times N(d_2) = 6$$

where:

$$d_1 = \frac{\ln \frac{400}{450} + (10\% + \frac{1}{2}\sigma^2) \times 0.25}{\sigma\sqrt{0.25}} \quad \text{and} \quad d_2 = d_1 - \sigma\sqrt{0.25}$$

Numerical methods, such as dichotomy or Newton's method, can solve for this equation and for our example would yield: $\sigma_{imp} \approx 23.5\%$ per annum.

Implied volatility can then be used to compute the theoretical value of other options with similar characteristics (strike close to $450, maturity close to 3 months) on the same underlying. On most markets, all the other parameters are known with certainty and options prices are actually quoted in implied volatility rather than price.

References and further reading

Black, F. and Scholes, M. (1973) 'The pricing of options and corporate liabilities'. *Journal of Political Economy* **81**(3): 637–654.

Wilmott, P. (2001) *Paul Wilmott Introduces Quantitative Finance*. John Wiley & Sons, Chichester.

Exercises

Exercise 1

'In Black–Scholes theory, the volatility risk of the derivative is hedged by selling $\delta = \dfrac{\partial f}{\partial S}$ units of the underlying, because the latter has a volatility risk proportional to the former. Since the drift coefficient μ of the underlying does not play any role, one may similarly hedge the volatility risk of the derivative by selling the same quantity δ of any other asset that follows a geometric Brownian motion with identical volatility parameter σ as the underlying.' Comment on this statement.

Exercise 2: historical volatility vs. implied

Describe a market situation where historical and implied volatility would be strongly divergent. *Hint*: Consider, for instance, exceptional events scheduled to take place at a future date which is known in advance.

Exercise 3

Determine the following limit cases of the Black–Scholes formulas and comment:

1. $T \to 0$.
2. $\sigma \to 0$.

Exercise 4: skew curve

Use a spreadsheet to compute the **skew curve** of the option market below, i.e. the graph of implied volatility σ as a function of strike K. The underlying is a nondividend-paying stock currently trading at €30, and the continuous interest rate is 2.50%. Maturity is 1 year.

Call/put & strike	Price (cents)	Call/put & strike	Price (cents)
C40	49.43	C45	15.19
P15	1.73	C35	137.07
P20	15.28	C30	327.41
P30	247.50	P25	76.81

Exercise 5*: Black–Scholes and forward contracts

The settings are those of the Black–Scholes model. *The two questions are independent.*

1. (a) Using an arbitrage argument, show that the value at time t of a forward contract with strike K and maturity T is: $FC_t = S_t - Ke^{-r(T-t)}$.
   (b) Verify that FC_t satisfies the Black–Scholes partial differential equation.
2. (a) Using an arbitrage argument, establish put–call parity: $c_t - p_t = S_t - Ke^{-rT}$.
   (b) Re-derive put–call parity using Black–Scholes formulas. *Hint*: Generalize the formulas at any time t and use $N(-x) = 1 - N(x)$.

Exercise 6

Within the Black–Scholes framework, is the following a possible value for a derivative security on an underlying asset S?

$$\text{For all } t \geq 0, \quad D_t = \exp(S_t)$$

Exercise 7: forward-starting call

The compensation scheme for the employees of MeToo.Com includes stock options, i.e. call options on the company's stock. The stock options are distributed every 6 months, on the basis of a purchase price equal to 120% of the stock price at issuance, and exercisable in 2 years. MeToo.Com does not pay any dividend, and the rate curve is flat at a continuous 5% rate.

1. As an employee of MeToo.Com, you just received 1000 stock options. You would like to find out the value of this bundle, and you gathered the following data:

Dow Jones Industrial Index (DJI)	10 000
MeToo.Com (MTC) closing price	$10.00
DJI 6-month historical volatility	20%
MTC 6-month historical volatility	35%
MTC 6-month $10 call implied volatility	25%
MTC 2-year $10 call implied volatility	32%
MTC 2-year $12 call implied volatility	30%

2. As the director of Human Resources at MeToo.Com, you just distributed 1 000 000 stock options to the company's employees. You plan a 10% increase for the next distribution.
   (a) Estimate the cost of this increase, stating your assumptions and risks incurred.
   (b) Silverman, Sacks & Co., a reputed investment bank, offers you to purchase 100 000 forward-starting calls on MeToo.Com, which will be struck in 6 months at 120% of the stock price and become exercisable 2 years later. The offer is at $136 000. Analyse this offer.

Exercise 8: relationship between delta, gamma and theta

Using the Black–Scholes partial differential equation, show that the delta, gamma and theta of a portfolio of derivatives worth Π_t at time t satisfy the equation:

$$\Theta + rS_t\Delta + \tfrac{1}{2}\sigma^2 S_t^2 \Gamma = r\Pi_t$$

The derivatives are on the same underlying asset S. Compare this result with the relationship between theta and gamma in Section 8.2.3 for a delta-neutral portfolio.

Problem*: Black–Scholes and dividends

We extend the assumptions of the Black–Scholes model to take dividends into account under the form of continuous payments at rate q, which are reinvested in the stock.

1. Let n_t be the number of units invested in the underlying after t years, starting with one unit at time $t = 0$. Show that $dn_t = qn_t\,dt$, and find an analytical expression for n_t.
2. Show that the forward price of the stock at time $t = 0$ and for maturity T is: $F_0 = S_0 e^{(r-q)T}$.
3. Infer the new pricing formulas for European calls and puts on dividend-paying stocks from this result.
4. Consider a portfolio of value P_t at time t which is short one unit of derivative worth $D_t = f(t, S_t)$ and long $\dfrac{\partial f}{\partial S}$ units of underlying. By 'value' we mean asset value and cash flows.
   (a) Show that: $dP_t = -dD_t + \dfrac{\partial f}{\partial S}dS_t + q\dfrac{\partial f}{\partial S}S_t dt$.
   (b) Applying the Ito-Doeblin theorem, show that the portfolio is riskless between t and $t + dt$.
   (c) Determine the Black–Scholes partial differential equation for dividend-paying stocks.

Solutions

Exercise 1

This statement is wrong. Consider for instance the effect of hedging calls on technology stocks with shares in property funds: even if they had the same volatility, it is quite intuitive that technology stocks and property funds are not exposed to the same sources of risks.

In Black–Scholes theory, it is crucial that the derivative and the underlying be exposed to the same source of risk (W_t):

$$dS_t = \mu S_t\, dt + \sigma S_t\, dW_t$$

$$dD_t = df = \left(\frac{\partial f}{\partial t} + \mu S_t \frac{\partial f}{\partial S} + \frac{1}{2}\sigma^2 S_t^2 \frac{\partial^2 f}{\partial S^2}\right) dt + \left(\sigma S_t \frac{\partial f}{\partial S}\right) dW_t$$

For instance, if $\dfrac{\partial f}{\partial S}$ is positive, the value of the derivative increases when the underlying is subject to a random upwards variation dW_t. Hedging the risk (W_t) with another asset following a geometric Brownian motion $dQ_t = \mu' Q_t\, dt + \sigma Q_t\, dW_t'$ would be an imperfect hedge, the efficiency of which depends entirely on the correlation between (W_t) and (W_t'). In particular, if correlation is nil, such a hedge would be totally inefficient.

Exercise 2: historial volatility vs. implied

Historical volatility is based on past prices; implied volatility is a forward 'bet' on future prices made by option buyers and sellers. These two can therefore be expected to be strongly divergent when the markets expect high uncertainty around a future date, for instance when a major election or vote takes place. A historical example was the referendum for independence which was held in Quebec, Canada in October 1995.

Exercise 3

1. $T \to 0$.

$$d_1 = \frac{\ln \frac{S_0}{K}}{\sigma \sqrt{T}} + \left(\frac{r}{\sigma} + \frac{\sigma}{2}\right)\sqrt{T} \xrightarrow[T \to 0]{} \begin{cases} +\infty & \text{if } S_0 > K \\ 0 & \text{if } S_0 = K \\ -\infty & \text{if } S_0 < K \end{cases}$$

and $d_2 = d_1 - \sigma\sqrt{T}$ has the same limit as d_1 when $T \to 0$. Whence:

$$c_0 = S_0 N(d_1) - Ke^{-rT} N(d_2) \xrightarrow[T \to 0]{} \begin{cases} S_0 - K & \text{if } S_0 > K \\ 0 & \text{if } S_0 \le K \end{cases}$$

$$p_0 = Ke^{-rT} N(-d_2) - S_0 N(-d_1) \xrightarrow[T \to 0]{} \begin{cases} K - S_0 & \text{if } S_0 < K \\ 0 & \text{if } S_0 \ge K \end{cases}$$

These are the call and put payoffs at maturity: $\max(S_0 - K, 0)$ and $\max(K - S_0, 0)$.

2. $\sigma \to 0$.

$$d_1 = \frac{\ln\frac{S_0}{K} + \left(r + \frac{\sigma^2}{2}\right)T}{\sigma\sqrt{T}} \xrightarrow[\sigma \to 0]{} \begin{cases} +\infty & \text{if } S_0 e^{rT} > K \\ 0 & \text{if } S_0 e^{rT} = K \\ -\infty & \text{if } S_0 e^{rT} < K \end{cases}$$

and $d_2 = d_1 - \sigma\sqrt{T}$ has the same limit as d_1 when $T \to 0$. Whence:

$$c_0 = S_0 N(d_1) - Ke^{-rT} N(d_2) \xrightarrow[T \to 0]{} \begin{cases} S_0 - Ke^{-rT} & \text{if } S_0 e^{rT} > K \\ 0 & \text{if } S_0 e^{rT} \le K \end{cases}$$

$$p_0 = Ke^{-rT} N(-d_2) - S_0 N(-d_1) \xrightarrow[T \to 0]{} \begin{cases} Ke^{-rT} - S_0 & \text{if } S_0 e^{rT} < K \\ 0 & \text{if } S_0 e^{rT} \ge K \end{cases}$$

$\sigma \to 0$ means that the underlying has no volatility, i.e. is riskless. In this situation, the underlying must grow at the riskless rate r, under penalty of arbitrage. The value of calls and puts is then entirely determined by the position of the strike relative to the forward price $S_0 e^{rT}$.

Exercise 4: skew curve

Using Excel's solver we find the following implied volatilities:

Call/put & strike	Implied vol.	Call/put & strike	Implied vol.
C40	23%	C45	22.5%
P15	30%	C35	23.5%
P20	27%	C30	24.5%
P30	24%	P25	25%

Visually:

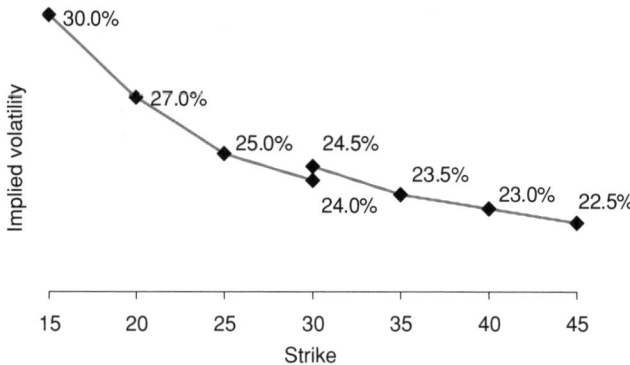

Note that the call and the put struck at €30 do not have the same implied volatility. This means that there is an arbitrage opportunity: sell the call, buy the put and hedge with a forward contract.

Exercise 5*: Black–Scholes and forward contracts

1. (a) The proof is identical to that in Section 4.2.2, using continuous interest rates rather than annual.
   (b) Let $f(t, S_t) = S_t - Ke^{-r(T-t)}$. Then:
   $$\frac{\partial f}{\partial t} + rS_t \frac{\partial f}{\partial S} + \frac{1}{2}\sigma^2 S_t^2 \frac{\partial^2 f}{\partial S^2} = -rKe^{-r(T-t)} + rS_t + 0 = rf(t, S_t)$$

2. (a) Put–call parity can be proved:
   - with a traditional dual arbitrage argument, assuming $c_t + Ke^{-rT} > p_t + S_t$ and $c_t + Ke^{-rT} < p_t + S_t$;
   - with a synthetic argument, noticing that a portfolio which is long call and short put has exactly the same payoff as a forward contract: $c_T - p_T = S_T - K = FC_T$; thus $c_t - p_t = FC_t$.
   (b) The Black–Scholes formulas are:
   $$c_t = S_t N(d_1) - Ke^{-r(T-t)} N(d_2)$$
   $$p_t = Ke^{-r(T-t)} N(-d_2) - S_0 N(-d_1)$$
   with:
   $$d_1 = \frac{\ln \frac{S_0}{K} + \left(r + \frac{\sigma^2}{2}\right)(T-t)}{\sigma \sqrt{T-t}}$$
   $$d_2 = d_1 - \sigma\sqrt{T-t}$$

Whence:

$$\begin{aligned}c_t - p_t &= S_t(N(d_1) + N(-d_1)) - Ke^{-r(T-t)}(N(d_2) + N(-d_2))\\ &= S_t - Ke^{-r(T-t)}\end{aligned}$$

Exercise 6

The value of admissible or tradable derivatives must verify the Black–Scholes partial differential equation:

$$rf = \frac{\partial f}{\partial t} + rS_t\frac{\partial f}{\partial S} + \frac{1}{2}\sigma^2 S_t^2 \frac{\partial^2 f}{\partial S^2}$$

But:

$$\frac{\partial f}{\partial t} + rS_t\frac{\partial f}{\partial S} + \frac{1}{2}\sigma^2 S_t^2 \frac{\partial^2 f}{\partial S^2} = 0 + rS_t e^{S_t} + \frac{1}{2}\sigma^2 S_t^2 e^{S_t} \neq re^{S_t}$$

The proposed derivative security cannot exist within the Black–Scholes framework: trading it on the market would lead to arbitrage opportunities.

Exercise 7: forward-starting call

1. The only relevant data is the closing price of MeToo.Com and the implied volatility of the 2-year call struck at $12:

$$\left.\begin{aligned}S_0 &= 10\\ K &= 120\% \times 10 = 12\\ T &= 2\\ r &= 5\%\\ \sigma &= 30\%\end{aligned}\right\} \xrightarrow{\text{Black–Scholes}} c_0 = 10N(d_1) - 12e^{-5\% \times 2}N(d_2)$$

$$d_1 = \frac{\ln\frac{10}{12} + (5\% + \frac{1}{2}(30\%)^2) \times 2}{30\% \times \sqrt{2}} \approx 0.0181 \rightarrow N(d_1) \approx 0.5072$$

$$d_2 = d_1 - 30\% \times \sqrt{2} \approx -0.4062 \rightarrow N(d_2) \approx 0.3423$$

$$c_0 \approx 1.3554$$

The value of a bundle of 1000 stock options is thus $1355.

2. (a) Using previous results, an increase by 10% × 1 000 000 = 100 000 stock options should therefore cost about $135 500. This estimate is made 'all other things being equal'. Since the strike is fixed only when the stock options are distributed, this cost will linearly increase or decrease with the stock price. Furthermore, an increase in volatility or rates would also result in a higher cost.

(b) The offer is only $500 higher than the previous estimate, which may seem surprisingly aggressive. However, we must be careful with the schedule: the estimate is 6 months forward, while the bank's offer is immediate. An equivalent offer for a payment in 6 months would be $136\,000 \times e^{5\% \times 0.5} = \$139\,443$. We can now calculate the implied volatility of this price and find 30.69%, which is reasonable.

Exercise 8: relationship between delta, gamma and theta

The Black–Scholes partial differential equation is:

$$rf = \frac{\partial f}{\partial t} + rS_t \frac{\partial f}{\partial S} + \frac{1}{2}\sigma^2 S_t^2 \frac{\partial^2 f}{\partial S^2}$$

where $f(t, S_t)$ is the value of any derivative. Substituting the differentials with their corresponding Greek letters:

$$rf = \Theta + rS_t \Delta + \tfrac{1}{2}\sigma^2 S_t^2 \Gamma$$

For a portfolio of N derivatives (on the same underlying) with values f_k and quantities q_k, we have:

$$\Pi_t = \sum_{k=1}^{N} q_k f_k(t, S_t)$$

Whence:

$$r\Pi_t = \sum_{k=1}^{N} w_k r f_k(t, S_t)$$

$$= \sum_{k=1}^{N} w_k \left(\Theta_k + rS_t \Delta_k + \frac{1}{2}\sigma^2 S_t^2 \Gamma_k \right)$$

$$= \sum_{k=1}^{N} w_k \Theta_k + rS_t \sum_{k=1}^{N} w_k \Delta_k + \frac{1}{2}\sigma^2 S_t^2 \sum_{k=1}^{N} w_k \Gamma_k$$

$$= \Theta + rS_t \Delta + \frac{1}{2}\sigma^2 S_t^2 \Gamma$$

where Θ, Δ and Γ are the Greek letters of the portfolio, and for a delta-neutral portfolio this equation becomes:

$$r\Pi_t = \Theta + \tfrac{1}{2}\sigma^2 S_t^2 \Gamma$$

When rates are not too high and the portfolio value is not too large, the expression on the left-hand side becomes negligible and we obtain the approximate relationship given in Chapter 8:

$$\Theta \approx -\tfrac{1}{2}\sigma^2 S_t^2 \Gamma$$

Problem*: Black–Scholes and dividends

1. Since dividends are reinvested in the stock at rate q, we have:
$$\frac{n_{t+dt} - n_t}{n_t} = q\, dt$$

Thus n_t satisfies the differential equation $\frac{dn_t}{dt} = qn_t$, whose solutions are of the form $n_t = n_0 e^{qt} + c$. Since $n_0 = 1$ we have $c = 0$, which yields the explicit expression:
$$n_t = e^{qt}$$

2. The identity $F_0 = S_0 e^{(r-q)T}$ is proved by an arbitrage argument. Suppose for instance that $F_0 > S_0 e^{(r-q)T}$. One may then sell one unit of stock forward at delivery price F_0, buy e^{-qT} units for $S_0 e^{-qT}$ financed by a loan at rate r, which will be repaid $S_0 e^{(r-q)T}$ at time $t = T$. The units held will grow to one because of dividend reinvestments, the strategy has zero cost and yields a positive profit $F_0 - S_0 e^{(r-q)T} > 0$ at $t = T$, hence it is an arbitrage. Similarly, supposing $F_0 < S_0 e^{(r-q)T}$ yields an arbitrage. Note that the assumption that the dividend rate q is known in advance is crucial: in practice, dividends are forecasted by equity analysts, which means that the arbitrage we just described actually entails risks, especially when long maturities are involved.

3. The formulas from the lognormal model are:
$$c_0 = e^{-rT}\left[F_0 N(d_1) - K N(d_2)\right]$$
$$p_0 = e^{-rT}\left[K N(-d_2) - F_0 N(-d_1)\right]$$

with:
$$d_1 = \frac{\ln \frac{F_0}{K}}{\sigma\sqrt{T}} + \frac{1}{2}\sigma\sqrt{T}, \quad d_2 = d_1 - \sigma\sqrt{T}$$

Since $F_0 = S_0 e^{(r-q)T}$, we have:
$$c_0 = S_0 e^{-qT} N(d_1) - K e^{-rT} N(d_2)$$
$$p_0 = K e^{-rT} N(-d_2) - S_0 e^{-qT} N(-d_1)$$

with:
$$d_1 = \frac{\ln \frac{S_0}{K} + \left(r - q + \frac{1}{2}\sigma^2 T\right)}{\sigma\sqrt{T}}, \quad d_2 = d_1 - \sigma\sqrt{T}$$

4. (a) Between t and $t + dt$, the change in value dP_t of the portfolio is equal to $-dD_t + \frac{\partial f}{\partial S} dS_t$ (change in value of one unit short of derivative and $\frac{\partial f}{\partial S}$

units long of underlying), plus the dividend payment at the continuous rate q applied to the value of the units of stock held: $q\,dt \times \dfrac{\partial f}{\partial S} S_t$.

(b) The Ito–Doeblin theorem yields:

$$dD_t = df = \frac{\partial f}{\partial t} dt + \frac{\partial f}{\partial S} dS_t + \frac{1}{2}\sigma^2 S_t^2 \frac{\partial^2 f}{\partial S^2} dt$$

Hence:

$$dP_t = -dD_t + \frac{\partial f}{\partial S} dS_t + q\frac{\partial f}{\partial S} S_t dt$$

$$= \left(-\frac{\partial f}{\partial t} - \frac{1}{2}\sigma^2 S_t^2 \frac{\partial^2 f}{\partial S^2}\right) dt + q\frac{\partial f}{\partial S} S_t dt$$

Since there is no random component in this equation, the portfolio is riskless between t and $t + dt$.

(c) Since the portfolio is riskless, its value must grow at the risk-free rate r under penalty of arbitrage:

$$dP_t = rP_t\,dt$$

Using $P_t = -D_t + \dfrac{\partial f}{\partial S} S_t$ and the equation for dP_t found above, we get:

$$r\left(-D_t + \frac{\partial f}{\partial S} S_t\right) dt = \left(-\frac{\partial f}{\partial t} - \frac{1}{2}\sigma^2 S_t^2 \frac{\partial^2 f}{\partial S^2} + q\frac{\partial f}{\partial S} S_t\right) dt$$

For this equation to hold, the expressions in front of each dt must be equal ('we divide both sides by dt'). Recalling that $D_t = f$ finally yields:

$$rf = \frac{\partial f}{\partial t} + (r-q)S_t\frac{\partial f}{\partial S} + \frac{1}{2}\sigma^2 S_t^2 \frac{\partial^2 f}{\partial S^2}$$

Appendix A: Probability review

A.1 States of nature; random variables; events

A.1.1 States of nature

The classical representation of uncertainty in finance consists of a set Ω of all possible future outcomes ω called **states of nature**: $\Omega = \{\omega_1, \omega_2, \ldots, \omega_n\}$. For example, a possible model for the future price in a year's time of stock Tiramigiù SpA currently trading at €100 in Milan could be:

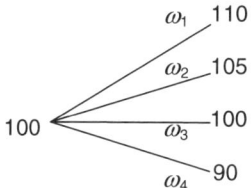

where ω_1 corresponds to the state of nature in which the stock price goes up €10, ω_2 corresponds to the state of nature where the stock prices goes up €5, and so forth.

The states of nature form the structure of uncertainty and only have an interpretative meaning. They should not be confused with the numerical values associated with them (thus one should *not* write $\omega_1 = 110$, $\omega_2 = 105, \ldots$).

It is possible to represent uncertainty with an infinite number of states of nature $\Omega = \{\omega_i \mid i \in I\}$, where I is the set of natural integers or real numbers. However, infinite models require a more sophisticated mathematical framework which is beyond our scope. We refer interested readers to a probability and statistics textbook at the end of this Appendix.

A.1.2 Random variables

A random variable is a function which associates a real number to each state of nature. In our example, the future price X of Tiramigiù SpA would be defined as: $X(\omega_1) = 110$, $X(\omega_2) = 105$, $X(\omega_3) = 100$ and $X(\omega_4) = 90$. We can then define the random payoff $C = \max(X - 100; 0)$ of a call option on Tiramigiù SpA struck at €100 (see Chapter 4 for the definition of a call option). C is in fact a random variable with $C(\omega_1) = 10$, $C(\omega_2) = 5$ and $C(\omega_3) = C(\omega_4) = 0$.

A.1.3 Events

It is often necessary to group several states of nature together into a 'meta-state' called an **event**. From a mathematical standpoint an event is simply a subset of Ω. In our example the event 'the stock price goes up' would be the subset $U = \{\omega_1, \omega_2\}$, and the event 'the payoff of the call is zero' would be the subset $Z = \{\omega_3, \omega_4\}$.

There exist standard notations for the most frequently used events associated to a random variable X.

- $[X = x]$: subset of all states of nature where X takes the value x.
- $[X \geq x]$: subset of all states of nature where X takes values higher than or equal to x.
- $[X \leq y]$: subset of all states of nature where X takes values lower than or equal to x.
- $[x \leq X \leq y]$, $[X > x]$, etc.

Events can be combined together through logical operators.

- $A \cup B$: 'A or B'.
- $A \cap B$: 'A and B'.
- $\bar{A}$: 'not A'.
- $\overline{A \cup (B \cap C)}$, etc.

A.2 Probability; expectation; variance

A.2.1 Probability

The second step in modelling uncertainty is to assign a **probability of occurrence** p_i to each state of nature ω_i. Intuitively, the number p_i corresponds to the chance between 0% and 100% of ω_i happening, and the sum of all probabilities must be 100%.

Following our example for the future price of stock Tiramigiù SpA in a year's time:

Appendix A

State of nature	ω_1: 'the stock price goes up €10'	ω_2: 'the stock price goes up €5'	ω_3: 'the stock price remains unchanged'	ω_4: 'the stock price drops by €10'
Probability of occurrence	$p_1 = 10\%$	$p_2 = 20\%$	$p_3 = 50\%$	$p_4 = 20\%$

The **probability of an event** A, denoted $P(A)$, is then the sum of the probabilities p_i associated to the states of nature $\omega_i A$. In our example:

- The probability of the event 'the stock price goes up' is: $P(A) = P(\{\omega_1, \omega_2\}) = p_1 + p_2 = 0.1 + 0.2 = 30\%$.
- The probability of the event $Z = [C = 0]$ ('the payoff of the call is zero') is: $P([C = 0]) = P(\{\omega_3, \omega_4\}) = 0.5 + 0.2 = 70\%$.

A.2.2 Expectation

The **expectation** or **mean** $E(X)$ of a random variable X is the weighted average of its possible values, with weights equal to the corresponding probabilities:

$$E(X) = \sum_i X(\omega_i) p_i$$

In our example, the expected future price of Tiramigiù SpA is:

$$E(X) = (110 \times 0.1) + (105 \times 0.2) + (100 \times 0.5) + (90 \times 0.2) = 100$$

This means that 'on average' we expect the price of Tiramigiù SpA to remain unchanged at €100 in a year's time. Keep in mind that this is only a calculation, not an event: there is in fact only a 50% chance that the stock price indeed remains unchanged in our model.

A.2.3 Variance

Variance and standard deviation measure the degree of instability of a random variable with respect to its expectation or mean. Specifically, the **variance** of a random variable X is the weighted average of its squared deviations from the mean:

$$\text{Var}(X) = \sum_i (X(\omega_i) - E(X))^2 p_i$$

Standard deviation is simply the square root of variance:

$$\sigma(X) = \sqrt{\text{Var}(X)}$$

In our example, the variance of the future price X of Tiramigiù SpA is:

$$\text{Var}(X) = (110 - 100)^2 \times 0.1 + (105 - 100)^2 \times 0.2$$
$$+ (100 - 100)^2 \times 0.5 + (90 - 100)^2 \times 0.2 = 35$$

And the standard deviation is:

$$\sigma(X) = \sqrt{35} \approx 5.91$$

This means that 'on average' we can expect the price of Tiramigiù SpA in a year's time will be away from its mean of €100 by ±€5.91. Again, keep in mind that this is a calculation: there is in fact a 30% chance that X will be away from its mean by ±€10 in our model.

A.3 Distribution; normal distribution

A.3.1 Cumulative distribution

The cumulative distribution F_X of a random variable X is the function defined for all real x by:

$$F_X(x) = P([X \leq x])$$

Following our example, the cumulative distribution for the future price X of stock Tiramigiù SpA in a year's time is given as:

$$F_X(x) = \begin{cases} 0 & \text{for } x < 90 \\ 0.2 & \text{for } 90 \leq x < 100 \\ 0.2 + 0.5 = 0.7 & \text{for } 100 \leq x < 105 \\ 0.7 + 0.2 = 0.9 & \text{for } 105 \leq x < 110 \\ 1 & \text{for } x \geq 110 \end{cases}$$

The graph of this step function is given below:

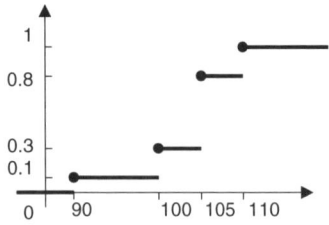

A.3.2 Continuous random variables

A random variable X is said to be **continuous** when its cumulative distribution is continuously differentiable, except perhaps in a finite number of points x. The derivative of F_X is called **partial distribution** or **distribution density** and is often denoted f_X. The formulas for the expectation and variance of X are given in Section A.5.

A.3.3 Normal distribution

We say that a random variable $\tilde{N}$ follows **a normal distribution with mean m and standard deviation σ** when its cumulative distribution is equal to:

$$F_{\tilde{N}}(x) = \frac{1}{\sigma\sqrt{2\pi}} \int_{-\infty}^{x} e^{-\frac{(u-m)^2}{2\sigma^2}} du$$

For $m = 0$ and $\sigma = 1$, $\tilde{N}$ is said to follow a **standard normal distribution**, and its cumulative distribution is often denoted N:

$$N(x) = \frac{1}{\sqrt{2\pi}} \int_{-\infty}^{x} e^{-\frac{u^2}{2}} du$$

Normally distributed variables are examples of continuous random variables. Their distribution density has a well-known bell-shaped curve which peaks at $x = m$, and the probability that their value lies between $m - \sigma$ and $m + \sigma$ is roughly 2/3, as illustrated below.

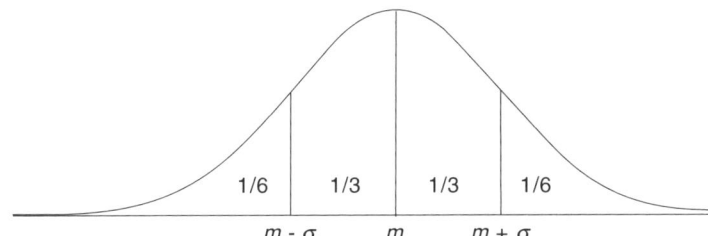

A.4 Independence; correlation

A.4.1 Independence

Two events A, B are said to be **independent** when:

$$P(A \cap B) = P(A) \times p(B)$$

Two random variables X, Y are said to be independent if any event A_X defined through X is independent from any event B_Y defined through Y. Examples of A_X and B_Y are: $[X = a]$, $[X > c]$, ..., $[Y \leq b]$, $[d < Y < e]$, ... and all their logical combinations.

A.4.2 Covariance and correlation

The **covariance** between two random variables X, Y is the weighted average of their joint deviation from their respective means:

$$\text{Cov}(X, Y) = \sum_i (X(\omega_i) - E(X))(Y(\omega_i) - E(Y)) p_i$$

The correlation coefficient between X and Y is a normalized measure of covariance between -1 and $+1$:

$$\text{Corr}(X, Y) = \frac{\text{Cov}(X, Y)}{\sigma(X)\sigma(Y)}$$

If X and Y are independent, their covariance and thus correlation is nil. Note that the converse is *not* true: one can find variables with zero correlation which are not mathematically independent.

A correlation coefficient equal to 1 means that there exists $a > 0$ and b such that $Y = aX + b$ with 100% certainty, and a correlation equal to -1 means that $Y = -aX + b$ with 100% certainty.

In our example, the correlation coefficient between the future price X of stock Tiramigiù SpA and the payoff C of the call on Tiramigiù is 0.72, as calculated below:

	X	C	p	$X - E(X)$	$C - E(C)$	$(X - E(X))(C - E(C))$
ω_1	110	10	10%	10	8	80
ω_2	105	5	20%	5	3	15
ω_3	100	0	50%	0	-2	0
ω_4	90	0	20%	-10	-2	20
E	100	2			Cov(X, C)	$8 + 3 + 0 + 4 = 15$
σ	5.91	3.32			Corr(X, C)	**0.76**

A.5 Probability formulas

A.5.1 Probability of events

$$P(\bar{A}) = 1 - P(A)$$

$$P(A \cup B) = P(A) + P(B) - P(A \cap B)$$

A.5.2 Expectation, variance and standard deviation of a discrete random variable

$$E(X) = \sum_i X(\omega_i) p_i$$

$$\text{Var}(X) = \sum_i [X(\omega_i) - E(X)]^2 p_i = E(X^2) - [E(X)]^2$$

$$\sigma(X) = \sqrt{\text{Var}(X)}$$

A.5.3 Expectation, variance and standard deviation of a continuous random variable

$$E(X) = \int_{-\infty}^{+\infty} u f_X(u) du$$

$$\text{Var}(X) = \int_{-\infty}^{+\infty} (u - E(X))^2 f_X(u) du = E(X^2) - [E(X)]^2$$

$$\sigma(X) = \sqrt{\text{Var}(X)}$$

A.5.4 Covariance and correlation between two discrete variables

$$\text{Cov}(X, Y) = \sum_i (X(\omega_i) - E(X))(Y(\omega_i) - E(Y)) p_i$$

$$= E(XY) - E(X) E(Y)$$

$$\text{Corr}(X, Y) = \frac{\text{Cov}(X, Y)}{\sigma(X) \sigma(Y)}$$

A.5.5 Properties of expectation, variance, covariance and correlation

$$E(aX + bY) = a\, E(X) + b\, E(Y) \quad \text{(linearity)}$$

$$\text{Var}(X) \geq 0$$

$$\text{Var}(aX + b) = a^2\, \text{Var}(X)$$

$$\text{Var}(X + Y) = \text{Var}(X) + \text{Var}(Y) + 2\, \text{Cov}(X, Y)$$

$$\text{Cov}(X, X) = \text{Var}(X)$$

$$\text{Cov}(X, Y) = \text{Cov}(Y, X) \quad \text{(symmetry)}$$

$$\text{Cov}(X, aY + bZ) = a\, \text{Cov}(X, Y) + b\, \text{Cov}(X, Z) \quad \text{(bi-linearity)}$$

$$-1 \leq \text{Corr}(X, Y) \leq +1$$

A.5.6 Transfer formula

- For a discrete variable: $\mathrm{E}\left(f(X)\right) = \sum_{i} f(X(\omega_i)) \, p_i$.

  In particular: $\mathrm{E}(X^2) = \sum_{i} (X(\omega_i))^2 \, p_i$.

- For a continuous variable: $\mathrm{E}\left(f(X)\right) = \int_{-\infty}^{+\infty} f(u) \, f_X(u) \, du$.

  In particular: $\mathrm{E}(X^2) = \int_{-\infty}^{+\infty} u^2 f_X(u) \, du$.

A.6 Chebyshev's inequality; Central Limit Theorem

A.6.1 Chebyshev's inequality

Let X be a random variable. Then for all $\varepsilon > 0$:

$$P(|X - \mathrm{E}(X)| \geq \varepsilon) \leq \frac{\mathrm{Var}(X)}{\varepsilon^2}$$

A.6.2 Central Limit Theorem

Let $(X_k)_{k \geq 1}$ be a sequence of independent, identically distributed random variables with mean μ and standard deviation σ. Then the cumulative distribution of the random variable $S_n = \dfrac{1}{\sigma \sqrt{n}} \sum_{k=1}^{n} (X_k - \mu)$ converges to that of a standard normal as n goes to infinity.

Further reading

Jacod, J. and Protter, P. (2002) *Probability Essentials*, 2nd edn. Springer, New York.

Appendix B: Calculus review

B.1 Functions of two variables x and y

B.1.1 Graph

The graph of a function of two variables $f(x, y)$ is a three-dimensional surface $z = f(x, y)$.

B.1.2 Continuity

A function of two variables is said to be continuous when for each point M_0 of the surface and every sphere centred on M_0 of arbitrary radius $\varepsilon > 0$ we can find a vertical cylinder of radius $\rho > 0$ whose intersection with the surface is included in the sphere... Formally: for all $\varepsilon > 0$ there exists $\rho > 0$ such that for all (x, y) satisfying $\sqrt{(x - x_0)^2 + (y - y_0)^2} < \rho$, we have: $|f(x, y) - f(x_0, y_0)| < \varepsilon$.

The two graphs below correspond to the functions $f(x, y) = \dfrac{xy^2}{|x|}$, $f(0, 0) = 0$ and $g(x, y) = \dfrac{xy}{x+y}$, $g(0, 0) = 0$, respectively. f is continuous, g is not.

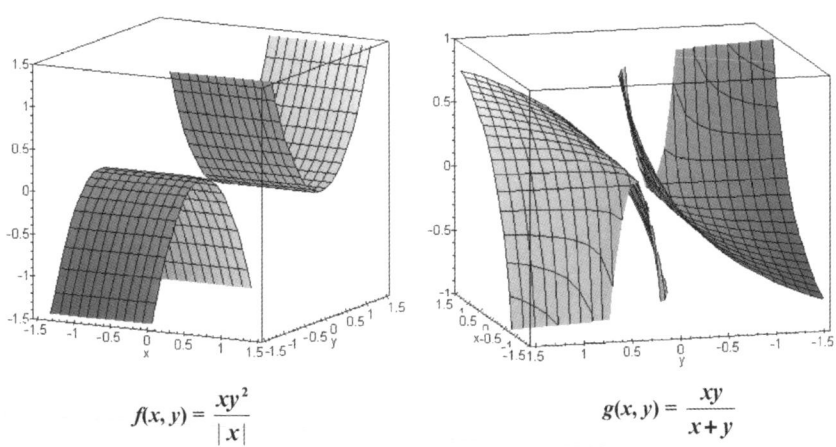

$$f(x, y) = \frac{xy^2}{|x|} \qquad g(x, y) = \frac{xy}{x+y}$$

B.1.3 Partial derivatives

The **partial derivative of f with respect to x** is the function of two variables denoted $\frac{\partial f}{\partial x}$ which one obtains by differentiating f with respect to x while holding y as a constant. The partial derivative of f with respect to y is defined symmetrically.

For example, the partial derivatives of $f(x, y) = x + (xy)^2$ are: $\frac{\partial f}{\partial x}(x, y) = 1 + 2xy^2$, $\frac{\partial f}{\partial y}(x, y) = 2x^2 y$.

B.1.4 Second-order partial derivatives

The partial derivatives of the partial derivatives are called second-order partial derivatives and denoted $\frac{\partial^2 f}{\partial x^2}$, $\frac{\partial^2 f}{\partial x \partial y}$, $\frac{\partial^2 f}{\partial y \partial x}$, $\frac{\partial^2 f}{\partial y^2}$.

B.1.5 Schwarz's theorem

If a function of two variables is twice differentiable and its second-order derivatives are continuous (in the sense of section B.1.2) then:

$$\frac{\partial^2 f}{\partial x \partial y} = \frac{\partial^2 f}{\partial y \partial x}$$

B.2 Taylor expansions

B.2.1 Taylor expansions for a function of a single variable x

First-order Taylor expansion

Let f be a continuously differentiable function of a single variable x, and x_0 a real number. A first-order Taylor expansion around x_0 is then given as:

$$f(x_0 + h) \underset{h \to 0}{\overset{(1)}{\approx}} f(x_0) + h f'(x_0)$$

For example, a first-order Taylor expansion for $f(x) = x^2$ around $x_0 = 1$ is: $f(1 + h) \underset{h \to 0}{\overset{(1)}{\approx}} 1 + 2h$.

Second-order Taylor expansion

Let f be a twice continuously differentiable function of a single variable x, and x_0 a real number. A second-order Taylor expansion around x_0 is then given as:

$$f(x_0 + h) \underset{h \to 0}{\overset{(2)}{\approx}} f(x_0) + hf'(x_0) + \frac{1}{2}h^2 f''(x_0)$$

For example, a second-order Taylor expansion for $f(x) = \sqrt{x}$ around $x_0 = 1$ is:

$$f(1 + h) \underset{h \to 0}{\overset{(2)}{\approx}} 1 + \frac{1}{2}h - \frac{1}{8}h^2.$$

B.2.2 Taylor expansions for a function of two variables x and y

First-order Taylor expansion

Let f be a function of two variables x and y with continuous partial derivatives, and (x_0, y_0) a pair of real numbers. A first-order Taylor expansion around (x_0, y_0) is then given as:

$$f(x_0 + h, y_0 + k) \underset{(h,k) \to (0,0)}{\overset{(1)}{\approx}} f(x_0, y_0) + h\frac{\partial f}{\partial x}(x_0, y_0) + k\frac{\partial f}{\partial y}(x_0, y_0)$$

For example, a first-order Taylor expansion for $f(x, y) = x + (xy)^2$ around $(1, 2)$ is:

$$f(1 + h, 2 + k) \underset{(h,k) \to (0,0)}{\overset{(1)}{\approx}} 5 + 9h + 4k$$

Differential notation

Denoting $dx = h$, $dy = k$, $df = f(x_0 + dx, y_0 + dy) - f(x_0, y_0)$, and omitting (x_0, y_0) in the partial derivatives we can write: $df = \frac{\partial f}{\partial x}dx + \frac{\partial f}{\partial y}dy$. Intuitively, this means that a small change in f will be the weighted sum of the changes in x and y, with weights equal to the partial derivatives.

Second-order Taylor expansion

Let f be a function of two variables x and y with continuous second-order partial derivatives, and (x_0, y_0) a pair of real numbers. A second-order Taylor expansion around (x_0, y_0) is then given as:

$$f(x_0 + h, y_0 + k) \underset{(h,k) \to (0,0)}{\overset{(2)}{\approx}} f(x_0, y_0) + h\frac{\partial f}{\partial x}(x_0, y_0) + k\frac{\partial f}{\partial y}(x_0, y_0)$$
$$+ \frac{1}{2}\left[h^2 \frac{\partial^2 f}{\partial x^2}(x_0, y_0) + 2hk \frac{\partial^2 f}{\partial x \partial y}(x_0, y_0) + k^2 \frac{\partial^2 f}{\partial y^2}(x_0, y_0)\right]$$

For example, a second-order Taylor expansion for $f(x, y) = x + (xy)^2$ around $(1, 2)$ is:

$$f(1 + h, 2 + k) \underset{(h,k) \to (0,0)}{\overset{(2)}{\approx}} 5 + 9h + 4k + 4h^2 + 8hk + k^2$$

Appendix C: Finance formulas

C.1 Rates and yields

Compounding of capital K at rate r over n periods: $K_n = K(1+r)^n$ (Chapter 1)

Conversion formula: $\left(1+r^{[\tau_1]}\right)^{\frac{1}{\tau_1}} = \left(1+r^{[\tau_2]}\right)^{\frac{1}{\tau_2}}$ (Chapter 1)

Continuously compounded interest rate: $e^{r^{[\tau]}_{[c]}} = \left(1+r^{[\tau]}\right)^{\frac{1}{\tau}}$ (Chapter 9)

Gross rate of return: $ROR = \dfrac{P}{E} = \dfrac{P_T - P_0 + I}{P_0}$ (Chapter 2)

Time of return: $TOR = \dfrac{P}{E} = \dfrac{1}{ROR}$ (Chapter 2)

Internal rate of return r^*: $-C_0 + \sum\limits_{i=1}^{+\infty} \dfrac{F_i}{(1+r^*)^{t_i}} = 0$ (Chapter 2)

Yield: $P = \dfrac{C_{t_1}}{(1+y^*)^{t_1}} + \dfrac{C_{t_2}}{(1+y^*)^{t_2}} + \cdots + \dfrac{N+C_T}{(1+y^*)^T}$ (Chapter 3)

Zero rate: $z(T) = \left(\dfrac{N}{p(T)}\right)^{\frac{1}{T}} - 1$ (Chapter 3)

Return of a portfolio of N assets: $R_P = \sum\limits_{k=1}^{K} w_k R_k$ (Chapter 5)

C.2 Present value; arbitrage price

Present value of a future cash flow C at time T: $PV = \dfrac{C}{(1+r)^T}$ (Chapter 1)

Present value of a cash flow table: $PV = \sum\limits_{i=1}^{+\infty} \dfrac{F_i}{(1+r)^{t_i}}$ (Chapter 2)

Net present value: $NPV = -C_0 + \sum\limits_{i=1}^{+\infty} \dfrac{F_i}{(1+r)^{t_i}}$ (Chapter 2)

Arbitrage price ('mark-to-market value') of a portfolio of N assets: $P = \sum_{k=1}^{N} q_k p_k$ (Chapters 3 and 5)

Arbitrage price of a bond: $P = \dfrac{C_{t_1}}{(1+z(t_1))^{t_1}} + \dfrac{C_{t_2}}{(1+z(t_2))^{t_2}} + \cdots + \dfrac{N+C_T}{(1+z(T))^T}$ (Chapter 3)

Arbitrage price of a fixed-income security: $P = \sum_{i=1}^{n} \dfrac{F_{t_i}}{(1+z(t_i))^{t_i}}$ (Chapter 3)

C.3 Forward and futures

Arbitrage price of a forward (or futures) contract (Chapter 4):

	No dividend or cash flow	Dividend rate q
At $t = 0$	$FC_0 = S_0 - \dfrac{K}{(1+r)^T}$	$FC_0 = S_0(1+q)^T - \dfrac{K}{(1+r)^T}$
At $t > 0$	$FC_t = S_t - \dfrac{K}{(1+r)^{T-t}}$	$FC_t = S_t(1+q)^{T-t} - \dfrac{K}{(1+r)^{T-t}}$
At $t > 0$, continuous rates (Chapter 9)	$FC_t = S_t - Ke^{-r_{[c]}(T-t)}$	$FC_t = S_t e^{q_{[c]}(T-t)} - Ke^{-r_{[c]}(T-t)}$

Forward price (Chapter 4):

	No dividend or cash flow	Dividend rate q
At $t = 0$	$F = S_0(1+r)^T$	$F = S_0 \left(\dfrac{1+r}{1+q}\right)^T$
At $t > 0$	$F(t, T) = S_t(1+r)^{T-t}$	$F(t, T) = S_t \left(\dfrac{1+r}{1+q}\right)^{T-t}$
At $t > 0$, continuous rates (Chapter 9)	$F(t, T) = S_t e^{r_{[c]}(T-t)}$	$F(t, T) = S_t e^{(r_{[c]} - q_{[c]})(T-t)}$

C.4 Options

Payoff of the call: $c_T = \max(0, S_T - K)$ (Chapter 4)

Payoff of the put: $p_T = \max(K - S_T, 0)$ (Chapter 4)

Appendix C

Binomial model: $\Delta = \dfrac{D_T^{(u)} - D_T^{(d)}}{S_T^{(u)} - S_T^{(d)}}$, $\quad D_0 = \Delta S_0 + \dfrac{D_T^{(?)} - \Delta S_T^{(?)}}{(1+r)^T}$ (Chapter 6)

Lognormal model: $D_0 = \mathrm{E}\left(\dfrac{D_T}{(1+r)^T}\right) = \mathrm{E}\left(\dfrac{f(T,S_T)}{(1+r)^T}\right)$ (Chapter 7)

Closed-form formulas for the European call and put (Chapter 7):

At $t=0$
$$\begin{cases} c_0 = \dfrac{1}{(1+r)^T}\left[F_0 N(d_1) - K N(d_2)\right] \\ p_0 = \dfrac{1}{(1+r)^T}\left[K N(-d_2) - F_0 N(-d_1)\right] \end{cases} \qquad \begin{cases} d_1 = \dfrac{\ln\dfrac{F_0}{K} + \dfrac{1}{2}\sigma^2 T}{\sigma\sqrt{T}} \\ d_2 = \dfrac{\ln\dfrac{F_0}{K} - \dfrac{1}{2}\sigma^2 T}{\sigma\sqrt{T}} \end{cases}$$

At $t>0$
$$\begin{cases} c_t = \dfrac{1}{(1+r)^{T-t}}\left[F(t,T) N(d_1) - K N(d_2)\right] \\ p_t = \dfrac{1}{(1+r)^{T-t}}\left[K N(-d_2) - F(t,T) N(-d_1)\right] \end{cases} \qquad \begin{cases} d_1 = \dfrac{\ln\dfrac{F(t,T)}{K} + \dfrac{1}{2}\sigma^2 (T-t)}{\sigma\sqrt{T-t}} \\ d_2 = \dfrac{\ln\dfrac{F(t,T)}{K} - \dfrac{1}{2}\sigma^2 (T-t)}{\sigma\sqrt{T-t}} \end{cases}$$

Black–Scholes partial differential equation: $rf = \dfrac{\partial f}{\partial t} + rS_t \dfrac{\partial f}{\partial S} + \dfrac{1}{2}\sigma^2 S_t^2 \dfrac{\partial^2 f}{\partial S^2}$ (Chapter 10)

Black–Scholes formulas for the European call and put (Chapter 10):

$$\begin{cases} c_0 = S_0 N(d_1) - K e^{-rT} N(d_2) \\ p_0 = K e^{-rT} N(-d_2) - S_0 N(-d_1) \end{cases}, \quad d_1 = \dfrac{\ln\dfrac{S_0}{K} + \left(r + \dfrac{1}{2}\sigma^2\right)T}{\sigma\sqrt{T}}, \quad d_2 = d_1 - \sigma\sqrt{T}$$

Note that in Black–Scholes r is a continuously compounded rate.

C.5 Risk

Historical volatility of returns: $\sigma_{periodic} = \sqrt{\dfrac{1}{N-1}\sum_{t=1}^{N}(r_t - \bar{r})^2}$ (Chapters 5 and 10)

Annualized volatility: $\sigma_{annual} = \sigma_{periodic} \times \sqrt{\text{number of periods per year}}$ (Chapter 5)

Sharpe ratio: $Sharpe = \dfrac{r_A - r_f}{\sigma_A}$ (Chapter 5)

Volatility of a portfolio of two assets (Chapter 5):

$$\sigma_P = \sqrt{\mathrm{Var}(w_1 R_1 + w_2 R_2)} = \sqrt{w_1^2 \mathrm{Var}(R_1) + w_2^2 \mathrm{Var}(R_1) + 2 w_1 w_2 \mathrm{Cov}(R_1, R_2)}$$

Volatility of a portfolio of N assets (Chapter 5):

$$\sigma_P = \sqrt{\mathrm{Var}(R_P)}$$

$$\mathrm{Var}(R_P) = \mathrm{Var}\left(\sum_{k=1}^{N} w_k R_k\right) = \sum_{k=1}^{N} w_k^2 \mathrm{Var}(R_k) + 2 \sum_{k=1}^{N}\sum_{j=k+1}^{N} w_k w_j \mathrm{Cov}(R_k, R_j)$$

$$\mathrm{Cov}(R_k, R_j) = \sigma_{R_k}\sigma_{R_j}\rho_{R_k,R_j}$$

C.6 Stochastic processes and stochastic calculus (Chapter 9)

Generalized Brownian motion: $dX_t = a\,dt + b\,dW_t$, $X_t = X_0 + at + bW_t$.

Geometric Brownian motion: $dX_t = aX_t\,dt + bX_t\,dW_t$.

Ito process: $dX_t = a(t, X_t)dt + b(t, X_t)dW_t$.

Ito–Doeblin theorem:

$$dY_t = df(t, X_t) = \left[\frac{\partial f}{\partial t}(t, X_t) + a(t, X_t)\frac{\partial f}{\partial X}(t, X_t) + \frac{1}{2}b^2(t, X_t)\frac{\partial^2 f}{\partial X^2}(t, X_t)\right]dt$$
$$+ \left[b(t, X_t)\frac{\partial f}{\partial X}(t, X_t)\right]dW_t$$

$$dY_t = df = \left(\frac{\partial f}{\partial t} + a\frac{\partial f}{\partial X} + \frac{1}{2}b^2\frac{\partial^2 f}{\partial X^2}\right)dt + \left(b\frac{\partial f}{\partial X}\right)dW_t$$

C.7 Greeks (Chapter 8)

δ or Δ (delta)	Γ (gamma)	θ (theta)	$\mathcal{V}$ (vega)	ρ (rho)
$\dfrac{\partial f}{\partial S}$	$\dfrac{\partial^2 f}{\partial S^2} = \dfrac{\partial \Delta}{\partial S}$	$\dfrac{\partial f}{\partial t}$	$\dfrac{\partial f}{\partial \sigma}$	$\dfrac{\partial f}{\partial r}$

Relationship between theta and gamma:

$$\Theta \approx -\frac{1}{2}\Gamma\sigma^2 S_t^2$$

Appendix C

	d_1 and d_2 coefficients
At $t = 0$	$d_1 = \dfrac{\ln \frac{S_0(1+r)^T}{K} + \frac{1}{2}\sigma^2 T}{\sigma\sqrt{T}}, \; d_2 = d_1 - \sigma\sqrt{T}$
At $t > 0$	$d_1 = \dfrac{\ln \frac{S_t(1+r)^{T-t}}{K} + \frac{1}{2}\sigma^2(T-t)}{\sigma\sqrt{T-t}}, \; d_2 = d_1 - \sigma\sqrt{T-t}$

	δ or Δ (delta)
At $t = 0$	$\Delta_{call} = N(d_1), \; \Delta_{put} = -N(-d_1)$
At $t > 0$	$\Delta_{call} = N(d_1), \; \Delta_{put} = -N(-d_1)$

	Γ (gamma)
At $t = 0$	$\Gamma_{call} = \Gamma_{put} = \dfrac{N'(d_1)}{\sigma S_0 \sqrt{T}}$
At $t > 0$	$\Gamma_{call} = \Gamma_{put} = \dfrac{N'(d_1)}{\sigma S_t \sqrt{T-t}}$

	θ (theta)
At $t = 0$	$\begin{cases} \theta_{call} = -\dfrac{\sigma S_0 N'(d_1)}{2\sqrt{T}} - \dfrac{K\ln(1+r)}{(1+r)^T}N(d_2) \\ \theta_{put} = -\dfrac{\sigma S_0 N'(d_1)}{2\sqrt{T}} + \dfrac{K\ln(1+r)}{(1+r)^T}N(-d_2) \end{cases}$
At $t > 0$	$\begin{cases} \theta_{call} = -\dfrac{\sigma S_t N'(d_1)}{2\sqrt{T-t}} - \dfrac{K\ln(1+r)}{(1+r)^{T-t}}N(d_2) \\ \theta_{put} = -\dfrac{\sigma S_t N'(d_1)}{2\sqrt{T-t}} + \dfrac{K\ln(1+r)}{(1+r)^{T-t}}N(-d_2) \end{cases}$

	$\mathcal{V}$ (vega)
At $t = 0$	$\mathcal{V}_{call} = \mathcal{V}_{put} = S_0 \sqrt{T} N'(d_1)$
At $t > 0$	$\mathcal{V}_{call} = \mathcal{V}_{put} = S_t \sqrt{T-t} N'(d_1)$

	ρ (rho)
At $t = 0$	$\begin{cases} \rho_{call} = \dfrac{KT}{(1+r)^{T+1}} N(d_2) \\ \rho_{put} = -\dfrac{KT}{(1+r)^{T+1}} N(-d_2) \end{cases}$
At $t > 0$	$\begin{cases} \rho_{call} = \dfrac{K(T-t)}{(1+r)^{T-t+1}} N(d_2) \\ \rho_{put} = -\dfrac{K(T-t)}{(1+r)^{T-t+1}} N(-d_2) \end{cases}$

Note: in all the above formulas it is assumed that the underlying asset S does not pay any cash flow.

Index

30/360 rule 1–2

American call 51
American put 51
annualization 4–5
approximate valuation of bonds 29–30
arbitrage opportunity 24–5
  absence of 25
arbitrage price 25–6, 32–3
  of forward contract 49–50
asset prices in continuous time 142–4

barrier option 92–3, 99–100
bear market 143
binomial model 85–90
  multiple-step 88–90
  one-step 85–8
Black–Scholes model 144, 167–74
Black–Scholes partial differential equation 167–70
bond markets 27
bonds 26–33
  approximate valuation 29–30
  arbitrage price 32
  convexity 43
  definition 26
  Treasury 26–7
  yield 27
  zero-coupon 27
bootstrapping 33
break-even point 125
bull market 143

call 51–53
  American 51
  European 51
  payoff 52
  put-call parity 53
call spread 59
closed-form formula 105–6, 171
time-value 106
Capital Asset Pricing Model (CAPM) 73–4
cash flow 14
Central Limit Theorem 107, 192
Chebyshev's inequality 192
closed-form formulas 105–6, 171
collar 59
compound interest rate 3–5
  annualization 4–5
  conversion formula 4
  equivalent 3
compounding table 3
continuously compounded interest rate 142–3
correlation 190
  of asset returns 70
cost of carry 62–3
coupons 26
covariance 190
covered short call 59
cumulative distribution 188

default risk 10, 28
delivery price (strike) 48
delta 126
delta-hedging 105, 126–7, 170
delta-neutral portfolio 126
derivative security
  categories 48
  definition 47–8
discount factors 34

discount rate 6, 104–5
discounting 5–6
distribution density 189
diversification 70, 71–2
drift 146, 168
dynamic hedging 125–32
dynamic strategy 170
dynamic trading strategy 127

European call 51
European put 51
exercise price (strike) 51
exotic derivatives 48
exotic options 51, 172
expectation 187
expected return 6
expiry maturity 51

face (nominal) coupon 141–2
face value 26
fair value 103
financial markets 24
financial security 23
fixed income security 32–3
forward contracts 48–51, 58
forward-neutrality 104
forward price 51, 58
forward rate 56–7, 63–4
fractioned rate 141
future contracts 48

gamma 128–30
  theta vs. 130–2
generalized Brownian motion 146–7
geometric Brownian motion 147
Greeks (sensitivities) 127–32
gross interest rate 2–3
gross rate of return 13

hedge ratio 170
historical volatility 172–3

idiosyncratic risk 73
implied volatility 174
infinite liquidity 25
interest 5

interest rate 2–5
  compound 3–5
  continuously compounded 142–3
  gross 2–3
internal rate of return (IRR) 15–16
Ito–Doeblin Theorem (Ito's lemma) 148, 152–3, 164–5
Ito process 147–8

knock-in barrier option 92
knock-out barrier option 92, 99–100

law of one price 25
leverage 78
lognormal model 103–8
long position 65
long volatility 172

mark-to-market 65
market risk 73
maturity 26, 48, 51
Monte-Carlo method 106–8

net present value (NVP) 14–15
nominal (face) coupon 141–2
nominal amount (face value) 26

optimal portfolio 73
options 48, 51–3
over-the-counter (OTC) 48

par amount 26
path-dependent 100
payoff 48, 49, 52
plain vanilla options 51–3
portfolio 23
  optimization 71–3
  price of 25–6
  valuation 65–6
  volatility 70
present value 5, 14
price
  arbitrage 25–6, 32–3, 49–50
  in continuous time 142–4
  delivery 48
  exercise 48
  forward 51, 58

of a portfolio 25–6
of a security 24
sensitivity 42–3
spot 51
price-to-earnings ratio (PER or P/E) 16
primary market 27
principal amount (face value) 26
probability density function 104
profit and loss (P&L) 125
put 51–53
   American 51–53
   European 51
   closed-form formula 105–6, 171
   pay off 52
   time value 106
put–call parity 52–3

random variables 186
rate of return (ROR) 13–14
return on investment (ROI) 13–14
risk 66–70
   and return of an asset 66–8
   and return of a portfolio 68–70
   -free asset 68
   -free rate 68
   neutrality 104
   premium 68
   specific (idiosyncratic) 73
   market (systematic) 73

secondary market 27
sensitivities (Greeks) 127–32
Sharpe ratio 68
short position 65
short sell 24
specific risk (idiosyncratic risk) 73

spot price 51
standard Brownian motion (standard Wiener process) 145–6
standard deviation 66
static trading strategy 127
stochastic calculus 147–8
stochastic processes 144–7
straddle 59
strike 48, 51
strips 31
synthetic short forward 59
systematic risk 73

table of future cash flows 14
theta 130–2
time, measuring 1–2
time of return 13–14
time value of options 106
Treasury bonds 26–7

underlying asset 47

value of a security 23–4
vanilla options 51–3
volatility 66
   historical 172–3
   implied 174

yield 27–30
   curve 28–9

zero-coupon
   bonds 27
   rate (yield) 30–31
zero-rate curve 31–2